THE AMERICAN LITERATURE SCHOLAR IN THE DIGITAL AGE

EDITORIAL THEORY AND LITERARY CRITICISM
George Bornstein, Series Editor

Palimpsest: Editorial Theory in the Humanities,
edited by George Bornstein and Ralph G. Williams

Contemporary German Editorial Theory, edited by Hans Walter Gabler, George Bornstein, and Gillian Borland Pierce

The Hall of Mirrors: Drafts & Fragments and the End of Ezra Pound's Cantos, by Peter Stoicheff

Emily Dickinson's Open Folios: Scenes of Reading, Surfaces of Writing, by Marta L. Werner

Scholarly Editing in the Computer Age: Theory and Practice, Third Edition, by Peter L. Shillingsburg

The Literary Text in the Digital Age, edited by Richard J. Finneran

The Margins of the Text, edited by D. C. Greetham

A Poem Containing History: Textual Studies in The Cantos, edited by Lawrence S. Rainey

Much Labouring: The Texts and Authors of Yeats's First Modernist Books, by David Holdeman

Resisting Texts: Authority and Submission in Constructions of Meaning, by Peter L. Shillingsburg

The Iconic Page in Manuscript, Print, and Digital Culture, edited by George Bornstein and Theresa Tinkle

Collaborative Meaning in Medieval Scribal Culture: The Otho Laȝamon, by Elizabeth J. Bryan

Oscar Wilde's Decorated Books, by Nicholas Frankel

Managing Readers: Printed Marginalia in English Renaissance Books, by William W. E. Slights

The Fluid Text: A Theory of Revision and Editing for Book and Screen, by John Bryant

Textual Awareness: A Genetic Study of Late Manuscripts by Joyce, Proust, and Mann, by Dirk Van Hulle

The American Literature Scholar in the Digital Age, edited by Amy E. Earhart and Andrew Jewell

---

DIGITALCULTUREBOOKS is an imprint of the University of Michigan Press and the Scholarly Publishing Office of the University of Michigan Library dedicated to publishing innovative and accessible work exploring new media and their impact on society, culture, and scholarly communication.

The American Literature Scholar in the Digital Age

EDITED BY

Amy E. Earhart and Andrew Jewell

THE UNIVERSITY OF MICHIGAN PRESS AND
THE UNIVERSITY OF MICHIGAN LIBRARY
ANN ARBOR

Published in the United States of America by
The University of Michigan Press and
The University of Michigan Library
Manufactured in the United States of America
∞ Printed on acid-free paper

2014 2013 2012 2011 4 3 2 1

A CIP catalog record for this book is available from the British Library.

Library of Congress Cataloging-in-Publication Data

The American literature scholar in the digital age / edited by Amy E. Earhart and Andrew Jewell.
p. cm. — (Editorial theory and literary criticism)
Includes index.
ISBN 978-0-472-07119-7 (cloth : alk. paper) — ISBN 978-0-472-05119-9 (pbk. : alk. paper)
1. Literature and the Internet—United States. 2. American literature—Research—Methodology. 3. American literature—Research—Electronic information resources. 4. American literature—Study and teaching—Methodology. 5. American literature—Study and teaching—Electronic information resources. 6. American literature—History and criticism—Electronic information resources. I. Earhart, Amy E., 1969– II. Jewell, Andrew (Andrew W.)
PS51.A64 2011
810.72—dc22 2010033750

Acknowledgments

This volume emerged from a powerful, energetic session of the Digital Americanists at the 2007 American Literature Association conference in Boston, Massachusetts. The quality of the papers, combined with the engagement of the audience, led us to believe that the profession was ready for a volume that considered the issues presented herein. We would like to thank the American Literature Association for its support of the Digital Americanists organization and of digital humanities projects more broadly.

We would also like to acknowledge the leadership that Kenneth M. Price has provided to the field of American digital scholarship. In addition to his pivotal work on the *Walt Whitman Archive* (http://www.whitmanarchive.org), Ken has taught and mentored many of the scholars represented in this volume, including its coeditors. His leadership inspires those of us working in the digital humanities to press for smart innovations in the field. Also, many readers of this volume may notice that the *Whitman Archive* has an enormous presence. This reflects not the undue bias of the editors or authors but the centrality of the *Whitman Archive* to the development of digital research in American literary studies in the past decade.

We also appreciate the support and leadership that Jerome McGann has provided to the broader digital humanities field and to many scholars, including ourselves. His early work in textual studies paved the way for later work in digital humanities, including his groundbreaking *The Complete Writings and Pictures of Dante Gabriel Rossetti: A Hypermedia Archive* (http://www.rossettiarchive.org) and the founding of NINES (http://www.nines

.org). Jerry's generosity is not to be understated. He has consistently used his position as senior scholar to support markedly innovative work and younger scholars.

Several additional people have provided advice and support to us as we conceived of and prepared this volume. We would like to thank the following people specifically: Brett Barney, Susan Belasco, George Bornstein, Maura Ives, James Harner, and Katherine Walter.

Contents

PART 2. MARKUP AND TOOLS: NEW MODELS AND METHODS FOR HUMANISTIC INQUIRY

PART 3. THEORETICAL CHALLENGES IN DIGITAL AMERICANIST SCHOLARSHIP

Introduction

AMY E. EARHART AND ANDREW JEWELL

Observing the title and concerns of this collection, many may wonder why we have chosen to focus on the *American* literature scholar; certainly the concerns of digital humanities are relevant across literary specializations. In fact, as other digital humanities scholarship demonstrates, the humanities as a boundary is itself suspect: it is not uncommon to see collaborations between a literary scholar, a computer scientist, and a librarian in digital humanities work. The artificial distinctions that have replicated the discipline divisions have become less relevant to those working in digital humanities, who often group around subject matter, not training. Add to this the increasing breakdown of national boundaries in literary studies, and perhaps it seems antiquated or anathema to reproduce *American* as a term with which to saddle a supposedly cutting-edge collection of essays.

Despite the pressures theoretical arguments put on "American" literary work, the profession continues to organize around traditional national models, and most scholars find it useful to self-identify as "Americanist" even as the term *Americanist* grows increasingly broad and disparate. This volume is meant to reach "Americanists" in the broadest sense. We have gathered a collection of essays from scholars working with American content in diverse and provocative ways. Some essays represent well-established work on canonical writers, others explore experimental ways of representing silenced cultural voices, and others look widely at the politics and methodology of our professional practices. What unites all of these essays is that they are concerned with the study of "American literature" and the interaction of that scholarly pursuit with digital technology.

Therefore, this book is not only or even primarily for those already professionally identifying with "digital humanities." Rather, it is aimed at the large and varied community of scholars and teachers who are interested in how digital media is altering the way that we approach the study of American literature and culture. Along with many of our colleagues, we believe that we will see the success of digital humanities not through the creation of a powerful subfield in humanities scholarship but through thoughtful integration of digital methodologies and models of collaboration in humanities research. It is also our belief that engagement with the digital humanities will happen by both those who call themselves "digital humanists" and those who reject the term. Already, scholars conduct and receive a large portion of their research digitally. Few scholars peruse the MLA bibliography in print, preferring access to the online database. JSTOR, Project Muse, and digital delivery of materials by libraries are becoming the norm for journal articles. With the University of Michigan's recently announced shift to a fully digital press, even the scholarly monograph is moving to a digital format. We expect that this trend will continue in the coming years, with digital media influencing all levels of scholarship. Not every scholar will create digital materials, but, eventually, all scholars will *use* some sort of digital materials. By gathering this collection together for our Americanist colleagues, we hope to further encourage the profession to consider how digital media is affecting all aspects of our scholarship and to recognize that there will be increasing benefits and challenges in the use of technology in scholarship.

As the following essays detail, utilizing digitization and computational power makes possible new ways of seeing, collecting, editing, visualizing, and analyzing works of literature. These new methods are at the core of professional academic life, altering not only what we can read through unprecedented access to textual information but also how we articulate our scholarly responses to materials. No longer is our scholarship limited to the print-confined genres of "essays" or "books" or "chapters." Digital publication means that our scholarship may take the form of sprawling "thematic research collections," algorithms that derive consequential meaning from enormous text corpora, or interactive visualizations of data derived from selected works of literature. Scholars are experimenting with 3-D visualizations, maps, images, movies, songs, spoken word, blogs, wikis, games, and more; in the next several years, we will likely see the normalization of new genres of scholarly production, and those new genres will emerge predominantly from interactions with digital media. Additionally, the digital medium reorganizes the publication models that supported most academic research in the past century. The regularized, relatively clean separations between writers and publishers, editors and designers, or distributors and researchers no longer exist, and this restructuring comes at a crucial time of transition for scholarly presses, as financial models for press viability show that we cannot continue to rely on print monographs as the gold standard of the profession.

Importantly, though, we do not create new models of scholarship simply because we *can* (or, at least, that should not be the reason). We explore digitally enabled models because manipulation of scholarly materials in the digital medium allows scholars to think about these materials in new ways, to develop new methods of working with repositories or collections, and to consider how visual interfaces might express ideas more meaningfully. Computational power can also bring into focus qualities of studied texts and objects we have never before ascertained, and new apprehensions will enable new insight. This power is the most exhilarating quality of digital scholarship: combining established forms (such as narrative prose) with new tools (such as manipulable, high-quality images of rare objects or computational analysis of large data sets) can result in better work. The digital medium, if utilized properly, can make insights more powerful, evidence more transparent, and communication more effective.

Our existing digital scholarship is, however, the incunabula of the form; the mature realization of digital humanities is yet to come. It may be that the heady, exploratory, embrace-the-new atmosphere of the early twenty-first century will persist and that a heterogeneous approach will continue to rule the day. Alternatively, we may see codification of new digital genres within the next decade and, with it, the adjusted, settled definitions of the role each participant plays in the new scholarly publication process. The history of institutional development suggests that forces will push scholars toward standardization of forms, and for those made nervous by the upswing in technical terminology within humanities circles, such stratification of roles would be welcome. However, before forms begin to become calcified and naturalized, we need to think carefully about the implications of the trends. It is extremely important that we engage in intensive discussion about digital scholarship right now, as what we imagine and create at this historical moment may be the model on which standardized forms are based.

While recognizing the powerful presence of certain kinds of digital scholarly forms, such as thematic research collections, this volume does not seek to limit the exploratory impulse driving many scholars interested in digital methods. Rather, we hope to encourage it. The diversity of our selection of essays for this volume is, we hope, a revealing snapshot of where we are in digital scholarship right now: contributors are thrilled by the possibilities, concerned about the glacial pace of professional infrastructure shifts, and eager to consider the intellectual implications of digital research. In selecting participants for the volume, we have looked to those who are involved in both the theory and practice of digital humanities. Our participants direct digital humanities research centers, edit archives and collections, and develop software and markup standards, as well as participate in the scholarly discussions about the field. We have also selected participants at varying stages of career—from entry-level assistant professors to endowed chairs—and from varied disciplinary paths, including librarians, humanities scholars, and technicians. We hope that these disparate voices will provide an entry into the topic and encourage questions from scholars who have not spent much time considering the impact of the digital on their work.

The digital approaches to American literary scholarship represented in this volume are not only a future potentiality but an important present reality. Digital scholarship is happening, and its future will be determined not by unknown and unseen forces but by those currently at work in the field. At this writing, however, it is still difficult for scholars in many academic departments to have digital scholarship properly evaluated during promotion and tenure reviews, and this resistance has pushed many of the more practical-minded to focus on traditional print scholarship, letting good—and often more ambitious—ideas for digital projects go unfulfilled. Departments and universities must work to develop clear tenure and promotion guidelines that address the shifting landscape of scholarly publishing. If we can open tenure and promotion criteria to consider a multiplicity of forms, we will nurture a new generation of innovative scholars and scholarship. The dominant model at many research colleges and universities requiring a single-author monograph for tenure and promotion is far too limiting and untenable in the current scholarly publishing climate.

To create a system that evaluates digital scholarship equitably, we need to build structures that promote confidence in the quality of new media materials. More specifically, we need to have reliable structures for peer review of digital content. Since much of born-digital content is self-published (i.e., scholars use the servers at their institutions to publish their digital content on the Web with no third-party entity validating the content prior to publication), the model of peer review must be expanded to evaluate such work. For many digital projects, peer-reviewed status can only come after the effort and resources have been expended to produce and publish the scholarship; the act of publication itself is not evidence of positive peer review. NINES (Networked Infrastructure for Nineteenth-Century Electronic Scholarship, at http://www.nines.org), a scholar-led organization founded by Jerome McGann and currently directed by Andrew Stauffer, is trying to address this issue. NINES has gathered various luminaries in Romantic, Victorian, and nineteenth-century American studies to serve as members of editorial boards, and these boards facilitate peer review of digital scholarship. Once vetted, the digital scholarly sites can boast a NINES logo signifying their peer-reviewed status and are also invited to aggregate their digital objects into the NINES search interface. If NINES can earn recognition as an important peer reviewer of nineteenth-century content, it has the potential to inspire alternative versions for other content areas.

To embrace digital approaches to humanities scholarship, we need to challenge traditional structures of our fields beyond just tenure and promotion criteria. We must revisit the very modes of scholarship production, the skill sets required for our scholarship, and the training of new scholars. Instead of replicating methods of work, we must match the work structure to the project. Some projects will continue to require sustained individual research. Other projects, including many outlined in this volume, are too big and require diverse skill sets demanding numerous participants in a collaborative group. We will need to reenvision the traditional training structures of graduate students, the future scholars in our fields, and the skills that they will require to produce scholarship in the new digital environment. This volume, we hope, is but an initial step in thinking through the inevitable impact the digital medium will have on the study of American literature and culture, one that shows the value of expanding our thinking about scholarly activities, methodologies, and questions.

PART 1

Shifts in Professional Practices

Collaborative Work and the Conditions for American Literary Scholarship in a Digital Age

KENNETH M. PRICE

Various commentators, playing off the naming scheme used for new software releases, have hailed the advent of Web 2.0, Humanities 2.0, and even Read 2.0.[1] In these recent coinages, Tim O'Reilly, Cathy Davidson, Peter Brantley, and others claim that a new stage of cultural development is within reach, a stage with fundamental implications for reading and scholarship. In these 2.0 versions of the Web, the humanities, and reading, collective intelligence, social networking, and collaboration are embedded within infrastructure and function. I remain skeptical, however, about how close we are to these hoped-for "second releases." Despite some remarkable accomplishments in digital humanities, we can more realistically and productively think of our work as Literary Scholarship 1.5 or, perhaps more boldly, as Literary Scholarship 2.0 Beta. We remain in a provisional, testing stage, and we should not overlook this critical step, either rhetorically or practically. In many regards, digital humanities remains in beta, as can be seen from the shortcomings that exist in our current models of collaboration within the field. These shortcomings point to issues that need to be addressed so that digital humanities can advance. Productive collaboration, both between individual scholars and with larger organizations and institutions, is a crucial precondition for progress in the humanities, especially in a digital context, and we are only beginning to see the enormous potential that collaboration holds for humanities research.

Those who celebrate digital work in its many forms—including, for example, the creation of databases, text-mining projects, online editions, computational text analysis, and map-based studies of textual distribution—sometimes suggest that the digital environment is inherently collaborative, while the print environment tends to be solitary. But more than the simple fact of collaboration, it is the *degree* to which there is conscious collaboration (as well as some difference in types of collaboration) that distinguishes digital scholarship from more traditional models. In a print environment, the field of literary studies is often seen as the domain for the solitary scholar: while there have been noteworthy collaborations, they are regarded as the exception rather than the rule. Monographs are prized, and solitary achievements are celebrated. However, this image of the self-sufficient scholar is largely an illusion, one that arises from our having become so accustomed to the collaborations of print culture that they are often nearly invisible, especially when we focus on the monograph or single-author article. But just how solitary is print production? Usually we hardly pause to question assumptions about print production or to think about some truly important collaborations: for example, the way book designers, proofreaders, copy editors, advisers, peer reviewers, and editorial boards shape the final product in cooperation with the author. The manufacturer of paper, the writer of advertising copy, the bookseller, and a host of others are agents, too, in different phases of the life cycle of an article or book. All contribute to highly complex systems of production, distribution, and preservation. To greater and lesser extents, these various agents within the publication system work with the scholar, yet they hover behind the scenes and rarely gain much visibility. To put the matter another way, the collaborative networks of traditional print publishing have become well established, so that while there is room for negotiation around the edges, the overall system is open more to refinement than to fundamental change.

This system of print culture has been developed over centuries through an elaborate division of labor. The corresponding functions in digital scholarship are far less defined, often out of necessity. For those creating electronic scholarly editions, for example, nearly every part of the process in digital scholarship is up for negotiation as new technical possibilities emerge, sometimes with great rapidity. Digital and print-based scholars share equally the obligation to master their subject matter, but digital scholars often find themselves also needing to retool or to create from scratch core components of the publication system: work flow, quality control, design, distribution, peer review, and preservation. I would argue, however, that these issues are not distractions taking a scholar away from real research but constituents of it. The relative stability of these aspects of print culture means that most print-based scholars engage with them more passively. There, scholars have a more circumscribed role, and they plug into a well-established system. Of course, the world of print is changing, too, because of economic pressures and the opportunities and perils of digital publishing. In fact, in discussions like this, the idea of sharply distinct print and digital environments serves now mainly as a heuristic device: it is rare to encounter a digital object not shaped in some way by print-based conceptions, and nearly all currently published print objects have been realized via digital communication and processing. But the fact remains that what is rendered invisible through familiarity in print culture is often the focus of intense attention and critique in digital scholarship. In short, there is a felt difference in the way scholars work when the ultimate product is electronic rather than print. Because scholars who collaborate in digital undertakings are more fully involved in questions of how their work will be created, presented, distributed, and maintained, they must master—or at least thoughtfully engage with—both the subject matter of their specialty and the practices of digital scholarship.

In the ordinary course of their work, digital scholars need to make a broad array of conscious decisions. Because digital scholarship is an evolving experiment that can still fail, the creation of digital works itself needs to be considered a focus for primary research, not merely a secondary issue of production.[2] Digital scholarship, while remediating the textual record and rethinking the possibilities of literary scholarship, raises practical and theoretical questions of great consequence. Of these, experiments with collaboration—across institutions and disciplines, with graduate students, with an expansive audience, with technology, and in other forms—are the most significant in terms of their potential for transforming the field of American literary study.

Collaborating with a Center

Many of the contributors to this volume have been affiliated with at least one of the following digital humanities centers: the Institute for Advanced

Technology in the Humanities at the University of Virginia (IATH), the Maryland Institute for Technology in the Humanities (MITH), and the Center for Digital Research in the Humanities at the University of Nebraska–Lincoln (CDRH).[3] These centers are staffed by a combination of humanists, librarians, computer scientists, professional staff, and student assistants. The centers strive to provide a rich intellectual environment that encourages scholarly development through collaboration. Even though scholars can be quite tech savvy, the quickly evolving nature of technology requires the assistance of experts in such matters as metadata and database design. In some cases, having an affiliation with a center may enable scholars to work with material at other institutions that would otherwise be inaccessible. Sometimes, the backing of a center and the promise of digitization are incentive for an institution's archives or special collections to loan material for use in a scholar's project.[4] Collaborations between scholars and centers have advanced digital humanities significantly. Such a model is new to literary studies, however, and it is developing as a problematically exclusive one. While certain scholars have ready access to expertise, others do not. Uneven access to resources, which greatly affects who can do digital humanities and where,[5] is not an issue we have had to address in such stark terms in other types of literary or humanistic scholarship. One solution for this problem would be for each institution of higher education to create a digital humanities center. That probably will not happen, however, because of cost and because some universities currently no doubt consider the field experimental and of marginal consequence. Clearly, across-the-board development would be expensive, perhaps too expensive to be undertaken.

Various individuals sometimes propose regional, national, and occasionally even international solutions to the need for improved infrastructure for digital scholarship. The three centers already mentioned—IATH, MITH, and CDRH—are sometimes able to support external projects, but their support is usually directed toward advancing the work of local faculty. A project such as the Software Environment for the Advancement of Scholarly Research (SEASR), funded by the Andrew W. Mellon Foundation, promotes the sharing of data in virtual work environments. SEASR attempts to overcome the problem of data stored in a range of incompatible formats. If successful, SEASR would provide a robust platform that would offer greater visibility for tools and applications now operating in widely scattered environments and that would allow scholars to overcome some of the limitations of their local infrastructure.

It is also possible that service providers will eventually emerge to shield humanists from technical issues, though the desirability of that result is open to question. The new organization Documents Compass, for instance, affiliated with the Virginia Foundation for the Humanities, provides services to help plan an edition, search for funding, and otherwise develop historical documentary editions in accord with best practices and with interoperability with other editions in mind.[6] Their advertising tagline—"We will take care of the details while you concentrate on your role as scholar"—promotes the documentary editing work of historians but does not conceive of electronic editorial work as being inextricably tied to the emerging discipline of digital humanities. What Documents Compass inaccurately describes as "details" involve decisions fundamental to the look, feel, functioning, *and* intellectual quality of an edition. Scholars who resist the technical aspects of digital humanities may find Documents Compass appealing, but I think this approach to collaboration is dubious.[7] Those scholars who wish to realize the potential of digital research in terms of presenting and analyzing literature will find that digital humanities questions inhere in these "details" and their often profound implications. For scholars to turn away from technical questions is risky because editorial, interpretative, and technical issues are intertwined in an electronic environment.[8] Further, the field of digital humanities thrives on pushing technology to be ever more responsive to the particular needs of humanistic questions. If we cede the field entirely to technical experts, it is less likely that the technologies will develop in such a way as to respond to the needs of humanists. At the same time, however, humanists must remain open to collaboration with technical experts and ready to consider the potential for existing applications and technologies to cross over for use in digital humanities; certainly not all of our tools and resources need be created from scratch since many innovative technical developments occur outside of the academy.

Collaborating with Fellow Subject Matter Specialists

The *Willa Cather Archive, The Vault at Pfaff's,* the *Walt Whitman Archive,* and other projects have created deep resources through collaborative labor. A multi-institutional, multischolar project can draw on expertise wherever it exists. Certainly the *Whitman Archive* has been fortunate to draw on key participants from the University of Nebraska–Lincoln, the University of Iowa, Duke University, and the University of Virginia, with important additional consulting work from individuals at Brown and Columbia universities. This distribution of work has had advantages, not the least being that various schools have helped share the cost of the project. But a dispersed project also faces the difficulty of coordinating effort. Because digital projects are remarkably dynamic, with the work of these projects often developing on a daily basis, the consequences of poor coordination can be immediate and severe but not always immediately rectified. Failures in coordination may require the redoing of work—at considerable mental and financial expense—or may result in misunderstandings about project goals.

Both open source tools and commercial ones abound now to aid a team-based approach to humanities research. Web conferencing and collaborative software or "groupware"—wikis, project management systems, Google Docs, and so on[9]—make collaboration more convenient than in the past, though they of course by no means relieve project directors of the need to coordinate collaboration, nor do they guarantee success. It is crucial for multi-institutional digital projects to develop a well-documented work flow, project-specific guidelines, and a system for communication. At the same time, scholars must be open to the revision of these systems, as new needs, ideas, and technologies emerge.

Collaborating with Librarians and Archivists

Librarians and archivists often control the source material scholars wish to work with, and their cooperation is critical if a project is to be preserved. Far more than humanities scholars, librarians and archivists have enthusiastically embraced digital scholarship, and they have often led in instituting guidelines for best practice. At some research institutions, librarians and archivists have full faculty status, and (speaking from my own experience with the *Whitman Archive*) there is much to be gained from striving to view a digital project from the perspective of library faculty so that mutual interests can be identified and collaborations forged.

Print-based scholars usually give little thought to the question of long-term preservation, and justifiably so, because that issue is already adequately addressed by the existing production system. The same is not true for digital scholars, however, who need to engage with librarians from the start. Print scholars recognize the value of acid-free paper and assume that any reputable book will be printed on good stock. They can take for granted that their work will last well into the future, and they do not question, much less help build, the system that lodges their books on the shelves of hundreds of climate-controlled libraries whose mission is to guarantee the life of the text for hundreds of years. In contrast, systems for the long-term preservation of digital scholarship require much more thought, both from the scholars who create the work and from the librarians and archivists who are charged with preserving (and sometimes distributing) it. Long accustomed to stable and finished products, librarians now face the challenge of preserving fluid, evolving, open-ended work.

Even with the elaborate efforts that have gone into undertakings such as the implementation strategies for preservation metadata of PREMIS and the digital content management system FEDORA,[10] some fundamental questions concerning long-term preservation of digital content remain unanswered. Scholars working alone and in idiosyncratic fashion—rather than collaboratively and in accord with international standards—are at high risk of having their work lost forever. Projects following international standards can certainly hope and perhaps expect that their core data will be preserved, but even the most circumspect digital scholar cannot assume that every facet of his or her work will endure; the look, feel, and behavior of existing Web pages, for example, depend on current browser capabilities and other factors and are far less likely to survive into the future than the files of which a work is composed. The challenges of preserving digital work (and migrating material as standards evolve) are enormous, and despite the progress made thus far, the long-term sustainability of the cultural record of our time remains in doubt. Creators of digital projects need to be in dialogue with librarians now about digital curation, both so that scholarship is created in forms that give librarians the best chance for collecting and preserving work and so that practices for doing so are developed with the needs of scholars in mind.

The challenges and rewards of scholar-librarian collaboration are illustrated by a recent grant-funded project of the *Walt Whitman Archive.* In that work, we have explored the promise of the Metadata Encoding and Transmission Standard (METS) as a means to coordinate and advance interoperability of metadata standards (TEI, EAD, TIFF, and MODS).[11]

Our experiment with METS sought to develop relationships between the *Whitman Archive* and librarians as well as to further conversation about possibilities for incorporating the content of the *Whitman Archive* into library systems for long-term preservation. Members of the multi-institutional research team—including faculty from CDRH, Columbia University, Brown University, and the University of Virginia—developed METS Profiles and METS instance records[12] for representative objects and tested the use of METS to manage the submission and retrieval of diverse collection materials in two different digital library catalogs, one at Brown and the other at Virginia. At the beginning of our undertaking, no project had developed a METS Profile for digital thematic research collections, nor had there been a demonstration of the effectiveness of METS as an ingestion tool for such collections.[13]

In part, the successful integration of digital thematic research collections into libraries hinges on how we conceive of these collections and on how they might be later repurposed. Such collections combine a comprehensive approach to content with a nontrivial element of scholarly shaping. They represent a perspective, an argument, a theme. This raises several important issues: To what extent can these intentions be discovered and reconstructed after the collection is cataloged by a library? How do these intentions affect the ingestion and retrieval processes? If a library wishes to archive or ingest the scholarly or interpretative dimension of a collection, is that dimension represented in the data and metadata alone, or is it instantiated as well through interface choices and features?[14] In the approaches to ingestion developed during the course of the METS project, Brown University attempted to preserve the look and feel of the *Walt Whitman Archive*'s digital objects, and the University of Virginia did not, the latter opting instead to preserve the atomized content only. For the *Whitman Archive,* the shaping and contextualizing of the data is key (rather than the mere delivery of the data itself), so the Brown approach has much to recommend it, despite the formidable difficulties associated with it.

Libraries are large systems that need authority, control, uniformity, and predictability, whereas digital research thrives on experimentation, expanding boundaries, and taking chances. These two cultures can work together, but there are some tensions inherent in the situation. One overlap for the two is in the need to follow standards of metadata, and there are research opportunities for librarians and literary scholars in this area.

Collaborating with Presses

Partnering with a university press can give a scholar access to a prestigious imprimatur and to expertise in design, quality control, advertising, and rights management. Currently, digital work coming out of university presses has a better chance of being reviewed than does other digital work, even that associated with a center, and it also has a better chance of being collected by libraries. Nonetheless, a collaboration with a university press ordinarily carries with it a key disadvantage, too. Presses are based on a model of cost recovery and usually cannot afford to make material openly accessible.

Some collaborations between presses and digital projects exist, however. The University of Virginia's Rotunda project is an important experiment, thus far partially successful. It has been most notable in reworking print editions of the Founding Fathers, making them now available online via subscription. Aggregating these volumes and making them cross-searchable is a big achievement. The likely impact of Rotunda's work with nineteenth-century American literary texts is less clear because of problems involving scale and pricing. It is expensive to buy a subscription to Rotunda, especially since ongoing maintenance fees are also required. Libraries will find it easier to justify this purchase for a project involving the Founding Fathers, given both the historical importance and the impressive mass of material that has been aggregated: in this case, the searchable whole is more valuable than the sum of its parts. For various reasons, Rotunda does not offer a similarly vast collection of nineteenth-century texts, though it has published several important digital editions of nineteenth-century American writers. With the coherence and functionality reduced, the justification for making the purchase seems less compelling. The model of restricted access also limits the audience at a time when many scholars are drawn to digital humanities partly by the promise of reaching more people than ever before.

Some work emerging from the university press community is consistent with open access. The University of Iowa Press, for example, has cooperated with the *Whitman Archive* in making copyrighted material freely available. Other publishers—the University of North Carolina Press, the University of Nebraska Press, and Blackwell Publishing—have also granted the *Whitman Archive* permission to make available the full texts of critical books. The amount of active collaboration in these arrangements is minimal, but that scholars are retaining online rights and that presses are granting those rights are steps in the right direction.

Collaborating with Graduate Students

Frequently, major digital projects provide graduate research assistants with real responsibilities and opportunities that far exceed those given to assistants on print-based projects. Graduate students sometimes grasp digital humanities more quickly than their faculty advisers and can thus take leadership roles earlier on a digital project than in a print environment. Indeed, most of the key players in digital humanities grew up in something like an apprenticeship system: they learned through doing and by being thrown into the ongoing labor of a project. In addition to this learning by doing, graduate students working on major digital projects can find themselves in immediate contact with a number of high-profile scholars in their fields, and these contacts are vital at the beginning of a career. For the project, the benefits of working with graduate students can be profound, since they are often creative and resourceful. But can we, in good conscience, train graduate students for a field that has an uneasy acceptance? Can we hope that we are developing leaders and pioneers in a field on an upward arc?

I believe that the answer to both of these questions is yes, but the key is to model for students the passionate pursuit of literary research questions; that development of scholarly passion, rather than mastery of one particular technology or another, is imperative. If graduate students are trained first to be excellent scholars, they will adopt the means necessary to answer their questions. Talented scholars have always been resourceful in drawing on the most expansive collection of materials possible and putting the best tools to work to achieve the desired ends. Increasingly, these means require technical approaches and innovation. Therefore, at the University of Nebraska–Lincoln, we supplement research assistantships and a learning-by-doing approach with coursework in digital humanities. In these courses, an expert introduces the students to some of the questions they could ask in their own digital scholarship.

But is it wise to encourage graduate students to begin their own digital projects when a monograph remains the professional gold standard? What does the career path of a digital humanist look like? The field is sufficiently new, flexible, and interdisciplinary that there is no single career path. Students who produce digital scholarship may be taking a risk, but they are also becoming more versatile, thereby increasing their career options and chance of success. With the number of literature PhDs exceeding the number of available positions, digital scholarship carries the cachet of being cutting edge, and institutions increasingly value the knowledge of graduate students working in this area. In the past, doctoral students in literary studies primarily sought jobs as professors. Graduate students trained in digital scholarship can continue to compete for those jobs but are also able to pursue jobs in libraries, digital centers, and publishing houses. Several students associated with the *Whitman Archive*, for example, have gained full-time employment as IT professionals; several other students have gained faculty appointments in libraries, digital centers, and English departments. Despite these and other success stories, digital literary scholarship is nascent enough that we must continue to work to improve its place in the academy and to increase the prospects for the next generation of scholars.

Collaborating with Computer Science Specialists

Thus far, my focus has been on humanists who have interests in technology. Another important collaboration, however, is that between humanists and computer scientists. The structure of U.S. universities usually separates humanists and computer scientists, with the latter often lodged in engineering schools. At the University of Nebraska–Lincoln, we have a fortunate and unusual situation in that the computer science department reports to both the dean of engineering and the dean of arts and sciences. The greater degree of communication between computer science and humanities faculty is starting to manifest itself in collaborative work on projects, internal and external grant support, and significant curriculum development.

What do computer scientists have to gain from collaborating with literary scholars? Humanities data is frequently fragmentary and ambiguous, and finding a way to make it tractable for computer analysis can help advance research in that field. Changes over time in the collection, digitization, archival, retrieval, dissemination, and communication mechanisms to meet the extraordinary range of human concerns and goals have further compounded the complexity of humanities data. These data are also inherently heterogeneous, with formats for humanistic information often varying for related data sets and distributed across multiple repositories at different institutions. For example, a literary scholar might wish to work with a large collection of electronic texts of poetry developed by various people according to different encoding practices. This same scholar might wish to study variants of these texts as given during poetry readings recorded in different formats at various times. To take another example, even a project such as MONK, which works with collections of texts created in various implementations of the TEI standard, has to deal with remarkably complex problems of aggregation and normalization for analysis.[15] Humanities data can have wide-ranging characteristics because of how they were generated (when, where, how, for which applications, by whom, and based on which personal biases) and the qualities of the original object from which the electronic data was created. The humanities therefore provide deeply mixed kinds of data for computer scientists. These data sets offer new opportunities for computer science professionals as they continue to explore the fundamental questions of their field—questions ranging from the study and analysis of algorithms and data structures to theories and practice of human-computer interaction. One of the advantages of such collaborations for humanists is access to expertise to help us develop new ways of exploring central interpretative questions.

Collaborating with Broad Audiences

Digital scholarship is enabled not only by the cultivation of lasting alliances with individuals and groups close at hand but also through less personal, more temporary interactions with distant—sometimes anonymous—collaborators. Peer review is a type of collaboration, and digital work rarely gets enough peer review before or after publication. For open-access sites, this is a problem primarily in terms of credibility in the academy. Tenure and promotion are tied to peer review, and without adequate review practices in place, some scholars are hesitant to invest effort in work that their colleagues may undervalue. Fortunately, scholar-directed initiatives are now under way to address this problem through organizations such as Networked Infrastructure for Nineteenth-Century Electronic Scholarship (NINES); the goal of NINES is to peer review and aggregate the best digital resources in nineteenth-century studies. One problem that may develop as NINES conducts peer review of digital scholarship is that it lacks resources to pay reviewers. This is problematic since the projects that reviewers might be asked to vet are sometimes vast and complex.

Print work requires extensive prepublication peer review because work cannot be altered once it is in print. In contrast, digital work, typically existing as work in progress, can be altered quite easily. In addition, in digital work, there is always the potential and often the reality of greater transparency; work in various stages of development is shared with scholars and with the public rather than waiting for the final product. Moreover, researchers publishing digitally can provide the full data sets on which conclusions are based, rather than merely the conclusions themselves.

If we can supplement public knowledge with what machines can do, we can begin to imagine how scholarship can advance through a dynamic interaction between automated systems, collections, and a judicious blend of the talents of ordinary users and scholars. In harnessing the potential of social computing, a key challenge is to involve an audience in the creation of content while maintaining academic rigor. The opportunities are enormous if we can utilize the interest, energy, and knowledge potential of social computing. A project like Wikipedia, though maligned at times, is also deeply impressive.[16] Many people are skeptical about public involvement in scholarly resources in the humanities, but we should remember successes in other fields. Professional astronomers, for example, certainly value the innumerable discoveries of novae, comets, supernovae, and variable stars made by amateur astronomers.[17] The value of the large amount of good information provided can, with the right checks in place, offset the potential damage of faulty information. Humanities scholars need to cultivate a greater openness as well. In this spirit, the *Whitman Archive* has made available both its encoding guidelines and Document Type Definition (the DTD establishes the grammar of the encoding). When projects make more of the process of their work transparent and available to users, others will be better able to build on and critique previous scholarship. To the extent possible, we should encourage commercial firms to make their data available for reuse. The promise of aggregating related texts—a root goal of TEI—can only be realized through greater openness.

With regard to the *Whitman Archive*, we have recently developed plans to seek user participation in addressing questions of attribution. In *Specimen Days*, Whitman mentions that he contributed to a Civil War newspaper: "During the war, the hospitals at Washington, among other means of amusement, printed a little sheet among themselves, surrounded by wounds and death, the 'Armory Square Gazette,' to which I contributed."[18] The *Armory Square Hospital Gazette* has not been adequately studied, nor have Whitman's contributions to it been identified. We are in the process of obtaining high-resolution digital scans of as many copies of this newspaper as can be located. We intend to create an interactive area at the *Whitman Archive* where the scholarly issue of attribution can be openly discussed and where various views can be aired.

As a freely available site, the *Whitman Archive* has attracted a global readership: user statistics show activity in all inhabited continents. In light of growing international interest, we have begun to refashion the *Whitman Archive* with a multilingual audience in mind. Most people first encounter Whitman in a non-English language, and if we wish to engage a world audience and also to assess, as part of our efforts, Whitman's international reception, we need to include translations and remakings of his work as it is absorbed in various cultures. This part of the *Whitman Archive,* now in the early stages of development, will depend on cultivating an array of international partnerships.

Collaborating with Machines

I began this discussion by suggesting that the collaborations that enable print scholarship have largely become invisible through familiarity and that the newness of digital scholarship tends to highlight the need for various kinds of collaboration. Even in digital scholarship, though, there is danger of taking at least one important collaborator too much for granted. We also need to think about how we collaborate with machines.

Although they are programmed by humans, who are also responsible for the creation of the data they store and process, machines can produce revealing results unforeseen by any human. The field of text analysis is a prime example. Here, the discovery of unforeseen patterns acts as a cue to further exploration (in some cases, then using very traditional techniques). For example, Tanya Clement has shown how visualizing patterns in Gertrude Stein's *The Making of Americans* has made possible new readings that were unavailable through ordinary means of analysis. Clement observes that the novel is not a "postmodern exercise in incomprehensibility"[19] but, instead, generates meaning through its patterns of repetition (the novel contains only 5,329 unique words out of its 517,207 total words). Through various types of visualization, Clement discovered two multiparagraph sections of approximately 500 words that share the same 495 words verbatim. Clement notes that "the long repeated section co-occurs in the Dalkey Archive Press 1995 edition on pages 443 and 480, respectively, making the midpoint between them page 462, which is also the exact center of this 924 page book."[20] Increasingly, a number of open source programs and applications, such as FeatureLens, are available and make scholarly collaboration with computers possible for both technical experts and nonexperts. These collaborations will undoubtedly contribute to significantly new readings of cultural texts.

Collaborating with Funding Agencies

Funding agencies are not ordinarily thought of as our collaborators, yet they are instrumental in the creation of many important projects. One point worth emphasizing is the considerable cost of large-scale digital projects. The way that most digital scholarship in American literature is funded contrasts with the way the traditional print monograph is funded. Many, if not most, scholars write and publish books without requiring support from funding agencies, but it would be next to impossible to build a project like the *Whitman Archive* without outside funds. It could be argued that a better comparison would be between the *Whitman Archive* and *The Collected Writings of Walt Whitman.* Although the *Collected Writings* did receive grant money, that project was able to proceed with far fewer infrastructure costs (e.g., no need to hire programmers and technical consultants), and the editors could reasonably hope for some cost recovery through book sales.

Recently, funding agencies—especially the National Endowment for the Humanities (NEH)—have put heightened emphasis on digital projects. Still, there are some difficulties in collaborating with funding agencies. As discussed earlier, humanities scholars and computer scientists are often separated physically and sometimes even administratively in U.S. universities (i.e., they are often in different colleges and report to different deans), and this split also manifests itself in the structure of the major funding agencies in the United States. NEH funds humanities projects, and the National Science Foundation (NSF) funds science projects; only in rare instances, such as Documenting Endangered Languages, is a program sponsored by both agencies.[21] (This split is in contrast to the Deutsche Forschungsgemeinschaft [German Research Foundation], which spans the interests of NEH and NSF in the United States.) It would be wise for both university administrators and funding agencies to promote interdisciplinary collaboration through grant opportunities to foster work that crosses traditional boundaries. Vital questions for digital humanists often reside at those border areas where computer science and the traditional humanities disciplines overlap. To secure funding that will allow for work by both humanists and computer scientists, principal investigators need to find those questions that exist at the intersection of the two fields and that will advance both.

Conclusion

This essay has sometimes emphasized problems because the "debugging" stage is crucial to the vitality of digital humanities. Tenure and promotion committees have a notoriously difficult time in the humanities with multiauthored projects (characteristic of digital humanities projects). Multiple authorship should not be more difficult for us to handle than it is for our colleagues in other fields where it is more common. As digital humanists, we need to be able to articulate the merits of collaboration, address the current shortcomings in our collaborative models so that our research and scholarship are intellectually sound and able to be preserved, and better understand and discuss how the technical "details" of this new scholarship are inextricably linked to major theoretical discussions, arguments, and interpretative acts.

Notes

1. Tim O'Reilly, "What Is Web 2.0[?]: Design Patterns and Business Models for the Next Generation of Software," http://www.oreillynet.com/pub/a/oreilly/tim/news/2005/09/30/what-is-web-20.html; Cathy N. Davidson, "Humanities 2.0: Promise, Perils, Predictions," *PMLA* 123, no. 3 (May 2008): 707–17; Peter Brantley of the California Digital Library organized a "Reading 2.0" conference in March 2006. I would like to thank the volume editors and Brett Barney, Matt Cohen, Elizabeth Lorang, Daniel Pitti, Yelizaveta Renfro, and Katherine Walter for helpful comments on this essay in draft form.

2. John Unsworth, "Documenting the Reinvention of Text: The Importance of Failure," *Journal of Electronic Publishing* 3, no. 2 (December 1997), available at http://quod.lib.umich.edu/cgi/t/text/text-idx?c=jep;view=text;rgn=main;idno=3336451.0003.201.

3. See http://www.iath.virginia.edu/; http://mith.umd.edu/; http://cdrh.unl.edu/.

4. The Paterson Free Public Library loaned the CDRH at the University of Nebraska–Lincoln what may be the only full run of the *New York Aurora*. The *Whitman Archive* made high-quality digital scans of one full year (November 1841 to November 1842) when Whitman was editor of the newspaper (for about six months of the year). We kept a copy of the scans for our use and provided a copy to the Paterson library as well.

5. For a broad overview discussing these centers, see Diane Zorich, *A Survey of Digital Humanities Centers in the United States* (Washington, DC: Council on Library and Information Resources, 2008), available at http://www.uvasci.org/current-institute/readings/dhc-survey-final-report-2008/.

6. See http://www.documentscompass.org/.

7. It should be acknowledged that there are potential disciplinary differences when considering the question of intellectual quality in digital resources. More specifically, the imperatives of historians developing documentary archives are not fully in step with those of literary scholars. For better or worse, the whole humanities/social sciences split might shape or be reinforced by entities like Documents Compass.

8. As those of us working on the *Whitman Archive* have discovered in the process of editing Whitman's poetry manuscripts, even an encoding standard as well-developed as the Text Encoding Initiative (TEI) does not come "preassembled" to address all of the features that a particular project sees as important. In fact, TEI frequently offers multiple alternatives for handling a given textual feature, and the better the editorial staff understands the subtleties of these alternatives, the better the likelihood that the resulting encoding will reflect their editorial perspective and goals. See http://www.tei-c.org/.

9. For a list of collaborative software applications, see http://en.wikipedia.org/wiki/List_of_collaborative_software.

10. See http://www.loc.gov/standards/premis/; http://www.fedora.info.

11. For Encoded Archival Description (EAD), see http://www.loc.gov/ead/. Tagged Image File Format (TIFF) is a widely supported file format for storing bit-mapped images. For the Metadata Object Description Schema (MODS), see http://www.loc.gov/standards/mods/.

12. In the METS standard, each digital object is represented by an instance record that organizes all of the metadata associated with that object. The METS board also maintains a registry of implementers, and those wishing to be included are required to submit a profile that describes in detail how their project has implemented the standard.

13. For more information on this project, go to http://cdrh.unl.edu/projects/pages/interoperability_metadata.php.

14. My articulation of these ideas is indebted to various remarks made by Julia Flanders in the course of our work on the Institute of Museum and Library Services grant exploring METS and the interoperability of metadata.

15. For information on MONK (Metadata Offer New Knowledge), see http://monkproject.org/.

16. Despite some well-documented problems, the range and accuracy of Wikipedia should not be discounted. See Roy Rosenzweig, "Can History Be Open Source? Wikipedia and the Future of the Past" (June 2006), http://chnm.gmu.edu/resources/essays/.

17. See, e.g., http://astronomy.swin.edu.au/sao/prospective/FAQ.xml.

18. Whitman, *Specimen Days,* in *Prose Works 1892,* ed. Floyd Stovall (New York: New York University Press, 1963), 1:288.

19. Tanya Clement, "'A thing not beginning and not ending': Using Digital Tools to Distant-Read Gertrude Stein's *The Making of Americans,*" *Literary and Linguistic Computing* 23, no. 3 (2008): 362.

20. Clement, "'A thing not beginning and not ending,'" 367.

21. Another example of cross-agency collaboration is a recent call for proposals for the "Digging into Data Challenge." In this case, the U.S. NEH and NSF are joining forces with the Joint Information Systems Committee of the United Kingdom and the Social Sciences and Humanities Research Council of Canada to encourage scholars to address the question "What do you do with a million books? Or a million pages of newspapers?" (e-mail correspondence from Brett Bobley, 16 January 2009).

Challenging Gaps: Redesigning Collaboration in the Digital Humanities

AMY E. EARHART

In 2008, Texas A&M University, like many universities in the United States, began to draft an academic master plan that sets long-range goals for research, teaching, and service and makes explicit that our scholarly production addresses the "grand challenges of society." A key criterion for gaining a place in the master plan is to demonstrate that a project or subject area displays collaboration across departments and colleges. As the Department of English prepared a written response to this challenge, I sat in meeting after meeting listening to humanities colleagues rehash the following points: (1) humanities work is undervalued by university administration and the larger society; (2) because our work is undervalued, we are not rewarded in the same way as science, business, or engineering faculty; and (3) our interdisciplinary scholarship should count as "working across departments and colleges," even when the work is conducted individually. While these complaints are not new, thinking through the issues clarifies a broader problem with humanities scholarship production. Instead of viewing such tensions as only interdisciplinary—humanities versus science—I realized that the tension was also intradisciplinary; those of us that work with digital humanities in traditional humanities departments are well aware of the resistance to collaboration or, more pointedly, the resistance of humanities academic reward structures to collaboration. Perhaps most important, I recognized that to engage with the issue of collaboration, the concept might need to be handled as a separate entity, removed from either interdisciplinarity or intradisciplinarity.

The blurring of interdisciplinarity with collaboration is one of the reasons we have not made greater strides toward reenvisioning collaboration in humanities scholarship. I want to separate these terms so that we might concentrate on collaboration without the shadow of interdisciplinarity, for a number of reasons. Chief among them is my belief that, as Cathy Davidson and David Theo Goldberg propose, interdisciplinarity has arrived.[1] While we can list multiple ways that interdisciplinarity has become accepted in the humanities—from MLA papers and sessions, job advertisements, scholarly publications, and the many humanities centers on campuses across the country—collaboration has not had the same impact. Davidson and Goldberg argue that "although humanists, for example, often engage in multiauthor, multidisciplinary projects (such as collaborative histories, anthologies, and encyclopedias) with the potential to change fields, universities and their faculties have been slow to conceive of new institutional structures and reward systems (tenure, promotion, etc.) for those who favor interdisciplinary or collaborative work."[2] This statement, however, suggests that multiauthorship and multidisciplinarity are equivalent. Instead, we must tease apart the two practices if we want to effectively engage them, particularly as the resistance to interdisciplinarity within the humanities seems to be fading. Collaboration continues to challenge disciplinary structures, and most tenure and promotion committees continue to look on collaboration as time diverted from "real" (individual) academic work. In response to this problem, the MLA Task Force on Evaluating Scholarship for Tenure and Promotion has called for the development of "a system of evaluation for collaborative work that is appropriate to research in the humanities and that resolves questions of credit in our discipline as in others,"[3] an admirable task, but one that appears to be a long-term goal rather than an immediate solution.

Numerous critics have directed our attention to the paradoxical emphasis on individual intellectual activity in the humanities. In "Collaboration and Concepts of Authorship," Lisa Ede and Andrea Lunsford examine the contradiction by pointing out that our reliance on the single author runs counter to the last quarter decade or so of critical theory: "The ideologies of the academy take the autonomy of the individual—and of the author—for granted. And they do so in ways that encourage scholars not to notice potential contradictions between, say, poststructural and postmodern critiques of originality and the academy's traditional injunction that a PhD dissertation must represent an original contribution to a discipline. In Pierre Bourdieu's terms, the result is a naturalization of contradictions that makes them appear not as contradiction but rather as cultural or disciplinary common sense."[4] A similar caution must be applied to modeling digital humanities collaboration. In structuring digital humanities projects, we tend to normalize collaboration and erase disciplinary difference, regardless of the very real collaborative problems many digital humanities practitioners report.[5]

Scholarship in the field, such as the important volume *A Companion to Digital Humanities,* tends to reenforce a representation of collaboration as stable and normative. The *Companion* devotes an entire section to the history of digital humanities, which it divides into the following fields: archaeology, art history, classics, history, lexicography, linguistics, literary studies, music, multimedia, performing arts, philosophy, and religion. Yet the structure of the *Companion* replicates the tension between interdisciplinarity and collaboration that I have pointed to in the larger humanities. Throughout the remaining sections of the book—titled "Principles," "Application," "Production," "Dissemination," and "Archiving"—an explicit discussion of collaboration is suspiciously absent, suggesting that we have achieved a working model of collaboration and that the various field divisions have learned effective methods of partnership. But the very organizing principle of the volume suggests the separateness of the disciplines; the disciplines are distinct, with little cross-border work that changes the original structures and practices of the particular field. The book's lone discussion about collaboration is found in Daniel V. Pitti's helpful essay "Designing Sustainable Projects and Publications," which situates collaboration as a piece of project management.[6] While the volume does show an awareness of collaboration and represents it as intrinsic to the work of digital humanities, the lack of explicit attention to the ways in which collaboration might occur and the barriers to collaboration within the humanities suggest that collaboration is a problem solved, rather than the looming issue it remains.

If we separate the issue of collaboration from interdisciplinarity, we are able to refocus our efforts on the successful development of collaborative models within the digital humanities. While critics such as Ede and Lunsford argue that certain areas in literary studies, such as rhetoric, writing, and composition, have begun to work collaboratively, the areas that continue to wield the most power, such as theory, remain focused on individual intellectual work. We might extend this model to other humanities fields, such as history and philosophy, where subfields that work collaboratively are resisted by those that hold the power within the greater discipline. Digital humanities should answer Ede and Lunsford's call to "make space for—and even encourage—collaborative projects in the humanities,"[7] as the large, project-based work of digital humanities necessitates a team of contributors. But Ede and Lunsford caution that in the rush to work collaboratively, we need to think about how ownership occurs and to be cautious that both work and rewards are evenly distributed.[8]

Anecdotal evidence points to unresolved tension in project collaboration. For example, at the "Digital Textual Studies, Past, Present, and Future" symposium held at Texas A&M University, Peter Robinson quipped that one approach to project development was to hire "trained experts," technologists who are able to work with humanist digital projects. At the same meeting, our special collections librarian, Steve Smith, joked that he was "only a librarian" but had some thoughts about digital humanities. While these comments were made as jokes in informal moments, they do suggest that there remains tension in the way that the varying participants think about their roles within project structures. As Kenneth Price argues in chapter 1 to this volume, the "details" of technology required for digital production are actually intimately entwined in the implications of technology decisions and rightly belong to all involved with a project. "Offshoring" technology work to trained experts creates a false dichotomy that will ultimately damage the scholarly worth of the materials that are produced. If we are to successfully develop projects, we must rethink our participants' interaction by creating models that reward exemplary joint project work. For a humanist, a paper with more than one author could be disregarded in the promotion process, particularly in fields such as history and english, whereas the opposite might occur for technologists housed in academic departments. As Julia Flanders stated in 2000, digital humanities work is "not part of the recognized practices of the standard disciplines; in fact, in some cases your discipline will disown you for undertaking this kind of work, and certainly won't grant you tenure for doing it."[9] While the resistance to digital work has changed since Flanders's 2000 talk, as evidenced by the increasing number of academic organizations recognizing digital humanities and the rising number of jobs in the field, traditionalists in the humanities continue to resist the work in part because of their resistance to collaborative scholarship.

In the search for viable forms of collaboration, some scholars have posited the use of a science laboratory model. "Labs are built around the process of discovery," writes Cathy Davidson, "and discovery is rooted in the practice of what is already known (past experiments, lab technique). A lab supports work that is new, and it concomitantly requires collaboration across fields and disciplinary subfields, as well as across generations."[10] While this is true in many labs, it is important not to romanticize the lab. Yes, research is shared across generations, but hierarchies are still in place. Linda and Michael Hutcheon agree that laboratory science provides a possible model of collaboration, but they remain cautious of adopting the model wholesale, as there is a "hierarchy implicit in that model," with its "stratified division of technical and intellectual labor."[11] As Ede and Lunsford remind us, "The sciences have a poor record of including women and members of minorities—or their perspectives—in research."[12] So, while we might look to the laboratory as a model, we need to be critical about its implementation in our field.

Where we might best utilize the lab model is as a created space "where no solitary thinker—no matter how brilliant or creative—could think through a complex problem as comprehensively as a group of thinkers from different fields, with different areas of expertise, different disciplinary training and biases, and from different intellectual generations."[13] I want to turn to the example of the *Walt Whitman Archive* (http://www.whitmanarchive.org) to clarify this point. The *Whitman Archive* is "an electronic research and teaching tool that sets out to make Whitman's vast work, for the first time, easily and conveniently accessible to scholars, students, and general reader."[14] While the *Whitman Archive*'s modest goals focus on providing scholarly materials, much like a print edition, the project has produced much more: (1) digital objects, (2) collaborative thinking from which scholarship emerges, (3) collaborative writing about the archive and archive production, (4) a new generation of digital humanities scholars, and (5) digital humanities tools and techniques. Those involved with the archive have treated the project as a laboratory in which to generate collaborative scholarship and to train future scholars. These outcomes are evident in the variety of individual and collaborative written documents published by those associated with the archive and the numerous tools and techniques that have been replicated in other digital projects.[15]

Nancy Nersessian's conceptualization of the research laboratory—as "not simply a physical space existing in the present, but rather a dynamic problem space, constrained by the research program of the laboratory director, that reconfigures itself as the research program moves along in time and takes new directions in response to what occurs both in the laboratory and in the wider community of which the research is a part"—might well describe the *Whitman Archive.*[16] The *Whitman Archive*'s longevity and continued relevance, in a rapidly changing field, reveals that codirectors Ed Folsom and Kenneth Price do indeed understand that the archive needs to respond to the evolving technologies and techniques that might be applied to digital materials, whether the transition from SGML to TEI, their ever-revised project interface, or the more recent spin-off, the map-based approach to Washington, DC, during the Civil War. A look through the *Whitman Archive* collaborators list suggests the number of scholars trained by the "Whitman lab." Scholars affiliated with the archive extend across generations (endowed chairs to undergraduate students), disciplines (humanities scholars, librarians, and technologists), and universities (the University of Iowa, the University of Nebraska–Lincoln, the University of Texas, Yeshiva University, Kent State University, the University of North Carolina at Chapel Hill, the University of Virginia, and the University of Georgia, among others). The *Whitman Archive* is indeed a formative laboratory, as it has expanded what might have remained a traditional humanities scholarly project to form a space for collaborative work that breaks disciplinary barriers so often imposed on humanities work. In effect, the Whitman lab is able to displace discipline by focusing on collaboration.

Considering digital humanities collaboration from the vantage point of a laboratory model allows us to examine one of the trickiest pieces of project development: money. Much as a science lab requires financial assistance, so do digital humanities projects. Kenneth Price has noted of "free" digital humanities materials, "When users visit a deep scholarly archive on the web they are experiencing the (mostly real) benefit of displaced costs."[17] Yet we have made very little headway into changing the infrastructure of humanities departments to support such work, to effectively model how we might move large numbers of digital projects from conception to prototype to evolved project. Digital projects remain rare, often the product of tenacious participants rather than a supportive academic environment. In the laboratory model, the science lab is often institutionally financed at start-up. Tying a new position to base funding allows scientists to purchase equipment and fund personnel necessary to the development of a project prototype that can then be used to secure external funds. This model has not made headway in the digital humanities, where we have, instead, relied on centers to funnel institutional support to select projects. Centers serve as valuable, even indispensable, resources for digital humanities project work, often providing funds, skills, and equipment that nurture projects. The center model has been very successful at a select number of institutions, but many others have resisted the model, arguing that the cost of such an entity is not justified. In part, the resistance comes from the lack of funds traditionally generated by humanities scholars. Since humanities scholars do not usually receive major research grants, the outlay of initial start-up expenditures for humanities work has often been considered a secondary priority to those disciplines that generate large external grants that often pay for a large percentage of universities' operating budgets.[18]

While those who work with a digital humanities center are fully aware of how crucial such an entity is for project generation, there is another possibility for scholars at institutions without centers. Jonathan Arac has argued that collaborative work within the humanities is best achieved through "distinctive intellectual projects,"[19] another possible route to successful project generation. Here we might return to the start-up model that is popular in sciences. Many science and engineering faculty come to institutions that do not have a center of expertise in their area. To fund their research, they often combine start-up funds with collaborative work to generate scholarship. By cabling together equipment and expertise, science and engineering faculty are able to develop models that allow them to achieve additional external funding. Regardless of the adopted model, digital humanities is not a free venture, and in order to produce successful projects, institutions must provide some form of funding or support.

While the laboratory might be transformed into a working model for digital humanities, those trained in the humanities approach scholarship in a markedly different manner than those trained in the sciences. Pitti states in his discussion of collaboration, "Given the dual expertise required [for digital humanities projects], scholars frequently find it necessary to collaborate with technologists in the design and implementation processes, who bring different understandings, experiences, and expertise to the work. Collaboration in and of itself may present challenges, since most humanists generally work alone and share the research's results, not the process."[20] Project partnerships often run into problems that boil down to differing opinions on the position of product or process to the project outcome. Humanists often focus on their immediate goals—"Let's mark up and put up X text"—while technologists are interested in developing new applications. Humanists tend to value the object and want to quickly master the technology necessary for putting the materials on the Web, while technologists tend to value the manipulations of the text. To technologists, the process and the failure may also produce interesting results or, at the very least, information that might be written up for publication, if in academia, or shared on preferred programmatic sites to gain reputation among peers, if a technologist. Obviously, there are individuals that are able to easily move across these boundaries, and there are projects that blur such distinctions, but when fields meet in digital humanities, the conflicts between project outcomes can quickly spiral into dissent, especially when project participants' goals are impacted by disciplinary reward structures. Some digital humanists, such as John Unsworth in his article subtitled "The Importance of Failure," locate process as key to the discipline of digital humanities. As Unsworth bluntly writes, "If an electronic scholarly project can't fail and doesn't produce new ignorance, then it isn't worth a damn."[21] Unsworth's charge reminds humanists working in the digital humanities of the value of experimentation and that we might challenge existing reward structures by producing scholarship, as broadly defined, in venues that best reward the participant, at each stage of the digital humanities project.

Concerns about collaboration within the digital humanities field are broad and difficult, and the approaches to solving such issues are amorphous, but I would like to suggest several ways that we might revise a model of collaboration. Most academic digital humanities projects involve three different groups: humanists, librarians, and technologists. There is no doubt that this working model has served our field, but we have not fully explored how other structures might benefit those who are not able to work with an academic support partnership. What if we restructure our groups to look both inside and outside of academia? Might we continue to maintain academic standards while incorporating external business interests and museums/libraries?

The participants in the *19th-Century Concord Digital Archive* (*CDA*) have begun to explore how such interactions might change the way that we envision the digital objects produced within academic projects.[22] While the archive is still in its infancy, early work suggests that the project will benefit from the tensions created by the varying participants' goals. The *CDA* is constructed as a shared space that gathers metadata and edited materials from the project group at Texas A&M University and visual materials housed at the Concord Free Public Library (CFPL). Many of the documents that are projected for archive inclusion are owned by the Concord Free Public Library Corporation. The William Munroe Special Collections of the CFPL is the primary archive of Concord history, life, landscape, literature, and people from 1635 to the present and, as such, is a major repository and interpretive agency. By linking the two entities in partnership, users will have integrated access to digital representations of the physical document (CFPL) and the technologically constructed, scholarly edited texts and user interfaces that allow interpretative scholarship (*CDA*). The edited texts housed in the *CDA* will be supplemented by the images housed on the CFPL Web site. This partnership allows the library to retain control of the digital images (important to funding and library restrictions), the user to gain access to original images, and the publication of an edited, searchable, interactive transcription on the *CDA*. In addition, the *CDA* will add metadata to materials currently held on the CFPL site, allowing the materials to be searchable with *CDA* interfaces and expanding the numbers of materials referenced by the site. While this approach allows a larger body of materials to be brought into the *CDA* and a more complete site for scholarly use, it does present tensions. Each object slated for inclusion requires negotiation and shared information. Communication is crucial for the success of the project, and we have participated in numerous meetings, phone calls, and e-mails to ensure that all parties are happy with the site development. But the continued negotiation has already proved to make the project smarter and stronger, with participants continually redefining and refining their understanding of the site and the materials that occupy it. This approach to project management represents a way in which scholars might gain access to primary materials while allowing museums to harness technical and scholarly expertise and, in the end, create a project that is stronger than one produced in isolation.

The other external partnership that digital humanities practitioners have not fully explored is the open source community. Funding agencies such as the National Endowment for the Humanities (NEH) and the Arts and Humanities Research Council (AHRC) have stated that the open source approach[23] to digital humanities work is necessary for both short-term financial support of projects and long-term success of digital humanities work. For example, the guidelines for NEH's Digital Humanities Start-Up grants includes the statement "NEH views the use of open-source software as a key component in the broad distribution of exemplary digital scholarship in the humanities."[24] AHRC's "Open Source Critical Editions" workshop asked its participants to explore "the possibilities, requirements for, and repercussions of a new generation of digital critical editions of Greek and Latin texts with underlying code made available under an open license such as Creative Commons or GPL."[25] However, both agencies have predominantly emphasized open archives and opening the internal code built for the project rather than asking scholars to consider the possibilities offered by tapping into externally produced open source software.

Even less attention has been given to structuring projects to invite participation *from* the open source development community. There are sterling examples of groups that have modeled open source methodologies in digital humanities, including the Text Encoding Initiative (TEI) movement, which has worked to standardize an XML appropriate to humanities projects, and NINES (the Networked Infrastructure for Nineteenth-Century Electronic Scholarship), currently developing open source tools for use by the broader community. Collex, a collections and exhibits tool of NINES, is open source and uses open source programs and models. According to Bethany Nowviskie, its creator, Collex is based on social networking models like Connotea and del.icio.us and other academic projects, such as MIT's SIMILE.[26] Further, the development of the software utilized the open source softwares Ruby on Rails and Solr, both of which have active development communities. Collex is available for developers on Subversion, a centralized site for sharing code and intended to develop participation from the developer community, which may lead to increased participation in the project. NINES is modeling the project on a standard open source approach: if you put the code out there, the developers will follow. The projects of NINES have become visible in the developer world, in part due to the participation of Erik Hatcher, a former employee of NINES and well known in the open source community for his work with Lucene. But is there a way in which we might model our projects that would further entice developers to participate in the project?

The BBC's Backstage movement (with the slogan "Use Our Stuff to Build Your Stuff") asks a (free) developer community to produce vast numbers of ideas and prototypes based on existing content feeds and open source software.[27] The noncommercial Backstage project "attempts to encourage and support those who have provided most of the innovation on the internet—the passionate, highly-skilled & public-spirited developers and designers many of whom volunteer their time and effort."[28] Interested developers are given the BBC content feeds as raw data and encouraged to share ideas and experimental prototypes through the Backstage Web site. A scan of the prototypes posted on the site indicates an interest in mapping, data mining, social networking, and visualization, among other topics. The models produced suggest that if digital humanities projects can leverage materials as raw data to an interested developer community, we might also benefit from such experimentation. Given the difficulty of finding and funding technologists for our projects, this should be a model that we consider. Further, the quality of the work on the Backstage site suggests that if digital humanists are willing to cede some control of their materials, surprising results that may benefit scholarship could occur.

Richard Miller's notion of boundary objects—where collaboration works through "an artifact that sits in the interface between two or more groups, and is a piece of shared knowledge and understanding"[29]—conceptualizes such an approach. An information scientist, Miller lists the following properties for boundary objects:

1. Must be coinvented
2. Should be developed in neutral territory
3. Should have a reasonable life
4. Must give a real use and meaning for all in the participating group

A project based on distributed expertise, where all participants have something to add, is appealing, but the challenge will be to build an object in the gap on which to hang the project. We know that projects need to have support from multiple participants to be generated; most humanists do not have the technological background to set up and run a project, nor do technologists have the editorial practice and content knowledge to deal with the humanities materials. The easy solution is to hire someone to get the project finished (a technologist), which allows the humanist to move on to the use of the digital materials. But this model limits the innovation that might occur in the project and encourages the project participants to work at cross-purposes as outcomes are not shared. It is far better to hash through the issues with equal players—with librarians who understand humanities and technology; humanists who understand the role of the library and technology; and technologists who are, at heart, humanists. It is in the action of the conflict, the negotiation and renegotiation, that the real work of shaping the project occurs and, of course, challenges Miller's positioning of the shared space as neutral.

Development of a project model that denotes boundary objects provides a way to allow a group to work around some of the conflicts that occur during project development. Many digital humanities projects are coinvented, but it remains difficult to create real use and meaning for all in the participating group. Developing a shared territory, whether disciplinary or spatial, could be a successful strategy for fostering equal participation and creation of a stronger project that benefits from the shared expertise of all partners. In the case of the *19th-Century Concord Digital Archive,* our Web site (http://www.digitalconcord.org) functions as our shared space. The jointly created site allows both partners to develop pieces of the project independently and to use the digital space as a place of interaction—a third space, if you will—between an academic entity and a library. The space forces the partners to produce materials that work toward a common outcome, while allowing individuals their separate sites in which to complete work that does not meet a common goal, always reminding participants of the intertwined nature of the project and participants. While the tensions between multiple partners could fragment a project, careful and constant negotiations of the project parameters—in effect, a smartly designed infrastructure—should produce a digital object or objects that meet shared outcomes. This model is apparent in other projects, including Collex, which gathers the metadata from numerous sites into a site that provides aggregated searching and collecting of the individual digital objects. These models suggest that digital humanities should more fully consider how to leverage the structured data that TEI and databases provide. Once the materials in the project are properly structured, multiple versions and uses of the materials might occur.

Instead of focusing on the particular site or project, digital humanities must begin to see multiple, interoperable uses of the data.

Gaps in project partnership might be solved with the development of shared knowledge of technologies and discipline to allow for more coherent project planning. I am not suggesting that all parties must have equivalent skills. Instead, those involved in a project must be able to understand the theory and practice of partners' disciplines so that all participants might shape the projects on which they work. I have sat in many meetings where humanists make comments like "Well, I wouldn't want to program—I mean why be able to do that?" or "Look, I just want to put up the texts. Don't ask me about the back end." While I understand where these comments come from—humanists are not trained to program, to mark up, to design databases—that does not excuse humanists from informed knowledge of the workings of their projects. It might be easy to farm out technology decisions to those who "know better," but then we are not taking advantage of the possibilities contained in a distributed knowledge system, nor are we assured that the final product will meet both humanities and digital (technology) goals. With shared knowledge, we can establish dialogue that assures the project works to deliver the content in a way that meets the goals of the humanist, librarian, and technologist. Alan Liu has argued that our target must be "to integrate information technology into the work of the humanities so fully and in so entangled a manner—at once as tool, perspective, and theme—that it would seem just as redundant to add the words "'computing,' 'digital,' 'media,' or 'technology' to 'humanities' as it was previously to add 'print-based.'"[30] While complete immersion is an admirable long-term goal, retraining is very time-consuming; therefore, an immediate collaborative model that allows all participants to share a threshold of knowledge might be an excellent stopgap solution. There are existing models of such interaction. TEI/XML, fairly standard in digital humanities, encourages the successful collaboration of all players—librarian, humanist, and technologist. To successfully mark a text, you must have knowledge of your subject matter, must have the technological skills to create validating TEI/XML, and must understand that TEI/XML is useful for interoperability and preservation of your work. Without an understanding of all three of the positions—that of the humanist, the technologist, and the librarian—you will not create a successfully marked text. Skills are based on a shared language and an understanding of concepts, and most digital humanists have, indeed, mastered the use of basic TEI/XML markup. As we work to build expertise in the field, we should expect digital humanities practitioners to have basic skills and theory of the creation and use of technologies.

As we think about developing shared skills across disciplines, we should also carefully review how we are training the future of digital humanities, our graduate students. Many digital humanities practitioners have taken the traditional research assistantship positions in our fields and used them as a way to immerse students in a project, creating, in effect, an apprenticeship for graduate students. If we return to the idea of the archive as a laboratory, we effectively find bench space for graduate students. But while we often give students tasks, we are less likely to allow the student to carve out a problem that might become the capstone of their PhD work. Nersessian argues that in a science laboratory, "a new participant must first master the relevant aspects of the existing history of an artifact necessary to the research, and then figure ways to alter it to carry out her project as the new research problems demand, thereby adding to its history."[31] She suggests that the student should be more intimately involved in deciding how and where she or he might participate within a project. A laboratory model creates a different role for faculty and graduate student, one that emphasizes interdependence, shared scholarship, and exchange of ideas—a closer working relationship for faculty and graduate student than the dissertation model currently in place. Nersessian's analysis of the laboratory indicates that while we must ask students to master basic skills by giving them particular tasks, we should also give students the power to develop their own piece of a project. If graduate students create projects that live in the boundaries, that benefit all partners, then we challenge power structures to form a collaborative environment that allows all participants to participate fully in the creation of a stronger final project.

A collaborative research approach would allow digital humanities to move away from the single authored dissertation (monograph) to a project or multiple paper–based product, a scholarly product more fitting for digital humanities and potentially more publishable, given current scholarly publishing issues. But is it too soon to change these structures? Should we first focus on increasing acceptance of digital work by tenure committees? What happens to the income stream that departments raise from teaching assistants? How will we position digital humanities graduate students in relation to traditional disciplinary fields? I have no easy answers, but I do think that we need to start a conversation about these infrastructure issues if we want to grow work in digital humanities.

In 1989, R. G. Potter called for a revision of literary studies: "What we need is a principal use of technology and criticism to form a new kind of literary study absolutely comfortable with scientific methods yet completely suffused with the values of the humanities."[32] We have still not adopted a model that selects the best of the two disciplines. While collaboration between varying disciplinary partners is appropriate now, our end goal should be, as Alan Liu suggests, a discipline where digital is represented within the term *humanities.* Projects like the *Whitman Archive* are leading the way by training future scholars to collaborate physically and intellectually, but we need institutional structures that participate in the training as well. This does not mean that we should merely mimic the institutional structures that we now have in place. "In general, we must acknowledge," says Liu, "the profession of the humanities has been appallingly unimaginative in regard to the organization of its own labor, simply taking it for granted that its restructuring impulse toward 'interdisciplinarity' and 'collaboration' can be managed within the same old divisional, college, departmental, committee, and classroom arrangements supplemented by ad hoc interdisciplinary arrangements."[33] We need to work together, in the shared spaces, to develop a model of collaboration that includes all participants, of varying disciplines and rank, both in and out of academia.

Notes

1. Cathy Davidson and David Theo Goldberg, "Manifesto for the Humanities in a Technological Age," *Chronicle of Higher Education* 50, no. 23 (2004): B7.

2. Davidson and Goldberg, "Manifesto," B7.

3. MLA Task Force on Evaluating Scholarship for Tenure and Promotion, "Report of the MLA Task Force on Evaluating Scholarship for Tenure and Promotion," in *Profession 2007*, ed. Rosemary G. Feal (New York: MLA, 2007), 9–71.

4. Lisa Ede and Andrea Lunsford, "Collaboration and Concepts of Authorship," *PMLA* 116, no. 2 (2001): 354–69, at 457.

5. Ede and Lunsford posit that a disciplinary turn to collaboration does not mean that collaborative practice becomes the one structure of scholarship within the field. Rather, multiple approaches need to be supported within the academies: "We hope to encourage scholarly work that interrogates these intersections and explores how demands of theory might be reconceived so that they allow for (or at least do not so deeply and

strongly discourage) collaborative, as well as individual, projects" (Ede and Lunsford, "Collaboration," 358).

6. Daniel V. Pitti, "Designing Sustainable Projects and Publications," in *A Companion to Digital Humanities,* ed. Susan Schreibman, Ray Siemens, and John Unsworth (Malden, Oxford: Blackwell, 2004), 471–87.

7. Ede and Lunsford, "Collaboration," 363.

8. Ede and Lunsford, "Collaboration," 364.

9. Julia Flanders, "Humanities Computing" (paper presented at the MITH Roundtable, University of Maryland, 2000), available at http://www.digitalhumanities.org/view/Essays/JuliaFlandersMITHSpeakersSeries (accessed 9 February 2009).

10. Cathy N. Davidson, "What If Scholars in the Humanities Worked Together, in a Lab?" *Chronicle Review,* May 28, 1999: B4. Jonathan Arac also calls for work that is "laboratory" based; see his "Shop Window or Laboratory: Collection, Collaboration, and the Humanities," in *The Politics of Research,* ed. E. Ann Kaplan and George Levine (New Brunswick: Rutgers University Press, 1997), 116–26.

11. Linda Hutcheon and Michael Hutcheon, "A Convenience of Marriage: Collaboration and Interdisciplinarity," *PMLA* 116, no. 5 (2001): 1364–76, at 1367–68.

12. Ede and Lunsford, "Collaboration," 363.

13. Davidson, "What If Scholars in the Humanities Worked Together," B4.

14. "About the *Archive,*" *Walt Whitman Archive,* http://www.whitmanarchive.org/about/index.html (accessed 9 February 2009).

15. For a list of related materials, see http://www.whitmanarchive.org/about/articles/index.html.

16. Nancy J. Nersessian, "The Cognitive-Cultural Systems of the Research Laboratory," *Organization Studies* 27, no. 2 (2006): 125–45, at 130.

17. Kenneth M. Price, "Dollars and Sense in Collaborative Digital Scholarship: The Example of the Walt Whitman Hypertext Archive," *Documentary Editing* 23, no. 2 (2001): 29–33, at 43.

18. Digital humanities offers the humanities scholar a chance to develop external support. While the amount generated from humanities funding might never equal the funding of science or engineering fields, upper administration does notice and often reward those that generate the funding.

19. Arac, "Shop Window or Laboratory," 122.

20. Pitti, "Designing Sustainable Projects," 471.

21. John Unsworth, "Documenting the Reinvention of Text: The Importance of Failure," *Journal of Electronic Publishing* 3, no. 2 (1997), available at http://dx.doi.org/10.3998/3336451.0003.201 (accessed 9 February 2009).

22. The participants include myself, the Concord Free Public Library, lead developer James Smith, the College of Liberal Arts at Texas A&M University, and the Map Room faculty and staff of Evans Library at Texas A&M University.

23. Bruce Perens defines *open source* as follows: "1) The right to make copies of the

program, and distribute those copies. 2) The right to have access to the software's source code, a necessary preliminary before you can change it. 3) The right to make improvements to the program" ("The Open Source Definition," in *Open Sources: Voice from the Open Source Revolution*, ed. Chris DiBona, Sam Ockman, and Mark Stone [Sebastopol, CA: O'Reilly, 1999], http://oreilly.com/catalog/opensources/book/perens.html).

24. National Endowment for the Humanities, "Digital Humanities Start-Up Grants," http://www.neh.gov/grants/guidelines/digitalhumanitiesstartup.html (accessed 9 February 2009).

25. Arts and Humanities Research Council, "Open Source Critical Editions Workshop Report." http://www.methodsnetwork.ac.uk/activities/act9report.html.

26. Bethany Nowviskie, "Collex: Semantic Collections and Exhibits for the Remixable Web" (2005), http://nines.org/about/Nowviskie-Collex.pdf (accessed 9 February 2009).

27. BBC Backstage is located at http://backstage.bbc.co.uk/.

28. "Backstage.BBC.Co.Uk," http://backstage.bbc.co.uk/archives/2005/01/about.html (accessed 9 February 2009).

29. Richard Miller, "Creating Boundary Objects to Aid Knowledge Transfer," *Knowledge Management Review* 8, no. 2 (2005): 12–15, at 13.

30. Alan Liu, "The Humanities: A Technical Profession," *ACLS Occasional Paper* 63 (2004): 13–22, http://www.acls.org/op63.pdf.

31. Nersessian, "Cognitive-Cultural Systems," 133.

32. R. G. Potter, introduction to *Literary Computing and Literary Criticism: Theoretical and Practical Essays on Theme and Rhetoric*, ed. R. G. Potter (Philadelphia: University of Pennsylvania Press, 1989), xxix.

33. Liu, "Humanities," 13.

Whitman's Poems in Periodicals: Prospects for Periodicals Scholarship in the Digital Age

SUSAN BELASCO

In March 2007, the *Walt Whitman Archive* announced the addition of *Whitman's Poems in Periodicals,* a digital documentary edition of the approximately 160 poems Whitman published in 45 periodicals (both magazines and newspapers) from 1838 until his death in 1892.[1] The edition presents in electronic form the images of pages from the originals or microfilm copies and assists scholars and students in understanding another side of Whitman's career as a poet—one who constantly sought publication in the popular periodicals of his day in order to broaden his audience. *Whitman's Poems in Periodicals* also provides fresh ways of understanding Whitman's publication practices and enhances our understanding of nineteenth-century practices of reading and writing more generally. Using this new edition, scholars can examine poems as they first appeared and investigate a number of issues, including the ways in which different periodical contexts shaped Whitman's writing and publication of particular poems, the relationship between the periodical publications and the various editions of *Leaves of Grass,* his revision strategies as poems moved from manuscript to periodical to book, and Whitman's engagement with regional, national, and international audiences.

Working on *Whitman's Poems in Periodicals* in the *Whitman Archive* has provided a rare opportunity to consider the ways in which textual scholarship, periodical study, and new technologies overlap. This essay takes

Whitman's Poems in Periodicals as a case study and explores some of the challenges for periodical scholarship in a digital environment, taking up the following questions: How does a digital archive provide greater access to periodicals, and in what ways might it limit or prescribe scholarly research? Are the editors of archives artificially limiting the possibilities for periodicals research? How can scholarly digitization projects for periodicals ensure that we preserve the innate qualities of the periodical—the eclectic juxtapositions and the opportunities for serendipitous discoveries—in our research?

Even the most casual student of Walt Whitman knows that the poet extensively revised earlier poems and added new ones to *Leaves of Grass* from its first appearance in 1855 through the six American editions published during his lifetime. He was the "king of revision," as a student once wrote on an exam in my undergraduate American literature survey. Typing the word *revision* into the search engine of the bibliography in the "Criticism" section on the *Walt Whitman Archive* brings up 67 separate studies of Whitman's many approaches to revision, and a recent online exhibit at the Library of Congress is aptly titled "Revising Himself: Walt Whitman and *Leaves of Grass*."[2] For decades, scholars have studied the changes Whitman made as he reworked and expanded *Leaves of Grass,* the major project of his life. They have closely studied Whitman's attention to the details of production, his fascination with print, and the transition of his poems from manuscript to printed page.[3] With the development of the *Whitman Archive,* it is now possible to examine many of the poetry manuscripts alongside the printed texts of the poems in the editions of *Leaves of Grass.* Far less studied are the poems that Whitman published in periodicals throughout his life. In fact, his relationship with periodical editors and readers began long before the appearance of the first edition of *Leaves of Grass.*

The emerging study of periodicals has prompted scholars to examine the significant impact that magazines and newspapers played in the literary marketplace of the nineteenth century. While earlier generations of scholars primarily focused on the books that American writers published, scholars in recent years have begun to examine the importance of periodical publication to writers, as well as periodicals themselves as texts of interest and significance. There are new studies of the periodical publications of a variety of writers, from Margaret Fuller to Charles Chesnutt, as well as studies of individual periodicals, such as the *Atlantic Monthly* and *Godey's*

Lady's Book.[4] These studies have provided a much greater understanding of the prominent role that periodicals played in the careers of virtually all nineteenth-century American writers. In many ways, the turn of the twentieth century into the twenty-first has been—to adapt a comment about the "golden age of periodicals" made by the British writer D. L. Richardson in 1844[5]—the golden age of periodical study. Although the focus in Whitman studies has almost always been on *Leaves of Grass,* Whitman provides a particularly noteworthy case study for the field of periodical literature and for the ways in which digital archives are both providing access to increasingly rare materials and creating new tools for research in American periodicals.

From the beginning of his career, Whitman was deeply engaged in the periodical marketplace. In some respects, his career more closely follows that of a much earlier generation of American writers who were printer-publishers. For example, Whitman's early career followed a path that is much more like that of Benjamin Franklin or Isaiah Thomas than that of his contemporary Henry Wadsworth Longfellow, a professor who retired to write full-time. At the age of 12, Whitman was apprenticed to Samuel E. Clements, editor of the *Long Island Patriot,* where he gained many of the skills of printing and learned firsthand the art and craft of producing reading materials from start to finish. He was even occasionally involved in the distribution side of publishing. In 1838, he owned, edited, and printed a weekly newspaper, the *Long-Islander,* copies of which he delivered to subscribers on horseback. By 1842, Whitman was writing regularly for and then editing the *New York Aurora.* Through his association with this newspaper, Whitman became a part of the newest trend in periodical publishing—cheap, daily newspapers selling for a penny or two. Boasting a circulation of more than 5,000, the *Aurora* was designed, as he wrote in an article on 26 March 1842, to "carry light and knowledge in among those who most need it" and to "disperse the clouds of ignorance; and make the great body of the people intelligent, capable, and worthy of performing the duties of republican freemen."[6]

As a young man, Whitman worked at a series of newspapers in a variety of jobs—as a compositor, a contributor, and an editor—and became well known in New York City as a journalist. In fact, in a brief identification of Whitman on one of its Web sites, the Library of Congress describes him as an "American poet, journalist, and essayist."[7] Few nineteenth-century American writers, especially poets, could match Whitman's range of experience with periodicals. Certainly, few writers could have described the details of printing and publishing as Whitman did in "Chants Democratic 3," published in the 1860 edition of *Leaves of Grass.*

> *The four-double cylinder press, the hand-press, the*
> *frisket and tympan, the compositor's stick and*
> *rule, type-setting, making up the forms, all the*
> *work of newspaper counters, folders, carriers,*
> *news-men.*[8]

In addition to gaining this firsthand, technical experience, Whitman wrote constantly, publishing hundreds of articles as well as some fiction in various newspapers and magazines.

Whitman's career as a poet began more slowly. Although he published several poems in periodicals before 1855, the poems that appeared in *Leaves of Grass* that year were very different from the mostly conventional verses he had written in the past. As he revised and expanded the volume during the following decades, he published additional poems in periodicals, often incorporating them into the next edition of *Leaves of Grass.* He frequently sought out editors of British magazines and newspapers, hoping to bolster and extend his international reputation as he grew older. Although there are bibliographies of Whitman's poems published in periodicals, the poems themselves have never been collected or edited. For students of Whitman, the need to preserve these poems is particularly pressing because many of the periodicals in which the poems first appeared are increasingly rare, some are in extremely fragile condition, and a few may no longer exist.

Whitman's Poems in Periodicals is a part of the "Published Works" section of the *Whitman Archive.* This section is divided into two categories: "Books," which includes U.S. and international editions of *Leaves of Grass;* and "Periodicals," which currently includes poetry but not yet Whitman's extensive journalistic writings and short fiction. On the main page of the poetry section (fig. 1), users can access two essays: a general introduction that provides an overview of Whitman's relationship with the periodical marketplace, and an editorial introduction that provides information about methodology, technological challenges, editorial policy, and scholarly apparatus. A third line on this page takes users to a bibliography with a year-by-year listing of the poems Whitman published, beginning with the earli-

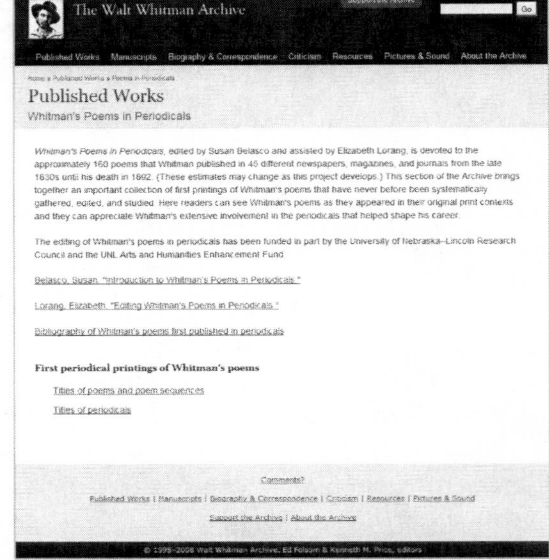

Fig. 1. Screen shot of the main page of *Whitman's Poems in Periodicals* in the *Walt Whitman Archive*, http://whitmanarchive.org/published/periodical/index.html

est poem for which we have a transcription, "Fame's Vanity," published in the *Long Island Democrat* on 23 October 1839.[9] The bibliography ends with what his friend Horace Traubel called Whitman's final poem, "A Thought of Columbus," published in *Once a Week* on 2 July 1892, almost three months after Whitman's death on 26 March 1892. Among other lessons that this bibliography teaches is the striking fact that Whitman's career as a poet began and ended with poems published in newspapers. The bibliography also permits users to move from the list to the poems by clicking on the titles or the names of the periodicals.

The main page of *Whitman's Poems in Periodicals* also provides two ways of studying the poems. By clicking "Titles of poems and poem sequences," users bring up an alphabetical list of all of the 160 poems in the edition. By clicking on a title, users can bring up any one of the poems. For example, clicking "Bardic Symbols" brings up a page that includes images of pages from the magazine in which it was published (the *Atlantic Monthly*), a transcription of the poem, and publication information. In this case, users can learn that "Bardic Symbols" underwent three revisions and title changes from the 1860 edition of *Leaves of Grass* through the 1881–82 edition, becoming, in its final version, one of Whitman's most famous poems, "As I Ebb'd with the Ocean of Life."[10]

While images of poems that appeared in magazines are fairly easy to present on the *Whitman Archive* because of the page size, poems that appeared in newspapers offer special challenges. In *Whitman's Poems in Periodicals,* newspaper poems include additional images for users, including an image of the entire page of the paper and, if necessary, a cropped image, since the poems are often difficult to locate on the large, multicolumned pages of most nineteenth-century newspapers. For example, clicking onto "O Captain! My Captain" brings up a page image of the *New-York Saturday Press,* where the poem can be easily read in the upper left-hand column because of the newspaper's relatively small format. Clicking onto "As the Greeks Signal Flame" brings up a transcription and two images: one of an entire page of the 15 December 1887 issue of the *New York Herald,* with its six dense columns of print; and a cropped image of the poem so that it can be more easily read. In both cases, readers can examine a single page of the newspaper and notice the other articles and news items that form the rich contextual background for Whitman's poems. In the case of "As the Greeks Signal Flame," for example, readers can readily see that the poem was a part of a nearly page-long tribute to John Greenleaf Whittier on his eightieth birthday, including a letter of appreciation of Whittier's work from Mark Twain.

The second way to study the poems is to click on "Titles of periodicals," which brings up a list of 45 periodicals—26 newspapers and 19 magazines—in which Whitman published poems. By clicking on a title in this list, users bring up a page that provides a brief historical introduction to the journal, magazine, or newspaper, including information about Whitman's relationship to the periodical, a clickable link to the poem within the periodical, and a bibliography of sources for further information about the periodical. Taken as a whole, this digital edition of Whitman's poems corrects many errors in earlier bibliographies and sources—in dates, page numbers, the titles of poems, and, in some cases, the titles of periodicals. One immediate advantage of an electronic edition is the ease with which one can correct such errors, including a few that we made ourselves during the process of collecting and preparing the poems for publishing on the *Whitman Archive.* Future plans include enabling users to link to manuscripts and printings in the editions of *Leaves of Grass.*[11] In the meantime, users can easily locate manuscripts and other printings by searching other sections of the *Whitman Archive.*

How does a digital archive provide greater access to periodicals, and in what ways might it limit or prescribe scholarly research? One of the points of pride for *Whitman's Poems in Periodicals* is the way in which we have provided new access to rare periodicals. But, as Elizabeth Lorang and I explain in our introductory essays in the archive, the process of locating and digitizing Whitman's poems has presented considerable challenges. In a recent article, "A Case Study in Using Historical Periodical Databases to Revise Previous Research," Sandra Roff correctly lauds the increasing number of digitized archives and collections of periodicals. As she points out, the *American Periodicals Series Online, 1740–1900,* now includes more than 1,100 titles.[12] She also calls attention to a number of other archives, such as the *Making of America* series (Cornell University), with its 35 titles; and *American Memory,* a Library of Congress initiative that includes 23 periodicals. Although other titles are beyond the scope of her study, additional collections come immediately to mind: Proquest's *Historical Newspapers;* the *National Digital Newspaper Program,* sponsored by the National Endowment for the Humanities and the Library of Congress; and individual archives, such as *HarpWeek,* the *Brooklyn Daily Eagle Online,* and the *Hartford Courant Online.* But, despite these important resources, anyone who thinks that most historical periodicals are available online would be surprised to learn how many periodicals—especially newspapers—have not been recovered in electronic formats. Further, many of these series are only available through expensive subscriptions, and many more have limited search features that preclude easy browsing of pages. Moreover, finding periodicals online is only the beginning of the work involved for a scholarly edition. Although there are many images of periodicals available on the Internet, many are inadequately documented and of poor quality. Our responsibility as editors included verifying the dates and page numbers for each poem and obtaining high-quality digital scans from the original printed form or, when nothing else was available, from microfilm.

Although some of the magazines in which Whitman published (e.g., the *Atlantic Monthly* or the *Century*) are widely available in print in most college and university libraries or in digital formats online, others in which he published are difficult to obtain. We used interlibrary loan, visited archives and special collections, and scanned or photographed full pages and full issues when they were available. An example of the difficulty is the very rare magazine *Truth,* established in 1881 and re-created in 1891 as a lavishly illustrated magazine of cartoons, humor, fiction, reviews, and poetry. According to our research, only about 20 libraries own copies of this magazine, and few of these are complete runs. Our efforts to locate the 19 March 1891 issue of *Truth,* which includes Whitman's poem "Old Chants," came to nothing until, by chance, I happened to see an episode of the PBS television program *History Detectives* that featured an investigation involving an advertisement in *Truth.* By contacting PBS, I was able to arrange for an image of the single page where the poem appeared, thanks to the generosity of a private collector interviewed on the program.

Another complication faced by any editor working on nineteenth-century periodicals is tracking down periodicals that were not systematically collected or those whose titles and publication circumstances changed. *Munyon's Illustrated World* and *Munyon's Magazine* represent a problem we have not yet resolved and remain one of the many mysteries in periodicals scholarship. As we explain on the *Whitman Archive,* very little is known about these magazines, and we have been unable to locate any complete files—or even any single issues. The titles do not appear in any index we have consulted, nor do they appear in *American Periodicals Series Online.* According to Frank L. Mott, J. M. Munyon, a Philadelphia editor, established *Munyon's Illustrated World* in 1884. Apparently hoping for a wider circulation, he changed the format to a family magazine with a new name, *Munyon's: A Monthly Magazine,* sometime in 1887. By Mott's account, the magazine reached a circulation of 100,000 before it ceased publication in 1894.[13] Whitman mentions J. M. Munyon in his notebooks and refers occasionally to his magazine by its original title, *Munyon's Illustrated World.*[14] According to Whitman's notebooks and letters and as listed in recent bibliographies, Whitman published in *Munyon's Illustrated World* a reprint of an earlier poem, "As the Greeks Signal Flame," in January 1888; a short essay, "The Human Voice," in October 1890; and a poem, "Osceola." But if Mott was correct about the timing of the name change for the magazine, all of Whitman's works would have been published in the renamed *Munyon's: A Monthly Magazine.* Another poem, "The Commonplace," was published as a manuscript facsimile in March 1891, but all we have been able to locate is a cropped image of the poem itself, labeled by the Library of Congress as from *Munyon's Magazine*—not a title mentioned by Mott or any other historian of American magazines. As we note on the *Whitman Archive,* we continue to research this magazine. In fact, we encourage users to contribute to *Whitman's Poetry in Periodicals* by offering information about rare periodicals on pages where our material is incomplete and by inviting investigations. Such invitations signal the collaborative venture of the *Whitman Archive,* which extends far beyond the contributions of staff members alone. Here, users can participate in a scholarly conversation and swiftly see the results, since we frequently add updates to the *Whitman Archive.*

Newspapers present additional challenges. First, of course, is the great difficulty of locating paper files of nineteenth-century newspapers. Many library collections routinely discarded paper copies after microfilm copies were made, and complete paper runs of newspapers are an increasing rarity today. While a few of the 26 newspapers in which we know that Whitman published poems still exist in paper form, many do not. Further, runs are often incomplete or missing items. Just as today, nineteenth-century readers often clipped copies of items out of newspapers to keep, and in the files of the Library of Congress, there are many unidentified clippings. Another problem is that hundreds of reels of microfilm are becoming too brittle for use. As any frequent user of microfilm knows, folds or creases in the original papers that were not straightened can eliminate lines of text and even entire sections of pages, making them unreadable. We have used microfilm when we had to, but in some cases, we have been extremely fortunate that libraries have been willing to allow us to use and scan their rare paper copies. For example, in 1842, Whitman published dozens of articles in the *New York Aurora,* as well as two poems, "The Death and Burial of McDonald Clarke" and "Time to Come," a revised version of one of his earliest poems, "Our Future Lot." The only complete run of the *Aurora* known to be in existence is at the Paterson Free Public Library of Paterson, New Jersey, which generously made the bound copies of the newspaper available to the *Whitman Archive* for scanning. Users of *Whitman's Poems in Periodicals* can therefore access page images from this newspaper that, until now, was only available to visitors to the library in New Jersey. Another mechanical challenge is the page size of many newspapers, such as the *New York Times* or the *New York Herald,* which present special problems for making scans and providing readable images. As I noted earlier, we have taken an additional step of providing cropped images for poems that appeared in newspapers where it is difficult to locate a poem on a particular page. Still, page size is an issue, and some of the images are not as clear as we would wish.

The many challenges we have encountered in mounting *Whitman's Poems in Periodicals* suggest some of the ways in which digital archives can provide greater access to periodicals. With our relatively narrow focus—collecting all of Whitman's poems that were published in a small group of periodicals from 1837 to 1892, we have consequently set limits on the scale of the project. Within the parameters of this project, though, we have created electronic access to several periodicals that were not previously digitized and some that were available only in highly specialized collections. For example, Whitman published "The Sobbing of the Bells," a poem commemorating the death of President James A. Garfield, in the *Boston Weekly Globe* on 27 September 1881. Only about a dozen libraries in the United States own some paper issues of this newspaper, and the only full run is in the Boston Public Library. The newspaper has never been microfilmed, and most of the copies that do exist are in very fragile condition. In fact, the well-worn copy of the *Boston Weekly Globe* we used for our edition was spotted on eBay and bought by an alert graduate student working for the *Whitman Archive.* As with the pages of the *New York Aurora,* the images that we include in *Whitman's Poems in Periodicals* are likely to be the only way that most users will ever see what the *Boston Weekly Globe* looked like.

It is important to remember that access to these rare periodicals is only possible because the *Whitman Archive,* devoted to a writer who has garnered enormous scholarly and popular attention, has received considerable institutional support and funding from a variety of sources, including the National Endowment for the Humanities and the Institute of Museum and Library Services. As a colleague once suggested at a conference, electronic archives continue, in many ways, to reinscribe the traditional canon of American literature, leaving out women and minority writers. While the works of major writers and periodicals are being digitized, there is limited funding for others. For example, scholars have no electronic or even microfilm access to the *New York Ledger,* the newspaper where Fanny Fern, among the most famous women writers in the nineteenth century, published her weekly columns from 1856 to 1872. In addition, while there are some Web sites that provide images of *Frederick Douglass' Paper* or the *North Star,* there is no reliable, searchable electronic archive of Frederick Douglass's periodicals. Some collections, such as *African American Newspapers* (available only by subscription), provide transcriptions but only a few page images. The list goes on and on, and the net effect is that research is indeed limited by the materials that scholars can readily and reliably access.

At the same time, are the *editors* of archives artificially limiting the possibilities for research? While access to periodicals provides one kind of limitation for research, the presentation of materials also affects the possibilities for research. Early in the development of *Whitman's Poems in Periodicals,* we took up the problem of how to present the poems in the periodicals on the *Whitman Archive.* From the beginning, our goal was to contextualize the poems, realizing, of course, that there were clear limits to what we could do and how much we could scan and transcribe. In addition, our object was to present an edition of Whitman's poems as they appeared in periodicals and not to create an archive of the periodicals themselves. A question that we constantly explored was how much of the periodical we needed to present in order to represent the context adequately. Further, the *Whitman Archive* has had an informal policy of not linking to other sites because of the problems with maintaining such links and ensuring that our links take users to other scholarly, carefully vetted projects. Our original plan was to include the title pages of periodicals, as well as tables of contents. This goal, however, had to be modified because of the great difficulty we had in locating and obtaining complete issues of most magazines and newspapers. We reluctantly decided on presenting page images of the poems within the periodical (typically, a single page). At the same time, as the project has developed, we have scanned entire issues as well as tables of contents and other pages from the periodicals. Although they are not currently available publicly on the *Whitman Archive,* we have kept electronic files of these images for future use.[15]

I have emphasized the problems and challenges for creating this edition, but in some cases, Whitman's poems did appear in periodicals for which there are accessible sources. Although sources like *American Periodicals Series Online* are available only by subscription and therefore not available for linking to the *Whitman Archive, Making of America,* for example, is a free resource. Whitman published poems in three magazines—the *Atlantic Monthly,* the *Galaxy,* and *Harper's Monthly Magazine*—that are available in the *Making of America* collection. Although our archive includes only the single-page images of the poems that appeared in these magazines, users could easily go to *Making of America* and call up the issues in which the poems appeared. Doing so, for example, would enable readers to see that "O Star of France" was published in an issue of the *Galaxy* (June 1871) that included several articles about French literature and politics, including an article about François Guizot, the French politician and writer who was removed from power during the French Revolution of 1848. The issue was published just as the Franco-Prussian War was ending, and Whitman's poem clearly participates in a larger context of international politics. At the same time, it is important to remember that online collections like the *Making of America* provide page images based on OCR that has not been edited for errors, which often limits the effectiveness of the search engine. Further, the periodicals in such collections are only as complete as the original sources. Unless, for example, a user had access to a paper copy of the June 1871 single issue, she or he would not know that the issue features a frontispiece portrait of Guizot, further underscoring the issue's focus on the situation in France in the aftermath of the war. The *Making of America* archive includes only what is in the volumes of the periodicals that were available to them for scanning. Because of long-held policies that the majority of libraries followed, the cover pages and front matter of the periodicals, including advertisements, were routinely stripped out in the binding process, making it impossible for users to examine what are now considered important historical documents. By examining the entire single issue of the *Galaxy* (even without the portrait of Guizot, as on the *Making of America* version) and/or by examining other periodicals of the same time, scholars obviously have access to much more information about the particular context for Whitman's poem.

But have we in fact limited the possibilities for research? In a special issue titled "Remapping Genre" in October 2007, the editors of *PMLA* included an essay by Ed Folsom, one of the coeditors of the *Whitman Archive*, entitled "Database as Genre: The Epic Transformation of Archives." In the essay, Folsom describes the *Whitman Archive* as a database, a place where all of Whitman's work is "freely available online: poems, essays, letters, journals, jottings, and images, along with biographies, interviews, reviews, and criticism of Whitman."[16] Folsom's essay was followed by a set of responses, including one by Meredith McGill, who suggestively argued that "digital projects such as *The Walt Whitman Archive* are significantly more dependent on print conventions than they need to be."[17] McGill turns directly to *Whitman's Poems in Periodicals* for one of her major examples, observing,

> Readers of the archive can summon an image of a poem as it appears on a page of the *Atlantic Monthly* or the *New York Herald*, but they cannot turn that page. Periodicals are marshaled as important contexts for Whitman's texts, but they are not independent nodes capable of launching a new investigation. The *Walt Whitman Archive* gestures toward the world outside Whitman's writing but zigs and zags mostly within itself. [18]

As I have suggested, the fact that users of *Whitman's Poems in Periodicals* cannot indeed "turn that page" has been a deliberate decision, made of necessity and by design. If there is a lesson to be learned from the creation of this documentary edition and the commentary of users, it is that, in many ways, we have been deeply rooted in the print tradition as we have approached this project. It is now time for us to consider how such a decision does indeed limit the kinds of research I have just outlined, in the example of using Whitman's "O Star of France" as a departure point for investigating the full context of his poem in the pages of the *Galaxy* and the many other periodicals carrying commentary on the end of the Franco-Prussian War.

As *Whitman's Poems in Periodicals* continues to grow and develop, new ideas and technologies can be used to broaden the ways in which students can access and study periodicals—with links to other sites and/or by using our own repository of scanned issues. Further, we need more flexible database structures to allow for users to collect, group, and sort information. We need more powerful, flexible search engines for use with texts that have been carefully edited, so that we can locate not just articles, stories, and poems, but also thematically related works. Finally, we need more online periodicals collections that provide actual page images in tandem with transcriptions that help us clearly understand how periodicals functioned for nineteenth-century American readers. At the same time, some of the burden must also fall on users to determine new research methods for negotiating scholarship in the digital age. Instead of wishing for an archive to be a complete environment, scholars might investigate tools like easily accessible browser plug-ins or add-ons that enable new methods for conducting research. A tool like WebMynd, for example, enables a user to develop an individualized archive of pages and Web sites and search them from one convenient location. Such tools are freely available and represent a new Web-based approach to research—not one based on the model of print conventions.

A final question concerns how scholarly digitization projects for periodicals ensure that we preserve the innate qualities of the periodical—the eclectic juxtapositions and the opportunities for serendipitous discoveries—in our research. One of the most challenging aspects of bringing periodicals online is the preservation of browsing—the hallmark, for centuries, of the ways in which we have read magazines and newspapers. Perhaps the most unusual of all the periodicals in which Whitman published is *Cope's Tobacco Plant*, the British trade journal published by the tobacco firm Cope Brothers and Company. Subtitled *A Monthly Journal, Interesting to the Manufacturer, the Dealer, & the Smoker, Cope's* appeared monthly from March 1870 through January 1881. The magazine was edited by the secretary of the printing department of Cope's Tobacco Factory, John Fraser, who was a collector of rare books and possessed an eclectic set of interests in philosophy, phrenology, beekeeping, smoking, and poetry.[19] Appealing to an audience of male readers, Fraser printed many articles about tobacco and tobacco products, including reviews of books on fishing and other topics of interest to men. Fraser was clearly interested in Whitman, who contributed "The Dalliance of the Eagles" to *Cope's*. It was published there in November 1880, the year before Whitman included it as one of the new poems in the 1881–82 edition of *Leaves of Grass*. But well before this poem was published, Whitman had an association with *Cope's* that has received very limited attention.

In addition to "The Dalliance of the Eagles," Whitman's history with *Cope's* included a poem attributed to (but not authored by) him, published in January 1872; his short prose piece in the form of letters, "Three Young Men's Deaths," in April 1879; a brief article on the poet Joaquin Miller's admiration for Whitman (December 1875); and a series of five biographical articles, written by an early Whitman biographer, James Thomson (May, June, August, September, and December 1880). Indeed *Cope's Tobacco Plant* paid a great deal of attention to Whitman, and the poet was clearly pleased about it. In a letter to Fraser on 27 November 1878, Whitman asked that copies of the magazine that included his work be sent to a number of British poets and writers, including William Rossetti and Alfred, Lord Tennyson. To what was obviously a question from Fraser about his sympathies with smoking, Whitman responded in the same letter,

I am *not* an anti-tobacconist—On the contrary have seen how impor-

> tant & valuable the sedative was in the extensive military hospitals of our Secession war—Still I do not smoke or chew myself—Sometimes wish I did smoke now in my old age & invalidism—but it is too late to learn—But my brothers & all my near friends are smokers, & I am accustomed to it—live among smokers, & always carry cigars in my pocket to give to special friends who prize them.[20]

Not only does Whitman's unlikely connection with this journal provide a fascinating glimpse into popular culture of the late nineteenth century, but it also presents some new avenues for investigation of Whitman's status in England in the 1870s and early 1880s.

Cope's is not available on microfilm, but we were able to obtain copies of the bound journal through interlibrary loan, and the University of Nebraska–Lincoln Libraries recently bought the complete run at auction. Having the paper copy of the journal was a great boon and a source of lively entertainment for those of us working on the *Whitman Archive. Cope's* is filled with articles and stories about smoking and tobacco and with poems on smoking, and it also includes colorful advertisement cards that can be detached from the pages, evidently designed for collectors. In the January 1872 issue, a group of poems appeared that celebrated smoking and were attributed to several poets, such as Henry Wadsworth Longfellow, John Greenleaf Whittier, and Walt Whitman.[21] One poem begins "Tobacco! Can I fail to love thee, seeing thee adopted in all lands." The contrast between this poem and "The Dalliance of the Eagles," which Whitman wrote and published in *Cope's,* could hardly be stronger. "Dalliance," with its vivid portrayal of two eagles copulating in the air, is erotically powerful, and the Boston district attorney in 1882 ruled it "obscene," along with some other poems from the seventh edition of *Leaves of Grass* (1881–82). Why and how "Dalliance" was published in *Cope's* remains a compelling topic for research.

The experiences we had in paging through the issues of *Cope's* as we prepared *Whitman's Poems in Periodicals* is an important reminder of the essential nature of periodicals themselves. Magazines and newspapers are open forms, encouraging readers to shift from articles to stories to poems and to read backward and forward within a single issue.[22] A few years before I began working on *Whitman's Poems in Periodicals,* I contributed to a special issue of *American Periodicals,* "Periodical Research in the American

Classroom." There, I wrote about the importance of preserving "eclectic juxtapositions and the opportunities for serendipitous discoveries" as we moved periodicals online.[23] By "eclectic juxtapositions," I meant the ways in which the pages of periodicals often place a variety of materials in close proximity—in a kind of cultural conversation in which we as readers are invited to participate. When we restrict ourselves to a single work isolated on a screen, we are violating the very nature of periodicals as collections of texts—not texts in isolation. We have tried to solve part of that problem by providing whole page images of newspapers in *Whitman's Poems in Periodicals,* so that users can observe, for example, that Whitman's poems in the *New York Herald* often followed the weather report. Closely related to the importance of maintaining juxtapositions is what I called "serendipitous discoveries," the preservation of browsing in periodicals that can result in the discovery of a poem attributed to Whitman or the understanding that a poem like "O Star of France" is a part of a particular cultural and political moment in history. We are well aware that we are not offering as many opportunities for experiencing the kinds of coincidences and discoveries that we experienced in paging through the issues of *Cope's.* But turning a page is, finally, a characteristic of print culture. Indeed, in an electronic environment, turning the page has limited meaning. In a virtual environment, it is simply not possible to turn the page, and there is nothing of the tactile feel of a periodical when a user comes to an electronic archive. Our task is to take the early forms of print culture and make them accessible for users who do not, for many reasons, have access to the originals. What we need now are new ways to access, search, and manipulate these preserved periodicals—important historical and cultural artifacts—for our research. Designing innovative ways to exploit the electronic environment is precisely the major challenge for periodicals research in the digital age.

Notes

1. *Whitman's Poems in Periodicals* can be accessed at http://www.whitmanarchive.org/published/index.html. Numerous libraries and collections have been involved in this part of the *Walt Whitman Archive.* First and foremost, I am grateful to Ed Folsom and Kenneth M. Price, coeditors of the archive, for inviting me to serve as the editor of *Whitman's Poetry in Periodicals.* I am especially indebted to University of Nebraska–Lincoln graduate student Elizabeth Lorang, who has served as the assistant editor since 2004 and is my valued partner in this project. At UNL's Love Library, we have

been helped enormously by Katherine Walter in Special Collections, the Center for Digital Research in the Humanities, and the staff of the Interlibrary Loan department. This project has greatly benefited from the invaluable work of several past and current UNL graduate and undergraduate students (Amanda Gailey; Ramon Guerra, now of the University of Nebraska–Omaha; Nicholas Krauter; Leslie Ianno; Jason McIntosh; Katherine Ngaruiya; and Janel Simons Cayer), as well as Brian Pytlik Zillig, associate professor and digital initiatives librarian, Love Library, UNL; and Brett Barney, research assistant professor, UNL Libraries, and project manager for the *Whitman Archive*. *Whitman's Poems in Periodicals* has been generously supported by grants from the UNL Research Council and the UNL Arts and Humanities Enhancement Fund. I am grateful to Linck Johnson, Elizabeth Lorang, and Kenneth M. Price for their helpful suggestions on an early draft of this essay.

2. "Revising Himself: Walt Whitman and *Leaves of Grass*," *American Treasures*, Library of Congress, http://www.loc.gov/exhibits/treasures/whitman-home.html.

3. See especially Ezra Greenspan, *Walt Whitman and the American Reader* (New York: Cambridge University Press, 1990), 63–87; Ed Folsom, *Whitman Making Books/Books Making Whitman: A Catalogue and Commentary* (Iowa City: Obermann Center for Advanced Studies, University of Iowa, 2005), http://www.whitmanarchive.org/criticism/current/anc.00150.html (accessed 11 November 2008); Susan Belasco, "*Leaves of Grass* and the Poetry Marketplace of Antebellum America," in *Leaves of Grass: The Sesquicentennial Essays*, ed. Susan Belasco, Ed Folsom, and Kenneth M. Price (Lincoln: University of Nebraska Press, 2007), 179–98; Ed Folsom, "What We're Still Learning about the 1855 *Leaves of Grass* 150 Years Later," in Belasco, Folsom, and Price, *Leaves of Grass*, 1–32.

4. See the journal *American Periodicals*, founded in 1991, which publishes history, criticism, and bibliography related to periodical study. Example studies include Mark L. Kamrath and Sharon M. Harris, eds., *Periodical Literature in Eighteenth-Century America* (Knoxville: University of Tennessee Press, 2005); Kenneth M. Price and Susan Belasco Smith, eds., *Periodical Literature in Nineteenth-Century America* (Charlottesville: University Press of Virginia, 1995); Ellery Sedgwick, *A History of the Atlantic Monthly: 1857–1909* (Amherst: University of Massachusetts Press, 1994); Aleta Feinsod Cane and Susan Alves, eds., *American Women Writers and the Periodical, 1837–1916* (Iowa City: University of Iowa Press, 2001); and Patricia Okker, *Our Sister Editors: Sarah J. Hale and the Tradition of Nineteenth-Century American Women Editors* (Athens: University of Georgia Press, 1995).

5. D. L. Richardson, *Literary Leaves*, vol. 1 (London: W. H. Allen, 1840), 51.

6. Walt Whitman, "The Penny Press," in *The Collected Writings of Walt Whitman: The Journalism*, vol. 1, *1834–1836*, ed. Herbert Bergman, Douglas Noverr, and Edward Recchia (New York: Peter Lang, 1998), 74. For a detailed study of Whitman's early life as a journalist, see Jason Stacy, *Walt Whitman's Multitudes: Labor Reform and Persona in Whitman's Journalism and the First "Leaves of Grass," 1840–1855* (New York: Peter Lang, 2008), 11–107.

7. "Today in History: May 31," *American Memory,* Library of Congress, http://lcweb2.loc.gov/ammem/today/may31.html (accessed November 11, 2008).

8. Walt Whitman, "Chants Democratic 3," *Leaves of Grass* (Boston: Thayer and Eldridge, 1860–61), 154, reprinted in *Walt Whitman Archive,* ed. Ed Folsom and Kenneth M. Price, http://www.whitmanarchive.org/published/LG/1860/poems/7.

9. Although bibliographies list "Our Future Lot" as published in the *Long-Islander* before 31 October 1838, we have not been able to locate any copies of this periodical and have no transcriptions or scans of this poem.

10. We are also in the process of providing editorial notes, such as for the poems Whitman published in the *New York Herald,* which is a model for the notes that we plan for all of the poems in the edition. For an example of the kind of scholarship that *Whitman's Poetry in Periodicals* is making possible and a detailed study of Whitman's poems in the *Herald,* see Elizabeth Lorang, "'Two more throws against oblivion': Walt Whitman and the *New York Herald* in 1888," *Walt Whitman Quarterly Review* 25 (2008): 167–87.

11. For further information about the methodology, editorial policy, and scholarly apparatus, see Elizabeth Lorang, "Editing Whitman's Poetry in Periodicals," *Mickle Street Review* 19/20 (April 2008), reprinted in *Walt Whitman Archive,* ed. Ed Folsom and Kenneth M. Price, http://www.whitmanarchive.org/published/periodical/technical_introduction/index.html.

12. Sandra Roff, "A Case Study in Using Historical Periodical Databases to Revise Previous Research," *American Periodicals* 8 (2008): 96–100.

13. Frank L. Mott, *A History of American Magazines, 1885–1905,* vol. 4 (Cambridge: Harvard University Press, 1957), 87–88.

14. See Walt Whitman, *The Collected Writings of Walt Whitman: Daybooks and Notebooks,* vol. 2, *December 1881–1891,* ed. William White (New York: New York University Press, 1978), 442; Walt Whitman, *The Collected Writings of Walt Whitman: The Correspondence,* vol. 4, *1886–1889,* ed. Edwin Haviland Miller (New York: New York University Press, 1969), 136n, 141n, 426; Walt Whitman, *The Collected Writings of Walt Whitman: The Correspondence,* vol. 5, *1890–1892,* ed. Edwin Haviland Miller (New York: New York University Press, 1969), 23, 120, 170n, 331.

15. For a discussion of this issue, see Lorang, "Editing Whitman's Poetry in Periodicals."

16. Ed Folsom, "Database as Genre: The Epic Transformation of Archives," *PMLA* 122 (2002): 1573.

17. Meredith McGill, "Remediating Whitman," *PMLA* 122 (2002): 1593.

18. McGill, "Remediating Whitman," 1594.

19. See Richard D. Altick, "Cope's Tobacco Plant: An Episode in Victorian Journalism," *Papers of the Bibliographical Society of America* 45 (1951): 333–50.

20. Walt Whitman, *The Collected Writings of Walt Whitman: The Correspondence,* vol. 5, *1890–1892,* ed. Edwin Haviland Miller (New York: New York University Press, 1969), 305.

21. In studying the pages of the journal for our use in *Whitman's Poems in Periodicals,* Elizabeth Lorang discovered this poem.

22. See Margaret Beetham, "Towards a Theory of the Periodical as a Publishing Genre," in *Investigating Victorian Journalism,* ed. Laurel Brake, Aled Jones, and Lionel Madden (New York: St. Martin's, 1990), 24–30.

23. Susan Belasco, "Juxtaposition and Serendipity: Teaching Periodicals in Nineteenth-Century American Literature," *American Periodicals* 12 (2002): 89–95.

Harriet Beecher Stowe's *Uncle Tom's Cabin:* A Case Study in Textual Transmission

WESLEY RAABE

"you must consider **it 's not** a matter of private feeling"
—Senator Bird in Harriet Beecher Stowe, *Uncle Tom's Cabin* (Boston: John P. Jewett, 1852), 1:121

"you must consider **it's** a matter of private feeling"
—*Uncle Tom's Cabin,* ed. Ann Douglas (New York: Penguin, 1981, 1986), 144

Vol. 1, pg. 121, l. 17
consider it's **not** a matter] JE HL
consider it's [*omit*] a matter] PG AC

In a recent essay, bibliographer Michael Winship remarks that he had "published a list of the textual corrections to only the first printing of *Uncle Tom's Cabin*" in volume 8 (1990) of the *Bibliography of American Literature* (*BAL*). "As far as I know," he continues, "this information has not been noticed by the editors of the many recent editions of the work."[1] That, for two decades, the many editors of Harriet Beecher Stowe's famous work have failed to address a list of corrections published in *BAL* merits reflection. The *Bibliography of American Literature,* "one of the monumental bibliographies of the twentieth century," is recognized as "an indispensable source" for the study of textual and publication history.[2] This study outlines the consequences of neglecting bibliographical scholarship, and it uses the methods of textual scholarship to reconsider the status of modern reprints and electronic texts in our own moment, when print and digital textuality are intermingled.

Machine-readable transcriptions that are derived both from facsimiles of early editions and from modern reprints are now widely available, so the detailed analysis of the textual transmission of reprints is a less onerous task than it was even a decade ago. Readily available electronic texts can be examined with the tools of textual scholarship to illuminate a line of descent for *Uncle Tom's Cabin* in the late twentieth and early twenty-first centuries, a line that includes versions of Stowe's text published both in print and digital form. While my attention to the accuracy of texts in reprint editions and digital archives mirrors a concern of the Anglo-American New Bibliography of the mid-twentieth century, online texts, even those texts prepared with the lower standards of large-scale digitization projects, should not be dismissed. They are a powerful resource for identifying textual variation, even for a textual scholar who seeks to prepare an authoritative edition. Another consequence of the use to which digital texts can be put—to which I here turn first—is that a scholarly apparatus is not a dry statement of fact but the evidence for the consequences of textual descent. A reading of the apparatus accompanying the online version of this essay shows that the same principles that explain textual descent in print apply also to electronic texts: scholars are advised to reconsider their uncritical preference for reprint books over electronic sources.

One of the early hopes for digital scholarship was that access to multiple documentary versions would limit the need to puzzle out the conventions of print apparatuses.[3] Some editorial work in American literature has delivered on that promise: the digital editions of *Typee* and *Clotel* under the Rotunda imprint of the University of Virginia Press are notable examples.[4] Nonetheless, a traditional print apparatus remains a useful method for presenting multiple versions of a text in highly condensed form, especially if the aim is to provide an overview of textual variation rather than a reading text. To present textual variants in a form that is both condensed and truthful will require a review of the concept of textual transmission that Walter W. Greg proposed in "The Rationale of Copy-Text." Greg's influential insight was to divide the features of printed texts into two classes. The "significant" features—which Greg designated *substantives*—"affect the author's meaning or the essence of his expression." The text's other features, those "affecting mainly its formal presentation," he designated *accidentals*.[5] If the authority for accidentals is presumed to lie with the personnel of printing houses rather than with authors, Greg's rationale offered a nuanced procedure for editorial work. The earliest printing is designated as the "copy-text" (the base text for the new editorially prepared text), but the copy-text holds presumptive authority only for the accidentals, because the punctuation and spelling of the earliest printing are more likely to reflect the author's practices. When a textual difference between an initial and a revised print is treated as substantive, neither version would have presumptive authority, so editors choose among substantive readings according to their judgment. Greg's distinction is a foundational concept for authorial intentionalist editing, and that tradition's refinement by Fredson Bowers, G. Thomas Tanselle, and others had "an unparalleled influence on Anglo-American editing in the twentieth century."[6]

Greg's distinction need not be reserved for appeals to authorial intention or to a preference for clear-text reading pages: it is useful for separating wheat from chaff when one wants to analyze textual descent of reprints that were prepared without authorial participation. If an author adds or removes a comma, at least some readers would be interested. But suppose a twentieth-century editor transcribes a nineteenth-century novel, and suppose further that this editor adds a comma, thereby converting a restrictive clause into a nonrestrictive clause. If the alteration is not reported, a reader is unlikely to realize that he or she has encountered an emendation or a transcription error. The editor's fault, if inadvertent, is understandable—if deliberate but not reported, it is regrettable—but few readers will notice. Greg's distinction between accidental and substantive variants can be applied regardless of whether one believes that a textual alteration derives from an author's intervention or from an editor's deliberate or inadvertent act.

The epigraph for this essay uses a transcription error in the Penguin edition (1981) edited by Ann Douglas to illustrate Greg's distinction, and it shows how a modernized apparatus entry—based on the initial book printing of *Uncle Tom's Cabin* (Jewett, 1852), two modern reprints, and an electronic text—conceals variation in typographical spacing. In the first pair of citations, from the Jewett and Penguin editions, the textual variant in boldface type includes both an accidental and a substantive difference. The Jewett edition has a thin space character before the apostrophe in the word "it 's," and the contraction is followed by the word "not." The Penguin text has no space before the apostrophe in "it's" and lacks the word "not." In the second epigraph citation, the conventions of print apparatuses provide greater information density: two lines represent four versions of the text. The pair of apparatus entries is preceded by a volume number, page number, and line number from the Jewett edition. The substantive variant "**not/** [*omit*]" is indicated with boldface type and bracketed editorial commentary. The variant is preceded by two pick-up words and followed by two drop-off words. Unlike the portion of the entry in boldface type, the "it 's/it's" pair has been silently modernized. In Greg's terms, "it 's/it's" is an accidental variant, and "**not/**[*omit*]" is a substantive variant. Because the accidental variant is excluded from the apparatus entry—"it 's" in the Jewett edition and "it's" in modern reprints are treated as the *same* word—the apparatus entry represents four documentary forms of Stowe's work in condensed form. Typographical space may bear meaning, but silent modernization of the Jewett edition's typographical spacing permits the apparatus entry to emphasize wording variation.[7] The final part of the apparatus entry is the series of sigla, which specify the sources for the texts: the Jewett edition is represented by the siglum JE, Kenneth S. Lynn's Harvard edition (1962) by the siglum HL, Ann Douglas's Penguin edition by the siglum PG, and the electronic text published in 1998 on Stephen Railton's *Uncle Tom's Cabin & American Culture* (*UTC & AC*) site by the siglum AC.[8]

This essay's accompanying online apparatus has entries in the style of the second quotation in the epigraph citation. The apparatus is not included in print form with this essay but can be acquired from the publisher's site or from the university repository.[9] This essay and the apparatus demand "jumping from the reading text to the apparatus," a specialized type of activity that Jerome J. McGann has characterized as radial reading.[10] But unlike a scholarly edition, which has a "text" to which the reader can refer, the apparatus refers not to an editorially prepared text but to the page numbers and lines in the 1852 Jewett edition. Readers may wish to consult facsimile page images for that edition from one of many publicly available digital archives.[11]

Using *Uncle Tom's Cabin* as the case, this study aims to prove that faith in the accurate transmission of print is as misleading as the distrust of texts in electronic form. The turn in literary scholarship away from bibliography and textual scholarship has almost inevitable consequences. The stubborn faith that texts are transmitted from one print form to another with mostly inconsequential alteration may confer unmerited authority on a printed text, and the conviction that digital objects are mutable and ephemeral leads to undeserved prejudice against scholarship in digital form. In fact, the assumption that a distinction between print and digital forms provides a useful guideline for scholarly authority, at least in the matter of textual accuracy, is nearly meaningless, as print and digital textuality may be thoroughly intermingled.

Electronic reprints that are prepared for scholars typically include a bibliographical header that provides the printed source from which an electronic text is prepared, a function comparable to a textual note in a print edition. A line of textual descent for *Uncle Tom's Cabin* can be established from such statements: Lynn based the 1962 Harvard edition on Jewett's two-volume 1852 edition. Douglas based the 1981 Penguin edition on Lynn's edition. The University of Virginia Electronic Text (EText) Center based its 1997 digital version on the Penguin edition, and Railton published the EText Center version on the *UTC & AC* site.[12] This line of textual transmission for *Uncle Tom's Cabin* in the second half of the twentieth century—of interest because these editions and electronic texts have influenced a generation of academic readers—is represented in figure 1.

Aside from sharing a line of textual descent, these editions and electronic texts are noteworthy in their own right. Lynn's introduction was an important early effort to advocate a place in the canon of American literature for Stowe's work, and the Belknap-Harvard imprint granted the text prestige.[13] Douglas affirmed the authority of Lynn's edition when she reprinted the Harvard text in the Penguin edition, an inexpensive mass-market paperback that has, for over two decades, remained attractive for classroom adoption. The widespread use of Douglas's edition made it an obvious source for one of the earliest electronic archives of literary texts, published by the University of Virginia EText Center. Railton, a faculty member in the same university's English Department, reissued the EText Center version as part of his ambitious and highly influential electronic archive.

The editors of these print editions are historians and cultural studies scholars, and the preparers of these electronic texts are an early generation of technically savvy humanities scholars and students. But they have minimal affiliation with bibliography and textual scholarship. Lynn's discussion of Stowe's famous footnote in chapter 12 is illustrative. Stowe attributed a

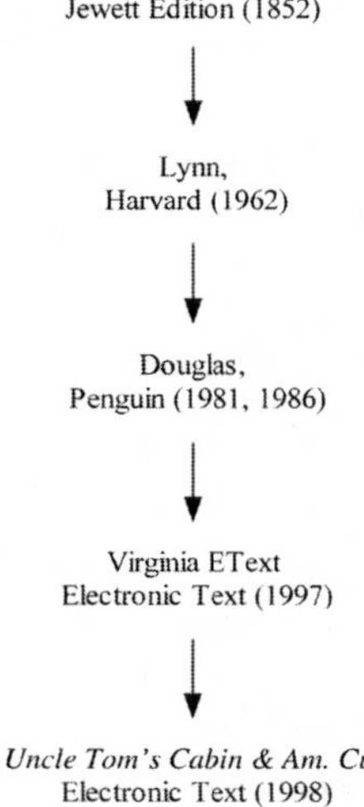

Fig. 1. Digital texts of *Uncle Tom's Cabin* as descended from print

quotation—that slave trade has "*no evils but such as are inseparable from any other relations in social and domestic life*"—to Dr. Joel Parker.[14] Lynn, in his editorial gloss on the footnote, states that "Mrs. Stowe attempted unsuccessfully to have this identifying note removed from the stereotype-plate of the first edition."[15] Lynn's note would be more clear if he had used the distinction between the terms *printing* and *edition* that is observed by bibliographers. The bibliographical concept of the "edition" includes all printings from substantially the same setting of type, and the "impression" or "printing" includes all copies printed as one set in a unit of time.[16] The stereotype plate was not altered for the first printing, but the footnote was removed in a later printing, which is part of the same edition. The alteration of the Parker footnote, as explained by E. Bruce Kirkham, is as follows: The footnote remained in printings of the first Jewett edition before the fiftieth thousand copy. Though the attribution to Parker was removed in the stereotype plates, it would continue to appear in previously printed sheets bound with later copies.[17] Another error that indicates Lynn's misunderstanding of the textual history of *Uncle Tom's Cabin* is his almost unqualified statement that there were "no alterations between the magazine version and the book version of her text," a statement that is demonstrably false, as Kirkham later proved.[18] Scholars may err, and it should be acknowledged that Lynn's edition preceded Kirkham's pioneering bibliographical scholarship on Stowe's work. But Kirkham's work should have undermined the authority of Lynn's 1962 edition among scholars: it did not. The Harvard edition is described as the "standard edition" in the Modern Language Association guide to teaching *Uncle Tom's Cabin* published in 2000.[19]

Kirkham established clearly, in the late 1970s, that the Jewett edition included an early corrected printing, and Winship, in *BAL*, expanded the list of known alterations in the Jewett edition.[20] *BAL*'s list of alterations is reproduced in the section of the online apparatus designated "Emendations in the Corrected Printing of Jewett Edition." This section of the apparatus uses the siglum JEU for the uncorrected first printing, the siglum JEC for the corrections made after the first printing of 5,000 copies, and the siglum JEC[2] for the Parker footnote. The corrections are generally small matters, but some have interpretive significance. The fourth chapter of Stowe's book, "An Evening in Uncle Tom's Cabin," displays the domestic happiness of the slave cabin. Uncle Tom, a slave on the Kentucky plantation of the Shelby family, is married to Aunt Chloe. Their youngest child, a toddler, is named "Mericky" in the uncorrected first printing (JE 1:42).[21] When Stowe changed the toddler's name to "Polly" in the corrected printing—Aunt Chloe uses the latter name for her daughter in chapter 44—the author aligned the child's name with other incidental characters named Polly. Two of the novel's named but invisible slaves, one on slave hunter Marks's list of human prey and one of the underservants in the St. Clare household, are named "Polly" (JE 1:107, 1:238). If a reader of the corrected printing first encounters Aunt Chloe's child as "Polly" instead of "Mericky," the text's subsequent Pollys are reminders of Aunt Chloe's fear that her youngest child could be sold away from her (1:145). Stowe's oversight during the work's composition—her inattention to (or indecision about) the name of Tom and Chloe's child—may indicate that her notion of Tom's family was not fully formed early in the work's serial composition. Another notable correction occurs in the final chapter, in the list of former slaves who reside as free men in Cincinnati. For one of these men, who is designated by the initial "W——," Stowe adds the man's net worth to the corrected printing (2:320). He who formerly lived as the property of another man has made himself into a property holder after achieving his freedom.

The textual alterations in sum indicate a significant (though not comprehensive) effort at authorial correction, and the attentiveness to punctuation in some corrections suggests that portions of the proofreading efforts were quite careful. Unpublished scholarship has indicated that later printings included additional corrections.[22] Of the 18 sites of correction identified in the apparatus on the basis of Kirkham's and Winship's scholarship, Lynn, by proofreading his transcription of the uncorrected printing, did independently emend three obvious errors. But the remaining corrections of accidental and substantive variants in the first Jewett edition—almost certainly requested by the author—do not appear in Lynn's edition.

The remaining lists of editorial emendations in the apparatus include both substantive and accidental readings. In contrast, the lists of transcription errors, unless otherwise noted, are selective and include only substantive readings. The following classes of accidental features are omitted silently from both parts of the apparatus: spaces preceding apostrophes or the negating word *not* in contractions; minor transcription errors (omitted or added commas, alterations of sentence capitalization in dialog); differing practices for chapter numbers and initial small capitals; modernization of spelling (diaereses, accents, and hyphens serve as pronunciation markers in the Jewett edition); and digraphs, ligatures, quotation marks, and em dashes. Print volumes have ligatures for ﬁ, ﬀ, ﬂ, ﬃ, and ﬄ, digraphs for œ, æ, Œ, and Æ, "smart quotes" and apostrophes, and em-length dashes. The electronic text substitutes unligatured letter sequences, straight quotation marks, and typewriter-style double hyphens for em dashes. The typographical features—as well as paper stock, type page margin, binding style, publisher imprint, editorial paratexts, and, for electronic texts, browser rendering—remain part of what Jerome J. McGann has called the "bibliographical codes."[23] But the palimpsestic quality of the modern print and digital age is most prominent in the *text* or information content, the part of the work that contemporary frameworks of technology and of law assume is transmissible from one material form to another.

If one credits Lynn with editorial emendations for three corrections that were also made in the Jewett printing, Lynn makes 32 alterations that might be considered emendations. If, among this group, Lynn's emendations of dialect are judged unnecessary or inadvertent, perhaps 20 alterations remain as intended acts of emendation. The list of all identified editorial emendations is provided in the section of the apparatus labeled "Lynn's Harvard

Text Emendations of Jewett Edition Text."[24] But the reprint edition that produced two or three dozen emendations also introduced 145 transcription errors. In chapter 12, "Select Incident of Lawful Trade," Stowe depicts the horror that slave auctions visit on families and condemns the silent acquiescence of the "enlightened, cultivated, intelligent man" (JE 1:199). The slave trader is supported by "public sentiment that calls for his trade." A transcription error in the Harvard edition replaces "sentiment" with "statement" (HL 137).[25] Stowe attacked even silent toleration of the slave trade. The Harvard edition error raises the level of action needed for complicity with lawful trade to "public statement." In another case, the Jewett edition offers a full explanation for an abrupt tonal shift in a section of St. Clare's dialog, but Lynn omits the entire line (JE 2:8; HL 226). Three transcription errors involve punctuation, and they seem to this reader to rise to the level of substantives. When Eva speaks to the St. Clare slaves a few days before her death, her sentences break off unfinished—the extent of the pause signaled by a fifth or sixth ellipsis dot. While conventional three- or four-dot ellipses do not appear elsewhere in Stowe's work, the extended ellipses may mark Eva's pauses meaningfully, as at least different from pauses indicated by the conventional ellipses dots in Lynn's edition.[26] When George Harris and family cross Lake Erie, the narrator in the Harvard text asks about the "electric word! What is it?" (394). In the Jewett edition, the question is not rhetorical, it is a question of definition. The antecedent should be "Liberty!" (JE 2:233). But the Harvard edition's most damaging error occurs in Stowe's sermon-like final chapter, when she emphasizes the importance of law: "If the laws of New England were so arranged that a master could *now and then* torture an apprentice to death, without a possibility of being brought to justice, would it be received with equal composure?" (JE 2:311). The Harvard edition omits the entire clause "without a possibility of being brought to justice" (453). While Stowe deplores violence, she condemns injustice more forcefully. Even if the dying Eva's pauses, signaled by extended ellipses, are considered accidentals, the 141 substantive transcription errors should have retired the Harvard edition from its role as a "standard edition." Its retirement from that role seems rather to have been based on other factors, the neglect of editions that have gone out of print and the proliferation of new editions for the classroom market. But its transcription errors remained part of the *text* of the twentieth-century *Uncle Tom's Cabin* even as the edition faded from view.

Douglas, who based the Penguin edition on Lynn's text, makes only minimal correction of errors in the Harvard edition. By my count, only six alterations of the Harvard text—listed in the apparatus under "Douglas's Penguin Text Emendations of Harvard Edition Text"—could be counted as emendations. Three obvious errors in the Harvard source text are corrected, including the curious repetition of "Chole" for "Chloe."[27] But the near absence of emendation suggests that the Penguin edition was proofread neither against the Jewett edition nor against Lynn's edition. In the portion of the Penguin edition that corresponds to volume 2 in the Jewett edition, not one alteration appears to qualify as an editorial emendation. As befits a minimally proofed text—or one corrected only by the publisher's copy editor—the edition is rife with transcription error. When Tom, in his apartment, prays aloud for Augustine St. Clare's deliverance from drink, St. Clare overhears him. He says that Tom's prayer "was n't very politic," but the Penguin edition has "wasn't very polite" (JE 1:267; PE 282). During the auction of the St. Clare slaves, Stowe notes that auction spectators are "handling" slaves, regardless of whether the person plans to buy: "Various spectators, intending to purchase, or not intending, as the case might be, gathered around the group, handling, examining, and commenting on their various points and faces with the same freedom that a set of jockeys discuss the merits of a horse" (JE 2:163). The public invitation to "handle" slaves, especially female slaves, appeals both to buyers and spectators: the latter may attend the auction merely for the opportunity to place hands on women and young girls. Stowe's subtle intimation, that slave auctions invite spectators to physically handle the human property on display, is omitted when the Penguin compositor's eye-skip turned the line into near gibberish: "Various spectators, intending to purchase, or not intending, examining, and commenting on their various points and faces with the same freedom that a set of jockeys discuss the merits of a horse" (PE 475). When the original line precedes Simon Legree's physical violation of Emmeline—she cries after he passes his hand over her "neck and bust"—the reader can recognize his act as characteristic of slave auctions in general (JE 2:165). The Penguin edition's faulty version puts unwarranted emphasis on Legree as a particularly heinous individual: in the reprint, his act can be read as anomalous or unusual, characteristic of his private nature rather than of slave auctions as a public institution.

In her introduction to the Penguin edition, Douglas labels Stowe a "careless writer,"[28] but as editor, Douglas is at least partly responsible for the carelessness with which Stowe's text appears. The apparatus lists 170 substantive errors in the Penguin edition. Because the Penguin text descends from the Harvard edition, the errors accrue. If the Penguin edition transcription errors are added to the Harvard edition set, with possible emendations subtracted, the substantive errors reported in the Penguin edition number 279: the reprint edition has approximately one substantive error every other page. Despite these faults, the Penguin edition has been cited as the text of *Uncle Tom's Cabin* in a wide range of scholarship—peer-reviewed articles, collections of criticism, and scholarly monographs.[29] To know that the Penguin edition has almost 300 substantive errors and to cite it nonetheless as the text of Stowe's work would be irresponsible, but Douglas's edition has shaped the reading of Stowe's work over almost three decades of scholarship and university classroom reading. A study of scholarly reading in the current moment must grapple with the edition that has served as a touchstone for scholarly work. The unwarranted faith in accurate textual transmission from book to book is perhaps matched only by an uncritical confidence that electronic texts are generally unreliable, the subject to which we turn next.

If an electronic text is derived from Douglas's Penguin edition, it will be unreliable. Stowe's text in its Penguin form entered digital culture at the EText Center and later at Railton's *UTC & AC* archive. The EText Center version of the text was considered for inclusion in the accompanying apparatus—and was consulted during its preparation—but it was excluded to address the greater prominence of the version published on the *UTC & AC* site. One of the tasks undertaken at Railton's project was to silently proofread the electronic text against a copy of the Jewett edition. That effort at proofreading the electronic text—against original early printings of the Jewett edition—caught many obvious errors. Thirty-nine errors were corrected, thirty-eight of them derived from transcription errors in either Lynn's Harvard edition or Douglas's Penguin edition. For example, the Penguin edition's "suveyed" and "suport" are corrected to "surveyed" and "support"; and the Harvard and Penguin editions' "Kenutcky" and "smoulding" are corrected to "Kentucky" and "smouldering."[30] However, the electronic text is unreliable because the Penguin source text was inaccurate, the optical character recognition (OCR) process introduced numerous errors, and silent proofreading is not an effective method to identify errors. The apparatus lists 69 errors that can be attributed to the OCR process, which replaced small capitals or italic type with roman characters, converted letter-punctuation combinations to another form, substituted letters, or combined two letters into one. For example, "barn-yard" becomes "bam-yard," "Butler" becomes "Butter," "burns" becomes "bums," and "har" becomes "bar."[31] In a comical case of a dropped letter *l*, Topsy's memento, Little Eva's hair, is described as a "fair soft cur" rather than a "fair soft curl" (JE 2:130). Due to a faulty process in the preparation of the electronic text, a large section of text dealing with Cassy's son Harry after he is sold into slavery is lost (2:208). To arrive at a reasonable count of the substantive errors in the *UTC & AC* text, emendations made in the Harvard or Penguin edition are subtracted from the total number of errors, as are emendations made while proofreading the electronic text. Errors from the Harvard and Penguin editions are also cumulative with the additional transcription errors during the OCR process. The text has 313 substantive errors, but the consequences of these errors are difficult to assess because scholars remain reluctant to cite electronic texts.

As an editor who has published two electronic versions of *Uncle Tom's Cabin* in its *National Era* newspaper form, one as part of my dissertation and one on Railton's *UTC & AC* site, I acknowledge my stake in scholarly attitudes toward electronic texts. If scholars rely on electronic texts for their own research but choose to cite print forms in their books and articles—a dark confession that trust in electronic resources is a matter of private, not public, feeling—scholarship published in electronic form will be viewed with suspicion. Having suggested several hundred modifications to the published electronic text on the *UTC & AC* site, I advise skepticism toward the authority of electronic texts. But such skepticism is uncritical if a scholar does not bring similar skepticism toward texts that are published in print form and toward his or her own ability to transcribe accurately. To copy and paste from a browser into a word processor is far wiser than to transcribe from a copy of a book propped on a knee before the keyboard. Those who tend toward skepticism of electronic texts—and trust of printed texts—should use the skepticism to advantage: copy and paste the electronic text, but then triple-check the electronic text by comparing it to page images, to physical copies, and to other printed transcriptions. Whether one's citation is print or digital becomes a vexed question, but such practices are more likely to make one aware that texts have histories, that modern reprints also alter historical texts. It remains the scholar's task to determine whether an alteration is significant. A textual scholar approaches a printed or digitally published text with a measured confidence that processes of transmission have altered the text, and these alterations, whether accidental or deliberate, are readable signs of cultural engagement with texts. The type of proof offered here, the elaborate apparatus on modern reprints, could be repeated for almost any electronic text derived from two different print exemplars. For Americanists, online databases provide vast resources for such study: *Early American Fiction, Making of America, Documenting the American South, Wright American Fiction,* Internet Archive, Google Books, and Project Gutenberg.[32] And the NINES tool Juxta puts textual comparison of multiple texts within the reach of scholars with basic digital literacy. After the scholar has overcome the reluctance to deal with the tools necessary to compare texts electronically and learns to compensate for the limitations of OCR or transcribed texts, the only hurdles that remain are the digital text projects that have inadequate provenance statements, that prevent copying, or that limit page views. Researchers can overcome these hurdles by careful assessment of transcription provenance or by addressing requests to the providers of hobbled resources.

Based on an early version of the evidence assembled in the apparatus, I provided Railton with a list of textual variants between the transcription of *Uncle Tom's Cabin* on the *UTC & AC* site and the transcription at the *Early American Fiction* project. He was disturbed at the number of errors but pleased for the opportunity to correct them. As of late 2006, he had corrected the text of the Jewett version on his site. Barring a mishap in the management of files—to prevent or recover from such mishaps is one of the primary responsibilities of digital projects—the electronic edition of *Uncle Tom's Cabin* currently available on Railton's site is far more accurate than the Penguin edition. This story has one more twist. Railton is also the editor of the 2008 Bedford/St. Martin's edition of *Uncle Tom's Cabin,* a companion to volume 1 of the *Bedford Anthology of American Literature* (2008). According to its note on the text, the Bedford edition is derived from the version published on *UTC & AC,* but the Bedford edition was in galleys when I shared the list of variants between the *UTC & AC* and the *Early American Fiction* text with the editor.[33] Railton corrected the two versions of the text independently. The current line of descent for the Jewett–Harvard–Penguin–*UTC & AC*–Bedford text is represented in figure 2.

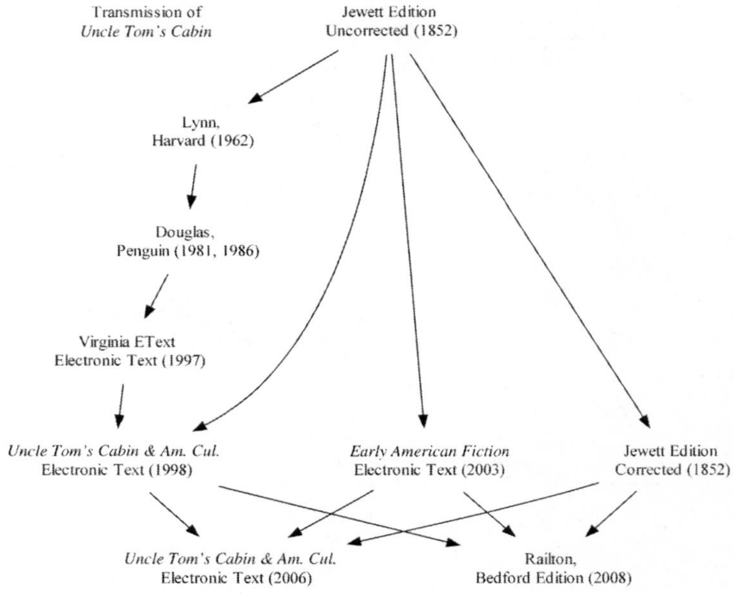

Fig. 2. Descent and intermingling among print and digital texts of *Uncle Tom's Cabin*

The practical consequences for this line of descent are simple from the perspective of textual authority, but the cultural authority of electronic texts has greater consequences. Each transcription based on a previous document will depart from the forms of the previous document and will have less textual authority. Three practices can improve the accuracy of a transcribed copy: proofreading against original documents, collating independent keyboardings of the same version electronically, and collating against other versions of the text. Oral proofreading is more effective than silent proofreading, but neither method is as accurate as independent keyboardings and electronic file comparison. Some textual scholars minimize the distinction between printed and electronic texts. G. Thomas Tanselle writes, "Printed and electronic renderings are thus not ontologically different; they may be made of different physical materials, but the conceptual status of the texts in each case is identical."[34] While this statement is true if texts are defined as an abstraction independent of documentary form—a key area of conflict between the position advocated by Tanselle and that advocated by McGann—the wider community of scholars has observed a sharp distinction between the authority of printed and digital objects. Concerns ancillary to this study of textual descent—scholarly reputation of the editor, publisher's imprint, price, editorial paratexts, and so on—arguably have greater cultural power than the ontology of the text.

Railton's *UTC & AC* archive may well have shaped scholarship in the decade of its online life—and I defer to work published elsewhere in this volume—but the evidence is difficult to find, as citation of the archive in published scholarship remains rare.[35] If scholars use the archive but cite print resources, their choice may reflect doubt about the authority of the text, but the choice possibly reflects an acceptance of widespread cultural concerns about the impermanence and mutability of digital resources. Scholars will heed cautionary advisories in the *MLA Style Manual* and the *Chicago Manual of Style*, respectively, that "electronic texts are not as fixed and stable as their print counterparts" and that "electronic content by its very nature will continue to be impermanent and manipulable."[36] The latest edition of the *MLA Style Manual* (2008) treats Web publication as occupying a continuum from print publication to live performance: of the former, a reader can be "reasonably assured that a copy in a local library will be identical to that consulted by an author," but of the latter, the reader must recognize that any version "is potentially different from any past or future version and must be considered unique." The revised MLA manual also indicates that URLs can be omitted from electronic sources, in part because of the troublesomeness of typing them into a browser—an anecdote that implies that transcription from a paper-based source is the imagined use of the URL.[37] The manual's rhetoric seems not to imagine clicking on or copying and pasting from a digital source. Despite a rhetoric that sometimes recalls the previous edition's bias toward print as the default medium, the new citation recommendation—that print should not be treated as the default publication form—is welcome. The decision no longer to require dates of access for electronic materials in the new format is commendable. In his probing analysis of digital media, Matthew Kirschenbaum offers a trenchant reason for resisting the former practice, because the "repeated and conspicuous emphasis on exactly when the source was checked is disruptive and serves to prejudice still-emerging perceptions of the stability (and reliability) of the medium."[38]

As the apparatus entries for the two-volume Jewett edition of *Uncle Tom's Cabin* make clear, any two copies of a book are potentially different. Despite my confirmation that not one of four copies of Lynn's Harvard edition and not one of four copies of Douglas's Penguin edition includes a substantive reading that differs from the apparatus, I cannot state with certainty that neither edition has been corrected. While a suspicion of print copies marks an allegiance to textual scholarship as a discipline, the suspicion of electronic sources is pervasive. At the founding sessions for the Digital Americanists at the 2007 American Literature Association conference, a number of professional anxieties were brought forward. Reference to online research resources—instead of print volumes and archival documents—is held by some senior scholars to reflect negatively on the quality of research. In other cases, authors citing online versions of books or articles omit URLs because they are aesthetically distracting (despite the insistence in the 1998 *MLA Style Manual* that URLs were necessary for electronic sources).[39] If scholars take the additional step of suppressing the electronic nature of a source—whether in unreflecting confidence that electronic texts are identical to print forms or in anguished concern that they may not be—the only method for reading such cultural practices is a detailed comparison of print and digital forms with the tools of textual scholarship.

But the practice of textual scholarship can also be harmed by an attitude of suspicion toward digital resources. A digital text prepared by OCR means, which is inadequate for many purposes, is uniquely able to complement other methods of text acquisition. In my own work on the New Edition of *Uncle Tom's Cabin* (1879), I collated my keyboard transcription against the Google Books OCR text. Although the OCR is faulty, the Google Books version is helpful for catching errors in original printings. For example, during Sam's speechifying, the 1879 edition has "pertistent," but while transcribing, I unconsciously corrected the error to "persistent."[40] So long as the resulting text is not spell checked or regularized, machine-dumb accurate OCR is a more reliable means of identifying this type of error than multiple keyboardings, silent proofreading, or oral proofreading. Errors that seem obvious once identified but are difficult to notice when typing or proofreading are possible candidates for correction by a publisher or an author. If another copy from the same edition has the error corrected, such cues may help to identify early and late printings and contribute to a more comprehensive account of the edition's printing history. While proofreading the Google Books text cannot substitute for a keyboard transcription from an original copy, a machine comparison of a keyboard transcription with a machine-readable transcription prepared from OCR should become a standard part of the process for preparing a scholarly edition, at least for works in common roman types of the nineteenth century.

My reading of the transmission of *Uncle Tom's Cabin* in modern reprints suggests a culture of professional scholarly studies in which we have become complacent about print textual transmission. In an era of expanded canons, we need to be reminded that texts, too, have histories. We ignore that history at peril of overlooking textual transmission in a discipline ostensibly concerned with texts and documents. If texts are no longer verbal icons—if they are shaped by interaction with material culture—why is scholarly citation so readily content that any poorly prepared reprint of one version of a text adequately represents the work? If the textual complexity of one of the preëminent works in the expanded canon of American literature is so poorly understood, we should expect that the canon's more recent additions present comparable complexity. As new reprint editions are based on texts that have been published in electronic form, our expectations for editors of classroom editions should be higher. Rather than merely proofing an electronic text found in a digital archive, scholars should demand, at a minimum, that editors of new print editions keyboard their text from images of original documents and use text comparison software to compare the transcription against the previous electronic publication. If Stowe's *Uncle Tom's Cabin* is an important work and if accuracy of quotation is a concern of the first order, a citation of a trustworthy electronic text is far preferable to citing the Penguin edition. The *Early American Fiction* site is more accurate than most print editions of *Uncle Tom's Cabin.* If the interest is the text that shaped reading at the moment of its publication, careful scholars would be wise to copy, paste, and double-check against page images on a reliable electronic source, a practice that is far more accurate than transcribing from a modern reprint. As our own scholarship is increasingly published electronically, we might look forward to a not-distant day in which the tools of textual analysis are more powerful by factors of thousands, when a scholar with an interest in quantifying the loss in contemporary practices of citation may have at her or his disposal both the tools and the corpus of scholarly criticism that are necessary to do the work justice.

Notes

I thank Stephen Railton and the University of Virginia Electronic Text Center for sharing electronic transcriptions that form the basis for the textual apparatus.

1. Michael Winship, "'In the four quarters of the globe, who reads an American book?'" in *Literary Cultures and the Material Book,* ed. Simon Eliot, Andrew Nash, and Ian Willison (London: British Library, 2007), 378 n. 19.

2. James L. Harner, *Literary Research Guide,* 4th ed. (New York: Modern Language Association, 2002), 368; James L. Harner, *Literary Research Guide,* 2nd ed. (New York: Modern Language Association, 1993), 381, 380.

3. John Lavagnino, "Reading, Scholarship, and Hypertext Editions," *Text* 8 (1995): 112.

4. Herman Melville, *Typee: A Fluid-Text Edition,* ed. John Bryant (Charlottesville: University of Virginia Press, 2006), http://rotunda.upress.virginia.edu:8080/melville/; William Wells Brown, *Clotel: An Electronic Scholarly Edition,* ed. Christopher Mulvey (Charlottesville: University of Virginia Press, 2006), http://rotunda.upress.virginia.edu:8080/clotel/.

5. W. W. Greg, "The Rationale of Copy-Text," *Studies in Bibliography* 3 (1950): 21.

6. Dirk Van Hulle and the MLA Committee on Scholarly Editions, "Guidelines for Editors of Scholarly Editions," in *Electronic Textual Editing,* ed. Katherine O'Brien O'Keeffe, Lou Burnard, and John Unsworth (New York: Modern Language Association, 2006), 42.

7. For a clear summary of fine distinctions in typographical spacing, see John Southward, *Modern Printing* (London: Raithby, Lawrence, 1924), 112.

8. Harriet Beecher Stowe, *Uncle Tom's Cabin: or, Life among the Lowly,* 2 vols. (Boston: John P. Jewett, 1852); Harriet Beecher Stowe, *Uncle Tom's Cabin; or, Life among the Lowly,* ed. Kenneth S. Lynn (Cambridge, MA: Harvard University Press, Belknap Press, 1962); Harriet Beecher Stowe, *Uncle Tom's Cabin: or, Life among the Lowly,* ed. Ann Douglas (New York: Penguin, 1981, 1986); Harriet Beecher Stowe, *Uncle Tom's Cabin: or, Life among the Lowly* (Charlottesville, VA: Stephen Railton, *UTC & AC,* IATH, EText Center, 1998), http://www.iath.virginia.edu/utc/uncletom/uthp.html.

9. The apparatus, entitled "Variants in Texts of *Uncle Tom's Cabin,*" is available from the publisher at http://www.press.umich.edu/pdf/raabe.pdf/ and also through the OhioLINK Digital Resource Commons at http://drcdev.ohiolink.edu/handle/123456789/3489.

10. Jerome J. McGann, *The Textual Condition* (Princeton, NJ: Princeton University Press, 1991), 120.

11. *Early American Fiction,* http://etext.virginia.edu/eaf/, provides a searchable text and facsimile page images from the Jewett edition. *Wright American Fiction, 1851–1875,* http://www.letrs.indiana.edu/web/w/wright2/, provides a searchable text and facsimile page images from microfilm. The Internet Archive provides facsimile page images in Acrobat PDF, searchable text, and other formats: see http://www.archive.org/details/uncletomscabin01stowrich and http://www.archive.org/details/uncletomscabin02stowrich.

12. Kenneth S. Lynn, "A History of the Text," in *Uncle Tom's Cabin* (Harvard, 1962), xxviii; Ann Douglas, textual note to *Uncle Tom's Cabin* (Penguin, 1981, 1986), 37; Stephen Railton, header to *Uncle Tom's Cabin* (EText Center, 1998), http://etext.lib.virginia.edu/toc/modeng/public/StoCabi.html; header to *Uncle Tom's Cabin* (Stephen Railton; *UTC & AC;* IATH; EText, 1998), http://www.iath.virginia.edu/utc/uncletom/uthp.html, 11 Mar. 2007. Railton states that the *UTC & AC* text was derived from the EText Center version (private communication).

13. On Lynn's introduction, see Claire Parfait, *The Publishing History of "Uncle Tom's Cabin," 1852–2002* (Aldershot, Hampshire, England: Ashgate, 2007), 187–89.

14. Stowe, *Uncle Tom's Cabin* (Jewett, 1852), 1:191.

15. Lynn in *Uncle Tom's Cabin* (Harvard, 1962), 135 n. 3.

16. Fredson Bowers, *Principles of Bibliographical Description* (Princeton, NJ: Princeton University Press, 1949; reprint, New Castle, DE: Oak Knoll Press, 1994), 37–39; G. Thomas Tanselle, "The Bibliographical Concepts of Issue and State," *Papers of the Bibliographical Society of America* 69, no. 1 (1975): 18–21.

17. E. Bruce Kirkham, "The First Editions of *Uncle Tom's Cabin:* A Bibliographical Study," *Papers of the Bibliographical Society of America* 65, no. 4 (1971): 372–73. Kirkham reports, based on his examination of multiple copies, that the footnote continues to appear in some copies of the Jewett edition identified by a sixtieth thousand slug on the title page.

18. Lynn, "A History of the Text," in *Uncle Tom's Cabin* (Harvard , 1962), xxvi; E. Bruce Kirkham, *The Building of "Uncle Tom's Cabin"* (Knoxville: University of Tennessee Press, 1977), 165–94.

19. Elizabeth Ammons and Susan Belasco, "Classroom Texts," in *Approaches to Teaching Stowe's "Uncle Tom's Cabin,"* ed. Elizabeth Ammons and Susan Belasco (New York: Modern Language Association, 2000), 7.

20. Kirkham, "First Editions," 373–74; Michael Winship and the Bibliographical Society of America, "Harriet Beecher Stowe," in *Bibliography of American Literature,* vol. 8 (New Haven: Yale University Press, 1990), no. 19343.

21. Parenthetical citations provide the Jewett volume and page number.

22. See Harry Earl Opperman, "A Bibliography and *Stemma Codicum* for British Editions of *Uncle Tom's Cabin,* 1852–1853" (PhD diss., Kansas State University, 1971), 417–18. Opperman examined a printing of volume 1 of the Jewett edition labeled eightieth thousand and a printing of volume 2 labeled seventy-fifth thousand. The italic type in the Parker quotation was changed to roman type. While I have supplemented Opperman's investigation by examining copies labeled sixtieth thousand and hundredth thousand, I cannot yet determine whether the other corrections identified by Opperman in volume 2 were associated with the alteration of the Parker footnote in volume 1. The apparatus reports only the corrections and alterations published by Kirkham and Winship.

23. McGann, *Textual Condition,* 60.

24. If an obvious error in the Jewett edition was inadvertently corrected during the keyboarding of the *Early American Fiction* text, the apparatus may not properly credit

an emendation to the editors of the Harvard or Penguin edition. An example occurs in JE 2:63, l. 21. The word *little* is spelled *litttle* (with three *t*'s) in the Jewett edition, but the spelling is corrected on the *EAF* project. This error is noted on the *Wright American Fiction* site.

25. For each set of paired passages, the parenthetical Jewett edition page number, with the siglum JE and volume number, indicates the apparatus entry. The Harvard edition page number, with the siglum HL, is provided parenthetically for cited passages.

26. JE 2:102, 103, 106; HL 295, 297.

27. JE 1:49, 141; HL 31, 98; PG 76, 163.

28. Douglas, introduction to *Uncle Tom's Cabin* (Penguin, 1981, 1986), 29.

29. A list of twentieth-century studies that cite the Penguin edition would overwhelm a bibliography. The following list is limited to twenty-first century studies that cite Douglas's edition as the text of *Uncle Tom's Cabin:* Ellen J. Goldner, "Arguing with Pictures: Race, Class, and the Formation of Popular Abolitionism through *Uncle Tom's Cabin*," *Journal of American and Comparative Cultures* 24, nos. 1–2 (2001): 71–84, http://search.ebscohost.com/login.aspx?direct=true&db=mzh&AN=2002531609&site=ehost-live; Rachel Naomi Klein, "Harriet Beecher Stowe and the Domestication of Free Labor Ideology," *Legacy* 18, no. 2 (2001): 135–52, http://muse.jhu.edu/journals/legacy/v018/18.2klein.pdf; Michael Borgstrom, "Passing Over: Setting the Record Straight in *Uncle Tom's Cabin*," *PMLA* 118, no. 5 (2003): 1290–1304, http://www.mlajournals.org/doi/abs/10.1632/003081203X67983; Christopher Diller, "Sentimental Types and Social Reform in *Uncle Tom's Cabin*," *Studies in American Fiction* 32, no. 1 (2004): 21–48; Barbara Hochman, "*Uncle Tom's Cabin* in the *National Era:* An Essay in Generic Norms and the Contexts of Reading," *Book History* 7 (2004): 143–69, http://muse.jhu.edu/journals/book_history/v007/7.1hochman.pdf; Caroline Field Levander, "'Let her White progeny offset her dark one': The Child and the Racial Politics of Nation Making," *American Literature* 76, no. 2 (2004): 221–46; Noelle Gallagher, "The Bagging Factory and the Breakfast Factory: Industrial Labor and Sentimentality in Harriet Beecher Stowe's *Uncle Tom's Cabin*," *Nineteenth-Century Contexts* 27, no. 2 (2005): 167–87, http://www.informaworld.com/10.1080/08905490500213410; Jeanne Elders Dewaard, "'The Shadow of Law': Sentimental Interiority, Gothic Terror, and the Legal Subject," *Arizona Quarterly* 62, no. 4 (2006): 1–30, http://muse.jhu.edu/journals/arizona_quarterly_a_journal_of_american_literature_culture_and_theory/v062/62.4dewaard.pdf; Linda Naranjo-Huebl, "'Take, Eat': Food Imagery, the Nurturing Ethic, and Christian Identity in *The Wide, Wide World, Uncle Tom's Cabin*, and *Incidents in the Life of a Slave Girl*," *Christianity and Literature* 56, no. 4 (2007): 597–631, http://search.ebscohost.com/login.aspx?direct=true&db=mzh&AN=2007651663&site=ehost-live; Kyla Wazana Tompkins, "'Everything 'cept Eat Us': The Antebellum Black Body Portrayed as Edible Body," *Callaloo* 30, no. 1 (2007): 201–24, http://muse.jhu.edu/journals/callaloo/v030/30.1tompkins.pdf; Marianne Noble, "Sentimental Epistemologies in *Uncle Tom's Cabin* and *The House of Seven Gables*," in *Separate Spheres No More: Gender Convergence in American Literature, 1830–1930* (Tuscaloosa: University of

Alabama Press, 2000), 261–81; Lauren Berlant, "Poor Eliza," in *No More Separate Spheres! A Next Wave American Studies Reader* (Durham, NC: Duke University Press, 2002), 291–323; Marianne Noble, *The Masochistic Pleasures of Sentimental Literature* (Princeton, NJ: Princeton University Press, 2000); Leland Krauth, *Mark Twain and Company: Six Literary Relations* (Athens: University of Georgia Press, 2003); Stephen Michael Best, *The Fugitive's Properties: Law and the Poetics of Possession* (Chicago: University of Chicago Press, 2004); Cindy Weinstein, *Family, Kinship, and Sympathy in Nineteenth-Century American Literature* (Cambridge: Cambridge University Press, 2004); Melissa J. Homestead, *American Women Authors and Literary Property, 1822–1869* (New York: Cambridge University Press, 2005); Sarah Robbins, *The Cambridge Introduction to Harriet Beecher Stowe* (Cambridge: Cambridge University Press, 2007).

30. Page numbers in the *UTC & AC* text match the Jewett edition. Compare JE or AC 1:115, 1:191, 2:54, 2:186; HL 79, 135, 258, 357; PE 137, 209, 372, 497.

31. JE and AC 1:39, 1:160, 2:11, 2:310.

32. *Documenting the American South,* University Library, University of North Carolina at Chapel Hill, http://docsouth.unc.edu; *Early American Fiction,* University of Virginia Library Digital Collections, http://etext.virginia.edu/eaf/; Google Books, http://books.google.com; Internet Archive, http://www.archive.org; *Making of America,* University of Michigan and Cornell University, http://quod.lib.umich.edu/m/moagrp/index.html; Project Gutenberg, http://www.gutenberg.org; *Wright American Fiction, 1851–1875,* Indiana University Digital Library Program, http://www.letrs.indiana.edu/web/w/wright2/.

33. Stephen Railton, preface to *Uncle Tom's Cabin* (Boston: Bedford/St. Martins, 2008), vi.

34. G. Thomas Tanselle, foreword to *Electronic Textual Editing,* ed. O'Keeffe et al. (New York: Modern Language Association, 2006), 1–6.

35. See Lisa Spiro and Jane Segal, "Scholars' Usage of Digital Archives in American Literature," in the present volume. Parfait's *Publishing History* does regularly cite the *UTC & AC* archive.

36. Joseph Gibaldi, *MLA Style Manual and Guide to Scholarly Publishing,* 2nd ed. (New York: Modern Language Association, 1998), 209; University of Chicago Press, *The Chicago Manual of Style,* 15th ed. (Chicago: University of Chicago Press, 2003), 644.

37. Modern Language Association, *MLA Style Manual and Guide to Scholarly Publishing,* 3rd ed. (New York: Modern Language Association, 2008), 212.

38. Matthew G. Kirschenbaum, *Mechanisms: New Media and the Forensic Imagination* (Cambridge, MA: MIT Press, 2008), 265.

39. Gibaldi, *MLA Style Manual,* 2nd ed. (1998), 210.

40. Harriet Beecher Stowe, *Uncle Tom's Cabin; or, Life among the Lowly* (Boston: Houghton, Osgood, 1879), 93, http://books.google.com/books?id=_eYRAAAAYAAJ. See note 24 for a similar case of inadvertent correction in the twice-keyboarded text of the *EAF* project.

Presentation of Archival Materials on the Web: A Curator's Model Based on Selectivity and Interpretation

LESLIE PERRIN WILSON

The World Wide Web has created great expectations among all types of archive users, academic literary scholars among them. These days, patrons and potential patrons—both on-site (in the repository) and from afar (via mail, e-mail, phone, and fax)—are quick to ask, "Is it available on the Internet?" or "Do you have plans to digitize it?" While the word *entitlement* has negative connotations best avoided in the discussion of a medium with the access-enhancing and arguably democratizing capabilities of the Web, the assumption underlying such queries is that the researcher has a right to comprehensive digital entrée to holdings and that creating such availability is a goal of all curators of significant archives.

In a perfect world, perhaps it would be so. If budget and staffing concerns were not a fact of life in libraries and archives everywhere, if such institutions were not frequently consulted by a range of users representing the full spectrum of technical fluency (from minimal searching ability to sophistication in locating and manipulating information on the Web), and if the private bodies that own so many of the collections valuable for scholarship could or would overlook the threat posed by Internet publication to maintaining their rights over their holdings, then there would be no impediment to the provision of full Web access. But even then, for those who preside over many archival and manuscript repositories, building a Web site would remain neither the only nor even necessarily the most important task at hand. As curator of the William Munroe Special Collections at the Concord (Massachusetts) Free Public Library (CFPL), I embrace the provision of Web access as one, but just one, of my responsibilities.[1]

The best many of us can do—the collective "we" being curators and archivists responsible for determining how to develop Web pages designed around the holdings under our care, simultaneously with implementing the policies of the administrative entities to whom we are accountable—is to follow a selective, interpretive approach based on our intimate familiarity with the content and strengths of our collections, the interrelationships among them, and the research requirements of the many types of patrons who use them. Moreover, however much full Web access to collections might improve the research capabilities of some users, we need to face the reality that a more limited strategy may, in fact, adequately fulfill our obligations to scholars working in the subject areas around which our collections are built, while at the same time respecting institutional missions and policies regarding the use of fiscal, human, and intellectual resources, as well as budgetary realities.

There may be overkill in the notion that if digitization is good, more digitization is better. The expensive wholesale scanning and mounting of materials is of doubtful value if full Web accessibility does not dramatically and measurably boost the incorporation of information from primary material into scholarship. Until it is clear that it actually, rather than potentially, opens up whole new worlds to a significant body of receptive and informed researchers and raises the caliber of scholarship substantially, those who manage rich collections on a tight budget may choose to combine a selective form of Web access with the more traditional methods of disseminating collection information that librarians and archivists have always practiced. I have sometimes, in jest, referred to this employment of technological possibilities to bring users to the archive through suggestive, rather than comprehensive, Web access as the "come hither" approach. The end result is mediation between the user's complete satisfaction by sources available on the Internet—a worthy goal that is not feasible for all repositories—and more traditional channels of direct contact between user and archive.

Site statistics on page hits and on the duration of visits may or may not reflect the meaningful use of digitized information once pages are constructed, but only the knowledge and experience of an informed human intelligence can apply judgment regarding content likely to be worth the expenditure of resources before it takes place. Restricted by frugal funding and staffing, we are forced to ask a question that would be irrelevant if limitless institutional resources were available: whether or not the research use of a proposed page or set of pages is justifiable given the cost involved. If data from a particular Web offering informs the degree work or published scholarship of only one or two people a year, do the pages meet a real demand?

Scanning archival and manuscript materials for Web presentation, constructing Web pages, and mounting them are labor- and equipment-intensive processes and frequently take more time and more personnel hours than anticipated. The suggestion that a repository will save money in the long run by digitizing holdings is bromidic and shows a serious disregard for what is involved. It is reasonable to question whether devoting the funding required to build any Web site—however informative and user-friendly—is a more compelling expenditure in terms of meeting the needs of an archival facility's multiple communities than are the other programs and services of the institution, such as responding to the demands of on-site patrons and those who communicate inquiries in various ways; the organization, arrangement, and description of unprocessed collections; the preparation of interpretive on-site exhibitions for the education and enjoyment of the local community and of visitors; departmental writing and publishing projects; the fulfillment of photograph orders for and negotiation of permission agreements with publishers; and so on. Web access may be harnessed to or undertaken in conjunction with some of these activities, but it does not supersede them.

Over time, I have grown increasingly aware of the whys and hows of developing institutional Web presence. Between 1995 (when the Concord Free Public Library started out with a dial-up connection and two pages mounted by a student from the Concord-Carlisle Regional High School) to the present time, we have mounted a significant cross section of our holdings on the Web (as of September 2008, the Web site size is 971 megabytes, of which 880 are for the Special Collections pages).[2] In the 1990s, we coded HTML by hand, then created and edited pages using Netscape Composer, later transitioning to Microsoft FrontPage, then to Dreamweaver 4.0, and then to Dreamweaver 8.0.[3] Our pages—which overall are simply constructed and form an intuitively navigable, reasonably searchable whole[4]—

draw steady visitation by various clienteles, including academic scholars in literature and history. Certain clusters of pages are consulted all the time, and those who use them report to me how valuable they are for research and teaching purposes.[5] I am proud of this ongoing work and accept the need to continue investing precious staff time to it.[6] But competing demands mean that it is not and will likely never be my department's first priority.

Those who champion a high degree of Web accessibility to archival collections hold up collaboration as a means of facilitating the digitization of materials. Collaboration of all kinds is, in fact, generally a good thing. Large, well-funded and well-staffed projects expand the body of readily available primary material and create digital possibilities for institutions in no position to construct sophisticated, searchable Web sites incorporating quantities of documents or information. The Library of Congress/National Endowment for the Humanities National Digital Newspaper Project forms a prime example.[7]

But collaboration is also difficult to implement. In relation to digital projects, partnerships still necessitate a significant investment of time and resources by participating organizations. Moreover, for small entities hoping to establish and reinforce Web presence and to bring more visitors to their own Web sites, it may seem a double-edged sword. Many such repositories would prefer to increase visitation to their own Web sites than to other URLs. In Concord at the moment, each institution and historic site is still actively engaged in discovering how best to use the Web to carry out and promote its particular mission. An intelligently designed, mutually beneficial digital collaboration will probably not take shape any time soon. Moreover, the feeling that specialized local knowledge and the ability to place materials in context are important in the presentation of materials has galvanized the determination to create access and explore ideas separately, through multiple institutional Web sites, each entity on its own terms. (In this, as in so many matters, Concord is known for its spirit of independence.) There is also the worry—not uncommon among small repositories—that privately held materials become vulnerable in various ways once consigned to storage on servers other than an institution's own and subject to policy making and decision making by parties dissociated from the local scene. In the morass that intellectual property issues have become, everyone hopes to avoid murky ownership and use issues.

Given these complicating factors, how does the Concord Free Public

Library resolve the dilemma of reconciling limited resources and big ambitions for providing access on a global scale? We design for our Web site informative sets of pages constructed around discrete, well-defined subjects, literary and other, showcasing carefully selected holdings or types of holdings most likely to be valuable to our patrons, without committing more resources than we can muster and without ceding control over how materials are presented and—to some extent—used. From the scholar's point of view, it is perhaps not everything that might be desired. But feedback on offerings of the Concord Free Public Library Web site suggests that we do reach our target audiences and that selective, interpretive access is one workable model for matching holdings with potential users.

Online exhibitions form a major way of letting scholars know the scope of holdings in specific, important subject areas. They also provide contextual information and encourage connections across collections and material types, both of which make them useful for purposes of teaching at the college level. Two examples of Concord Free Public Library online exhibitions especially relevant to the work of the literary scholar and teacher are "Emerson in Concord," mounted in 2003 in commemoration of the 200th anniversary of the birth of Ralph Waldo Emerson, and "Earth's Eye" (Walden Pond images), created to mark the 150th anniversary in 2004 of the first publication of Henry David Thoreau's *Walden.*[8] The former was presented first as an on-site display in the Concord Free Public Library art gallery, prior to mounting on the Web; the latter was created as a solely online exhibit, with no gallery component. Both were prepared with a mixed audience in mind—generalist as well as specialist—and both include extensive interpretive text. Neither is exhaustive in presenting relevant holdings from the library's collections—they simply indicate the types of materials we can provide to document their respective subjects.

Designed, prepared, and constructed entirely by Special Collections staff, "Emerson in Concord" and "Earth's Eye" each feature an opening narrative, a listing or listings of images on display, and separate pages for each image and any accompanying identification and context. Additionally, the Emerson exhibit also provides separate narratives for each thematic section of the display. The Walden exhibition includes a map with numbered locations from which users can click to pages throughout the display to view images of places mentioned in the narrative, as well as links within the narrative itself from which appropriate images may also be accessed directly.

The navigation of each display is relatively simple. Users can move to any of the numbered pages via the item listings and can move back and forth within the pages, to the previous and next image and to the narrative(s). The separate item pages of the Walden display also include links back to the opening Special Collections page—a feature we realized was desirable after the Emerson exhibit was mounted. Both exhibitions draw heavy use by Web visitors. The exhibits alert scholars that there are significant Emerson- and Thoreau-related manuscripts, printed books, ephemera, maps, photographs, artwork, and other materials in the William Munroe Special Collections, and they motivate some to contact us directly about displayed holdings and other related materials we might have.

The *Concord Historic Buildings* Web site[9]—launched in 2006 and still under construction—represents another type of documentation-focused digital project of interest to academic literary scholars as well as to other audiences. Conceived and prepared by Special Collections staff but constructed with the services of a hired consultant, it showcases six historic Concord structures, of which five are still standing.[10] Although the overt purpose of the *Historic Buildings* pages is to offer information about the six buildings and about the built landscape in general (not coincidentally, with particular focus on the landscape familiar to the nineteenth-century Concord authors), the curatorial decision to undertake it was motivated by a desire to answer the underlying question of how we know what we know today about the history of specific local structures.

This site is consulted not only by academic researchers but also by students, from the elementary through the college level. It textually and visually tells the story of the six selected buildings. Each of the buildings was chosen for inclusion because its history is traceable through rich and varied documentation. The deliberate choice of particularly well-documented structures for the pages ensures that the site reflects the ways in which many kinds of archival source material interlock to paint an accurate picture of the landscape over time.

Each building is presented through a lengthy opening narrative and a number of separate pages telling the structure's story one primary document at a time. As with our online exhibitions, navigation is straightforward, with some modifications for those pages. Instead of an up-front item listing, there is a separate "index" (linked to the narrative and to each separate item page) with thumbnails of all the numbered images for a building.

This index allows users to scan the complete contents of the site visually before investing time in navigation. The *Historic Buildings* pages also allow the visitor to click easily to the Concord Free Public Library main page as well as to the opening Special Collections page.

If personal response is an accurate gauge of a Web site's efficacy (as opposed to the cut-and-dried reporting of site statistics), the selective and interpretive *Historic Buildings* pages have successfully created an informative interface between archive and users. Scholars who have worked productively in Concord literature and social history for decades have reported discovering in those pages potential research materials they had not previously known existed, as well as exploring there topics and ideas that they had not considered but found interesting and useful in some way.

To be sure, some materials and the kinds of use they invite demand comprehensive, rather than selective, access. In building Concord's Special Collections pages, we take this into account in offering some pages that constitute either the complete representation of an archival or manuscript collection in great demand or the provision of all the information or data in a single, much-used document or body of documents. This is the case with our *Henry David Thoreau Land & Property Surveys* pages, which make every one of our nearly 200 manuscript surveys by Henry David Thoreau available in digital form, at high resolution.[11] We sought and obtained funding for this site, designed it carefully, and hired a consultant to manage scanning and construction, because, in original form, the surveys have always been much-requested by literary scholars, historians, and others and therefore were clearly worth the investment involved in digitization. Moreover, Web access makes it far easier to view the collection in entirety—which is how most scholars want to use it—than it is possible to do on-site with the manuscript surveys, many of which are large and awkward to handle, even one at a time. Also, digital enhancement of faint pencil markings simplifies the decipherment of Thoreau's scrawl, making the scanned versions more informative than some of the originals. That the resulting pages are consulted every day and that some recent groundbreaking scholarship has drawn heavily on them have more than justified what it took to construct them.[12]

Mounted in 2006, *The Wheeler Families of Old Concord, Massachusetts* provides an example of a single-item Concord Free Public Library resource, the full contents of which are made available on the Web. It is an updated, online version of an important and heavily consulted genealogical source of the same title, compiled by George Tolman in 1908.[13] (The Concord Free Public Library holds Tolman's original manuscript and some of the notes and working papers that preceded the finished manuscript.) The information contained in the Wheeler page is relevant for genealogical research and also for the basic identification of local people for literary and historical studies. Because a continuous stream of Wheeler-related inquiries is directed to the Special Collections (this early Concord family was prolific, if nothing else), the decision to mount the genealogy was clear-cut. For Web publication, the work was transcribed but not scanned, since it is the data within, rather than the subtleties of the original manuscript, that interest researchers. Transcription and updating were accomplished by a knowledgeable local resident and Wheeler descendant, thereby keeping the library's investment to a minimum.[14] As mounted, the file is best searchable through use of the find-in-page feature of whatever browser a genealogist or scholar may be using.

The pages of the *Searchable Antebellum Concord (Mass.) Town Reports* comprise an offering based on full, rather than selective, presentation of a significant run of the basic yearly publication issued by the town government.[15] These pages contain both digital images of all surviving Concord municipal reports from 1834 up to the Civil War—a body of information of interest to literary scholars and historians—and a search function streamlined from a full index created through OCR software. (As discussed shortly, the Concord Free Public Library's recently formalized partnership with the *19th-Century Concord Digital Archive,* centered at Texas A&M University, will enhance the searchability of the town reports, allowing the scholar to move back and forth with ease between our page images and data within the fully transcribed and edited versions of these public records in the *Concord Digital Archive.*) Other such library projects are in planning or under implementation, among them the *Antebellum Concord (Mass.) Newspaper* pages and the mounting in transcribed form of the nineteenth-century diary of Concord lawyer John Shepard Keyes—a key document for many studies, ripe for a project that will save the original manuscript from repeated handling and the scholar from the seemingly dreaded necessity of using microfilm. Although these data-rich pages are not interpretive, they represent selectivity in the sense that a decision was made to implement them as opposed to other potential projects based on Special Collections holdings.

Online finding aids form a final major category of Concord Free Public Library Web offerings that demand some discussion, despite the fact that they do not make Special Collections holdings directly accessible on the Internet. They describe archival and manuscript collections in sufficient detail for researchers to determine whether they might be relevant to their topics of exploration, leading the scholar to the repository when possibly pertinent material is identified. It could be argued that they constitute the most important Web offering we provide, although certainly not the most glamorous, aesthetic, or entertaining. In well-managed archives, finding aids have traditionally formed the primary access tools into complex collections of personal papers, family papers, organizational and governmental records, and also some artificially generated collections. They may be prepared for fully processed (organized and arranged) collections, for partially processed collections, and even for unprocessed collections, although it is difficult to describe seriously chaotic materials with any degree of precision. At the Concord Free Public Library, we prepare finding aids for and allow researcher use of fully processed collections only. At this point, we have approximately 150 finding aids online, mounted in HTML and searchable via Google and, to some extent, by other major search engines.[16]

It has been suggested, many times and in many contexts, that if curators and archivists scanned all the contents of all our collections for Web access and searchability, it would be unnecessary to undertake the processing and description of collections at all. Let me assure anyone who thinks this that an access product from collections that have not been organized and analyzed for content would make little more sense than microfilm from unprocessed collections, even taking into account searchability via OCR. Processing, description, and the preparation of machine-readable cataloging (MARC) records are still primary basic curatorial functions and feed into all other aspects of repository operation and management. Why should this be so? The answer lies in two of the major characteristics of organically generated archival and manuscript collections.

First, such collections are typically more valuable to the researcher in their entirety than for any one of the individual documents they contain. While a single letter from one correspondent to another may provide exactly the information a researcher seeks, the whole sequence of letters between the two correspondents generally offers at least useful context and sometimes additional key documentation. In some instances, the data sought by the researcher is obtainable only cumulatively, by piecing together bits of information culled from multiple letters. If these letters are not intelligently arranged and described, the efficiency of the scholar consulting either originals in hard copy or scanned versions on the Web is affected. Indeed, the disorganization of a collection sometimes prevents the discovery of crucial connections between separate pieces of data within a collection.

Second, organic collections often do not present information through a uniformly consistent vocabulary. In one of the Concord Free Public Library's collections of Bulkeley family papers, for example, the Bulkeley name appears spelled in at least five different ways. In other collections, widely recognized terms for the types of documents included (e.g., deeds, wills, and rights of dower) appear nowhere in the text of the documents themselves. The intervention of human intelligence is necessary to provide a controlled vocabulary. However, it can be very difficult for even highly trained personnel to apply concise and consistent descriptive terminology to related documents ordered without rhyme or reason.

But though it does not obviate the organization, arrangement, and description of archival and manuscript collections, the Web is tremendously effective in disseminating finding aids—the products of those processes. Whether an institution creates and mounts them using Encoded Archival Description (EAD) or, more simply, HTML, their availability on the Web greatly enhances access even without the scanning of a single document. At far lower cost than digitization would involve, both scholar and repository benefit. In fulfilling their basic collections management responsibilities before thinking about high-tech solutions to backlog and other problems, curators and archivists will find it much easier to accurately assess the real advantages and possibilities of digitization.

The reader may suspect by this point that the Concord Free Public Library is not cutting-edge in its technological practices for enhancing access to Special Collections holdings. Even though we make the most of the opportunities open to us, we represent something like the lowest common technical denominator in methodology and in the application of equipment and software. When we undertake projects that exceed our capabilities, we bring in consultants with equipment and expertise superior to our own. We tend to depend on existing mechanisms to create access, most especially for searchability, for which we rely largely on the services of Google (a Google search box is mounted directly on our pages) and other major search indexes. We recognize that this system is imperfect. The Concord Free Public Library Web site is built hierarchically, in multiple levels. Google's Web crawling seems not to extend fully down the many levels of the site and therefore does not draw on names and words several tiers below the opening pages of our various offerings. The user searching for a specific term that appears on one of the individual item pages of the *Historic Buildings* pages may come up empty. The search function built into the *Antebellum Concord Town Reports* offsets this disadvantage for one specific set of pages. Even so, unless the questing scholar already knows that the library's Web site is a rich source of Concord-related information and heads there without benefit of Googled results, he or she may never discover that potentially relevant material is within reach. We pay for our economies of methodology in fewer hits to our Web site than the data within it ought to draw, while the Web user sometimes pays in remaining unaware of resources available for research. In taking advantage of Google's services, we are obliged to accept Google on its own terms.

Google does not make it easy for the Webmaster who maintains a modest site to find out how to improve the searchability of indexed Web pages. It is impossible to make telephone contact with a real, live Google employee to discuss practical options for enhancing ranking in search results. From Google's perspective, accessible information on this topic carries the potential for abuse in the form of ranking manipulation. But for a small institution trying to build Web presence, this reluctance to give advice hinders understanding of the mix of factors that influence page ranking. To be fair, the Google Website Optimizer pages offer help. There is also a Google-sponsored YouTube video on how to optimize searchability.[17] Other Web sites, too, provide information about how page rankings are established and how to improve them, and personal communication with knowledgeable others in the field can be helpful.

But page structure and key features of an institution's Web pages are often long-established by the time anyone thinks seriously about page ranking. Well-endowed nonprofits and commercial concerns may employ the services of consultants on search engine optimization to improve ranking for a site already developed, but smaller operations are unlikely to have the means to do so. It would serve an institution's interests far better to know from the outset of Web site development the key elements—including the number of links to and from other sites and the deliberate and effective use of metatags—that feed into the PageRank algorithm that determines Google search ranking.[18] Archives with established Web sites may want to consider enhancing the header to information on their pages. To increase the number of links to an existing Web site, it may be useful to set up a blog. But whatever methods are chosen to enhance Web visibility, the continuing creation of new content-rich pages remains paramount for a repository seeking to make important collections available to a broader research constituency.

Parallel to problems with the indexing of HTML-created pages on Web sites like the Concord Free Public Library's, Google's failure to comprehensively index Open Archives Initiative (OAI) records has concerned archivists, librarians, and curators for some time.[19] The CFPL is committed to the preparation of MARC records for OCLC for its archival and manuscript holdings as well as its printed holdings, and MARC records have long formed an important means of access to Special Collections materials. This issue therefore represents a significant additional limitation on Google's ability to reflect what is available to researchers across our collections on a given topic. To the detriment of scholarship, many patrons do not realize that Google search results do not constitute the "one-stop shopping" of resource identification. The fact that Google's purposes and those of the scholarly and archival communities do not completely mesh makes it imperative for scholars to realize and for archivists continually to remind them that they must employ multiple search services and strategies to determine whether or not the material they seek is out there somewhere, in an archival facility if not on the Web.

Had anyone suggested to me five years ago that the Concord Free Public Library might enter into a formal Web partnership with Texas A&M University (TAMU), I would have thought the possibility remote. Indeed, when Amy Earhart (assistant professor of English, TAMU) first approached me in 2005 regarding CFPL involvement in the *19th-Century Concord Digital Archive* (*CDA*),[20] I did not think that anything would come of it. I had been approached before by representatives of agencies and organizations proposing what were couched as Web "collaborations" but were, in reality, not much more than one-sided attempts to appropriate and use unique CFPL holdings—materials unavailable through any other venue—to promote agendas other than the library's. There is sometimes a very thin line between collaboration and exploitation, but the two are never synonymous. I had consequently declined all such overtures. I must always keep in mind the Concord Free Public Library Corporation's policy of maintaining its rights over its holdings, a factor that does not typically form a consideration for would-be Web site builders who—however innocently—fail to grasp that true collaboration takes into account the purposes, needs, and concerns of the several parties involved. All cooperative ventures—digital partnerships included—require hard work to ensure a balanced, reciprocal arrangement in which those involved each get something they want in the process of furthering some larger, more disinterested goal.

But Earhart was serious, thoughtful, and persistent about her *19th-Century Concord Digital Archive.* It soon became clear to me that she was willing to hammer out a meaningful way for Texas A&M and the Concord Free Public Library to join forces. After two years of discussions and negotiation by two institutional lawyers, the Concord Free Public Library chose to partner with Texas A&M in this important project to increase the accessibility of Concord-related documentation to the scholarly community.[21] The key shift in thinking that allowed the library to enter into the collaboration was the focus on shared searchability of archival resources as the guiding principle, rather than the provision by one institution of materials to be used and interpreted by the other. The *CDA* will allow integrated access to digital representations (housed on the CFPL's server) of some original documents owned by the library and to Earhart's transcribed, edited texts of those materials.

As indicated, the searchability of the Concord Free Public Library Web site has its shortcomings. Since searchability is the essence of the *CDA*/CFPL partnership, the library's involvement in the project meets a very real institutional need while serving Earhart's purposes in creatively utilizing technology to build a combined digital and textual archive geared toward academic scholars in a variety of disciplines. The *CDA* shows great promise for simultaneously encouraging solutions to the challenges inherent in presenting archival materials on the Web; for enlarging the usefulness and the actual use of the library's selective, interpretive Web site; and for increasing scholars' chances of locating digitized material pertinent to their studies—all without either signatory institution slighting the mission or impinging on the rights of the other. The collaboration works on a practical level because each committed party has entered into it in a spirit of mutual, intelligent self-interest, tempered by care to extend common courtesy and characterized by an "eyes wide open" acknowledgment of and willingness to confront problems, limitations, and conflicts. Texas A&M enjoys rather more funding, staffing, and technical resources than the Concord Free Public Library has at its disposal, while the CFPL holds archival riches without the use of which the *CDA* has relatively little of a visual nature to show, given the simple fact that TAMU does not systematically document Concord. A certain balance of power—always healthy in cooperative efforts—has thus been built into the partnership from its inception. Beyond pragmatism, however, the *CDA* has been informed by an underlying idealism—a sense of the possible—regarding both the value of primary documentation and the creation of access to it on the Web. In many ways, it exemplifies collaboration.

The digitization of the Concord town reports has served as a prototype for the joint TAMU/CFPL preparation of materials for presentation through the *CDA.* I hope for and fully anticipate an increase in the use of the *Antebellum Concord Town Reports* pages on the CFPL Web site as a result of the collaboration. The interactive capabilities envisioned and under development by Earhart will provide a gateway for the user to access through a single search both the digital images on the CFPL pages and the fully transcribed text on the *CDA* site. Once relevant material is located, the scholar will be able to conduct additional searches through either the search box on the CFPL pages or—for searches combining the data from the specific set of pages with information from other, distinct *CDA* pages—through *CDA* search features. As value added, the greater sophistication of the *CDA* search options may well draw a more than typically informed user—one knowledgeable about navigational tools and techniques—to the CFPL Special Collections pages, thereby heightening the chances that searches there will effectively identify potential resources for scholarship.

Regardless of the outcome of collaboration between the Concord Free Public Library and Texas A&M University, however, the curatorial balancing act that constitutes my job will not change. My multiple responsibilities in managing Concord's collections have increased both through the local provision of selective Web access to archival holdings and through involvement in a collaborative project that—if all goes as planned—will increase the scholarly audience likely to benefit from the effort we put into creating such access. As much as I would like to pursue what is purely possible, I can never completely forget what we can actually undertake, given the complexity of the working situation. I will continue to follow a selective and interpretive approach in developing the Special Collections pages of the Concord Free Public Library Web site, although now also with an eye toward the purposes of the *Concord Digital Archive.* I like to think that my necessarily practical approach does not preclude inspiration and inventiveness. Representing Concord as I do, I cannot resist closing with a quotation from Emerson, who in the essay "Illusions" wrote, "'Tis the charm of practical men that outside of their practicality are a certain poetry and play."[22] As the final word, however, it may be more apropos to note that I was able to locate that quotation only with the aid of the online version of Eugene Irey's concordance to Emerson's essays on the Concord Free Public Library Web site.[23]

Notes

1. The Concord Free Public Library, established in 1873, has operated through a joint public/private form of management since its founding. The William Munroe Special Collections—one of six library departments and the major archive of Concord history, life, landscape, literature, and people from 1635 to the present time—is privately held and administered by the Concord Free Public Library Corporation, as distinct from the Town Library Committee. Each year, the Special Collections staff of three (a full-time curator, a part-time staff assistant, and a part-time technology associate, aided by intermittent volunteer and intern help and occasionally by paid consultants) provide on-site service to between 1,500 and 2,000 researchers and answer countless inquiries by mail, e-mail, phone, and fax. The clientele is varied, ranging from local public school children working on hometown history projects to academics researching dissertations, articles, and books and professional authors writing on Concord-related topics. Special Collections holdings include the full gamut of archival and rare book materials—personal papers, family papers, records and publications of local organizations and government, printed volumes, pamphlets, broadsides, ephemera, newspapers, maps, scrapbooks, photographs, works of art, a few artifacts closely related to archival and manuscript holdings, oral history tapes and transcripts, cassettes (audio and video), CDs, and more.

2. The Concord Free Public Library Web site is accessible at http://www.concordlibrary.org/, the specific pages for the William Munroe Special Collections at http://www.concordlibrary.org/scollect/scoll.html. The library's home page was formerly hosted by the Minuteman Library Network, then was part of the Town of Concord Web site, and became independent in 2007.

3. Thanks to Robert C. W. Hall (technology associate in Special Collections and Webmaster for the Special Collections pages) for providing information relating to the CFPL Web site, its history, and its construction.

4. We registered our site with Google—the search engine for the pages—in 2005.

5. The most heavily consulted are the *Henry David Thoreau Land & Property Surveys* pages at http://www.concordlibrary.org/scollect/Thoreau_Surveys/Thoreau_Surveys.htm. The *Concord Historic Buildings* Web site at http://www.concordlibrary.org/scollect/BuildingHistories/index.html is used extensively in the elementary, high school, and college classroom.

6. The time involved includes my own; that of Robert Hall, who handles all of the department's digital work and edits, mounts, and maintains its pages; and that of Constance Manoli-Skocay (staff assistant), who selects and organizes some archival material for Web access and contributes interpretive text to the Special Collections pages.

7. See http://www.loc.gov/ndnp/.

8. "Emerson in Concord" is accessible at http://www.concordlibrary.org/scollect/Emerson_Celebration/Opening_page.html, "Earth's Eye" at http://www.concordlibrary.org/scollect/Walden/Walden.htm. The introductory essay to "Earth's Eye" was written by W. Barksdale Maynard, author of *Walden Pond: A History* (New York: Oxford University Press, 2004).

9. The *Historic Buildings* pages, at http://www.concordlibrary.org/scollect/BuildingHistories/index.html, were constructed in part through the Bradley P. Dean Memorial Fund. Consultant Tracey Zellmann of NautilusOne is constructing the site to CFPL specifications.

10. The structures are the Town House, Middlesex Hotel (no longer standing), Damon Mill, Concord Free Public Library, Anderson Market Building, and Thoreau/Alcott House. The pages for the Town House, Middlesex Hotel, Damon Mill, Concord Free Public Library, and Anderson Market are mounted, and those for the Thoreau/Alcott House remain to be done.

11. See n. 5 for the URL. Funding to digitize the Thoreau surveys and to construct the pages was provided by AT&T. Our consultant for this project was Deborah Bier of Windfall.

12. See, e.g., Patrick Chura, "Economic and Environmental Perspectives in the Surveying 'Field-Notes' of Henry David Thoreau," *Concord Saunterer*, n.s., 15 (2007): 37–64.

13. See http://www.concordlibrary.org/scollect/wheeler.htm.

14. Joseph C. Wheeler transcribed and edited the Wheeler genealogy for the CFPL Web site.

15. The temporary URL is http://www.nautilusone.biz/CFPL-Search/intro.html.

16. The opening page for our finding aids is at http://www.concordlibrary.org/scollect/Fin_Aids/index.html. At this point, perhaps 60 to 65 percent of our archival and manuscript holdings are processed, described, and represented by online finding aids.

17. The Website Optimizer pages are accessible at http://www.google.com/website

optimizer, the YouTube video at http://www.youtube.com/watch?v=5GK0aQrCDEo. Google also offers a tool for feedback on page visibility at http://www.google.com/webmasters/tools/, a video titled "Search Friendly Development" at http://code.google.com/events/io/sessions/SearchFriendlyDevelopment.html, and a video titled "Site Review by the Experts" at http://code.google.com/events/io/sessions/SiteReviewsExperts.html.

18. Thanks to consultant Tracey Zellmann (http://www.nautilusone.biz/) for sharing information about search engine optimization. Also, there is a useful, well-documented essay on the subject on Wikipedia, at http://en.wikipedia.org/wiki/Search_engine_optimization.

19. Kat Hagedorn and Joshua Santelli, "Google Still Not Indexing Hidden Web URLs," *D-Lib Magazine* 14, no. 7/8 (July/August 2008), http://www.dlib.org/dlib/july08/hagedorn/07hagedorn.html (accessed 31 July 2008).

20. See http://www.digitalconcord.org/.

21. The partnership was formalized in 2007.

22. Ralph Waldo Emerson, "Illusions," in *Conduct of Life* (Boston: Houghton Mifflin, 1904), 317.

23. See http://www.concordlibrary.org/scollect/EmersonConcordance/index.htm.

Scholars' Usage of Digital Archives in American Literature

LISA SPIRO AND JANE SEGAL

In 2006, Texas A&M University hosted a "Digital Textual Studies" symposium that brought together some of the leaders in the field. The participants explored the ways in which digital humanities could open up new pathways in research, such as through plotting Whitman's movements in Civil War Washington on a GIS map or enabling the analysis and manipulation of digital facsimiles of William Blake's *Songs of Innocence and Experience*. Yet in the midst of this enthusiasm lurked a discomfiting sense that the digital humanities remained a marginalized field little understood by "traditional" scholars. As Morris Eaves, one of the editors of the *William Blake Archive*, asked at the symposium: Are humanities scholars actually using thematic digital research collections, which bring together resources focused on a particular research theme? If so, how are they using these resources, and what impact are they having on humanities scholarship?

We investigated these questions by focusing on scholars working in nineteenth-century American literature and culture. Our study[1] had three components:

1. A survey of scholars in American literature, culture, and history, conducted in April 2007, about how they use digital resources to support their research, as well as follow-up interviews with selected scholars, also conducted in April 2007.
2. A bibliographic analysis to determine whether scholarly works published

between 2000 and 2008 use leading scholarly digital collections—specifically, whether Whitman scholars cite the *Walt Whitman Archive* (*WWA*, http://www.whitmanarchive.org), whether Dickinson scholars reference the *Dickinson Electronic Archives* (*DEA*, http://www.emilydickinson.org), and whether researchers working on *Uncle Tom's Cabin* cite *Uncle Tom's Cabin & American Culture* (*UTCAC*, http://www.iath.virginia.edu/utc/).

3. A survey of Whitman, Dickinson, and Stowe scholars, conducted in May 2007, about why they did or did not cite the digital archives previously mentioned, as well as follow-up interviews with selected scholars, conducted from May to June in 2007.

By taking this multifaceted approach, we were able to profile Americanists' general attitudes toward digital resources, evaluate how often they cite digital collections, analyze their perceptions of the ways that digital collections have influenced their work, and examine specific examples of how digital collections are shaping scholarly discourse. We have found that scholars are open to—indeed, increasingly reliant on—digital resources, particularly electronic journal collections such as JSTOR and Project Muse; however, few scholars cite digital collections in their work. The *WWA*, the *DEA*, and *UTCAC* serve as models for digital scholarship, but it will likely take time for these innovative resources to be fully integrated into research.

Prior Studies of Humanities Scholars and Computing

Some see the Web as enabling new forms of humanities research, while others see hype. According to Patrick Leary, the Web enables scholars to track down allusions and references quickly, discover connections in unexpected sources, and build connections with other scholars and with enthusiastic amateurs.[2] Matthew Kirschenbaum contends that digitized text collections serve scholarly reading practices such as "not reading," or gleaning what is important about a text without reading it closely, and "distant reading," or using text mining and visualization to detect patterns in texts.[3] Yet others caution that the potential of digital resources to transform research has been exaggerated. For instance, Anthony Grafton argues that many archival resources and other materials have not and likely will not be digitized and that scholars will continue to find much value in examining the actual physical objects for details such as marginal annotations and even the scent of the page.[4] Others point to cultural and institutional barriers limiting scholars' adoption of new technologies, particularly the conservatism of tenure committees and the lack of institutional support for digital scholarship.

On the whole, our research corroborates earlier studies showing that humanities scholars have adopted e-mail, word processing, and online library catalogs and journal collections as standard tools and resources, even as they have been reluctant to venture into newer uses of computing for research and publication. According to a 2001 anthropological study, humanities scholars employ technology to extend and adapt traditional research functions, but they are not convinced that digital editions are useful, and they are confused about how to cite them.[5] Obstacles to more sophisticated use of digital resources include the lack of leadership by prominent scholarly organizations, the need for better analytical and technical tools, the absence of ways to preserve digital work, copyright and permissions issues, a paucity of sustainable business models, and the dearth of specialists.[6] In 2006, the MLA reported that 40 percent of departments have no experience in evaluating articles in electronic format and that 65.7 percent have no experience with electronic monographs. As Jerome McGann argues, the institutional resistance against publishing and peer-reviewing online is "widespread, deep, and entirely understandable."[7]

American Studies Scholars' Usage of Digital Resources

To understand how digital resources are affecting humanities scholarship, we turned to scholars themselves, focusing on those in American literature and culture. In April 2007, we invited subscribers to two discussion networks in American studies—H-AMSTUDY and H-USA—to take a survey examining how they use digital resources. Eighty-five people responded, including faculty members, graduate students, museum professionals, and independent scholars in fields such as literature, history, museum studies, and religious studies.

On the whole, we found that American studies scholars have begun to rely on digital resources, particularly electronic journals. For the most part, scholars are not transforming their core methodologies, but they are using digital resources to make research more efficient. Survey respondents most commonly used journal articles (97 percent) and electronic texts (95 percent); only 12 percent used blogs, and 4 percent used simulations. The scholars surveyed primarily employed digital resources to consult secondary materials, such as commentaries and bibliographies (91 percent); to quickly find and retrieve passages using search engines (83 percent); and to gain access to unique or hard-to-find materials (83 percent). Far fewer employed digital resources to "explore new modes of interpreting text" (26 percent) or to "use analytic tools" (22 percent).

Perhaps the most compelling survey results came in response to the open-ended, free-text question "Do you think that the availability of electronic resources has transformed humanities scholarship? If so, how? If not, why not?" On the whole, our survey respondents view the Web as benefiting research by making many more resources accessible, enabling searching across vast databases, fostering online communities, and supporting the democratization of knowledge. Yet some respondents worried that scholars would overlook nondigital resources and ignore the physical object, build arguments based on a few constrained search terms and predetermined hypotheses, miss the serendipity of discovery in archives and the stacks, and undervalue libraries.

Narrowing the Question: Citations of the *Walt Whitman Archive, Dickinson Electronic Archives,* and *Uncle Tom's Cabin & American Culture*

After creating a general profile of how Americanists perceive digital resources, we examined citations of digital collections in scholarly literature from 2000 to 2008. To make our research project manageable, we focused on three thematic digital research collections: the *Walt Whitman Archive,* the *Dickinson Electronic Archives,* and *Uncle Tom's Cabin & American Culture.* We selected these three collections because they are well-regarded, mature scholarly digital collections focused on nineteenth-century American literature, a field in which one of the authors has demonstrated expertise.[8] Founded in 1995 by Whitman scholars Kenneth M. Price and Ed Folsom, the *WWA* is an electronic research and teaching tool that includes every print edition produced in Whitman's lifetime, his manuscripts, criticism, material by/about Whitman's disciples, and related cultural materials. The *DEA* was founded in 1994 by Dickinson scholar and executive editor Martha

Nell Smith in collaboration with fellow scholars in the Dickinson Editing Collective, including Lara Vetter, Ellen Louise Hart, Marta Werner, Tanya Clement, and Jarom McDonald. It aims to contribute to scholarship and teaching by "exploring and virtually reconstructing Dickinson's textual, social, historical, and geographical worlds." The collective claims, "Our editions place the manuscripts themselves at the center of critical attention."[9] Founded in 1998 by Stephen Railton, an expert on nineteenth-century American literature, *UTCAC* attempts to use electronic technology to enable its users to explore the role of *Uncle Tom's Cabin* in American culture. *UTCAC* documents the novel's significance by gathering "pre-texts" such as works on sentimental culture and minstrel shows; versions of *Uncle Tom's Cabin;* and responses to the novel, including reviews, songs, movies, and 3-D cultural artifacts, or "Tomitudes."

To measure the impact of the *WWA,* the *DEA,* and *UTCAC,* we examined how often each was cited in scholarly works on Whitman, Dickinson, and *Uncle Tom's Cabin* that were published between 2000 and 2008. To narrow our focus, we looked at works cited in bibliographic essays on the authors in *American Literary Scholarship* between 2000 and 2004 (the last date available at the time we did our research). For works from 2005 to 2008, we searched the *MLA International Bibliography* for "Walt Whitman," "Emily Dickinson," or "*Uncle Tom's Cabin.*"[10] We chose not to include reviews or dissertations, and we eliminated from our bibliographies works not available at our library (Rice University's Fondren Library) and difficult to acquire through interlibrary loan, which comprised only a small percentage of the total.

Somewhat surprisingly, few scholars cited these digital collections in their bibliographies, although citation of the *WWA* and *UTCAC* appears to be increasing. Only 12 percent (36 of 294) of the works in our Dickinson bibliography and 21 percent (65 of 317) of the works in our Whitman bibliography cited the digital collections, while 10 percent (8 of 82) of the works in our *Uncle Tom's Cabin* bibliography cite *UTCAC.* Whereas 17 percent of works on Whitman published in 2003 cited the *WWA,* that percentage had increased to 47 percent in 2007, largely due to the fact that *Leaves of Grass: The Sesquicentennial Essays,* a collection of 19 essays by Whitman scholars edited by *WWA* editors Kenneth M. Price and Ed Folsom and coeditor Susan Belasco, used the *WWA* as its authoritative source for all six editions of *Leaves of Grass.* Likewise, citation of *UTCAC* seems to be increasing; it was not cited at all between 2000 and 2006, but the percentage of citations increased to 12 percent in 2006 (2 OF 17) and 33 percent in 2007 (5 OF 15) and 2008 (1 OF 3).

Of course, by focusing on works included in *American Literary Scholarship* or indexed by the MLA, we missed some significant books and articles. When we searched JSTOR, Project Muse, Google Scholar, Google Books, and Amazon Book Search for the names of the digital collections on November 7, 2007, we found an additional 19 works citing the *WWA,* 40 works citing the *DEA,* and 20 works citing *UTCAC.* Typically, these are works that were published before 2000 or after 2006 or that focus on fields besides literary study, such as history, teaching, library science, or digital humanities. Even with these additional sources, citation of these digital collections remains fairly low.

Further investigation revealed that far more scholars *consult* digital collections than *cite* them. After identifying which scholars did and did not cite the digital archives, we invited them to take a survey based on the survey we had already administered to American studies scholars. This survey also gathered information about why they did or did not cite the digital archive. Eleven Dickinson, 8 Whitman, and 3 *Uncle Tom's Cabin* (*UTC*) scholars responded to our surveys of scholars who did cite the digital collections, while 25 Dickinson, 20 Whitman, and 12 UTC scholars completed our surveys of scholars who did not cite the digital collections. We also invited respondents to participate in a follow-up conversation and were able to speak with 7 Whitman scholars, 2 Dickinson scholars, and 1 *UTC* scholar, as well as 1 scholar who has published on both Whitman and Dickinson.[11]

Whereas 58 percent of the scholars we surveyed said that they frequently *use* digital resources, only 26 percent said that they *cite* them frequently. Why are so few scholars citing the *WWA,* the *DEA,* and *UTCAC*? Respondents to our surveys were reluctant to answer this question. The most common response was "I wasn't aware of the archive at the time that I did my research," although most skipped the question altogether. In follow-up interviews, the following additional reasons emerged: scholars do not believe they need to cite the digital version of a work; they are confused about requirements for citation; they believe that it is preferable to cite from a standard print edition, which is thought to have more credibility and be more permanent; and they are required to cite particular print editions by journals.

Of course, scholars will not cite digital collections if they do not know about them. Our citation analysis included works published as early as 2000, so the research for such articles was conducted even earlier, perhaps before the digital collections gained notice among scholars. Awareness seems to remain a problem for *UTCAC*. Although 76 percent of the Dickinson scholars and 90 percent of the Whitman scholars we surveyed were aware of the *DEA* and *WWA*, only 46 percent of *UTC* scholars knew about *UTCAC* at the time of our survey. Why are so few scholars aware of *UTCAC* when compared to the other digital collections? Whereas the *DEA* and *WWA* were launched in the mid-1990s, *UTCAC* was established in 1998, so it has had less time to gain an audience. While the *DEA* and *WWA* each focus on a single author, *UTCAC* organizes itself around a single work. Although there are large and active scholarly communities focused on Dickinson and Whitman and journals devoted specifically to those authors, the Stowe community is smaller and lacks its own journal. Indeed, there are far fewer publications on *Uncle Tom's Cabin* than on Whitman and Dickinson. Over 40 percent of the articles on our Whitman bibliography and about 10 percent of the articles in our Dickinson bibliography were written by contributors to these digital archives. In contrast, the developer of *UTCAC* has concentrated on building the archive and has only recently begun to publish articles that cite it.

Whether scholars discover collections on their own depends on the search tools they are using. If scholars used WorldCat, they would probably find the *WWA*, the *DEA*, and *UTCAC*, since all three are cataloged there. They would be less likely to discover the resource if they employed their university's library catalog, since according to WorldCat as of November 2008, only 52 libraries have cataloged the *DEA* or *WWA* and only 45 have cataloged *UTCAC*. The *MLA International Bibliography* only began indexing digital research collections in 2006, and all three collections are included in the most recent edition. If scholars used Google or Wikipedia to do research, they would be in luck: all three digital collections rank in Google's top 10 results, and all three are cited in multiple Wikipedia articles. (Of course, Wikipedia typically is not recognized as a scholarly research source, but 36 percent of the Whitman, Dickinson, and *UTC* scholars taking our survey acknowledged using it.)

Even though thematic research collections have been created by leading scholars, print continues to carry more scholarly authority than digital sources. As a Whitman scholar we interviewed said, "The average literary scholar can't tell the difference in quality between digital sources, maybe because there are not the scholarly vetting operations that they've learned to maneuver in the print world. They seem to view all digital resources as equal and therefore poorer than print resources." Moreover, whereas acid-free paper has a long life span, Web pages seem ephemeral, and scholars worry that lack of institutional support will mean that scholarly Web sites will disappear.

Not only are scholars confused about how trustworthy digital resources are, but they also do not always know the conventions for citing online sources. As a Whitman scholar we interviewed explained, "For many years, how to cite online sources was not quite clear—that's still the case. In my own work, if I have something as print source and online, I would go with print because I knew that how to cite it wasn't going to change. . . . When that settles down and there's a standard, people may be more likely to cite electronic sources." Although MLA guidelines call for electronic sources to be documented, many scholars believe that they do not need to cite the online collection where they found a digitized resource; instead, they cite the original print edition, even if they only examined the version online. As one Whitman scholar suggested, "If you want to talk about the text of a poem in the 1871 edition, why would you cite the *Walt Whitman Archive* when you could cite the print, even if you looked at the text online? It carries more scholarly weight to cite the print. What you're looking at online is just a facsimile of the text." Furthermore, as Ed Folsom, editor of the *Walt Whitman Quarterly Review* and codirector of the *Walt Whitman Archive,* noted during the discussion following our presentation at the 2007 American Literature Association conference, scholars may be reluctant to include long, unwieldy URLs in their bibliographies, since URLs such as http://www.whitmanarchive.org/disciples/traubel/WWWiC/4/med.00004.21 often do not fit into one line in a bibliography.[12]

Along with fears that online resources are of poorer quality, some scholars worry they will be tarred as poor researchers if they do research online. A Whitman scholar we interviewed speculated that doing research online may be thought lazy: "Maybe people feel that not citing the digital resource makes it look like they've done old-school nitty-gritty research rather than just get online and do what anyone could do." Even if they believe that the online edition is superior, scholars tend to cite from standard editions. As a Whitman scholar acknowledged, "There is the lingering sense of obligation to cite approved editions. . . . As things stand now, I use the Web site, then track down the citation in a print volume."

Indeed, some journals insist that scholars cite specific print editions. One journal insisted that a Whitman scholar early in his career cite the NYU Press edition of *Leaves of Grass*—not necessarily out of any bias against electronic editions, but because that edition was part of its house style. Although this scholar said in an interview that he is not "looking to ruffle any feathers," he has decided to cite from the *WWA* in his forthcoming book, partly out of an ethical obligation to credit his real source, partly because it is easier to cite full-text editions as they appear in the *Whitman Archive* than in the NYU Press edition.

Evaluating the Impact of Digital Collections on Scholarship

Although we had hoped to find examples of scholars drawing on the *WWA*, the *DEA*, and *UTCAC* to create innovative digital scholarship—scholarship that takes research in new directions through the use of digital resources and tools—the archives themselves stand as perhaps the best examples of digital scholarship in their fields. Even as scholars come to rely on online journal articles and primary source materials, there are still few examples of cutting-edge digital scholarship that demonstrate innovative use of electronic resources. Nevertheless, digital collections support traditional research methods and open up new areas of inquiry by making possible rapid search and retrieval, stimulating discussions about editorial methods, and enabling scholars to do work that was previously limited by difficulty in accessing information. According to Whitman scholars, the *WWA* is stimulating a growth in manuscript studies and making possible deeper usage of key resources. For Dickinson scholars, the *DEA* has contributed to the growth of interest in Susan Dickinson and the ongoing debate about editorial methods. *UTC* scholars suggest that *UTCAC* provides wider access to multimedia materials and raises awareness of the novel's broad cultural significance.

The Impact of the Walt Whitman Archive on Scholarship

Although evidence of the *WWA*'s significance is thus far subtle in the published record of Whitman scholarship, scholars credit it with contributing to the increasing prominence of manuscript and textual study of the poet. Scholars we surveyed called the *WWA* a "major source," "indispensable," "the first place that I go to do research on Whitman," even "the most important development in the history of Whitman studies." In evaluating the *WWA* as a resource for research, scholars not citing the *WWA* gave it an average score of 4.31 out of 5, while scholars who cited the *WWA* gave it a 5.

By providing ready access to previously hard to access resources such as Whitman's manuscripts, notebooks, and journalism, the *WWA* hopes to transform scholarly discourse about the poet. The *WWA* keeps Whitman scholarship up to date by hosting newly discovered documents, such as an interview with Whitman that was rediscovered by Nicole Kukawski and a manuscript about race that was found by *WWA* staff member Brett Barney in 2002. When scholars do cite the *WWA,* they often reference nineteenth-century reviews and "Live Oak, with Moss," a rediscovered poem that is best understood through facsimiles of the manuscript made available through the *WWA.* One interviewee commended the *WWA* for "making primary sources available that were either not available before or were severely limited in availability because they were not digital." An interviewee from Britain speculated that the *WWA* would have a "potentially big" impact for people like him, since he would not have to travel across the Atlantic to work at archives and could "access new materials sooner rather than later." By making it possible to search across Whitman's works, the *WWA* has made the research process more efficient and reduced transcription errors. As an interviewee said, "Instead of flipping through a book for a word, I can find it instantly. If I want to cite a passage, I can cut and paste it—without introducing error in process."

Perhaps more profoundly, scholars credit the *WWA* with contributing to the increasing prominence of manuscript and textual study of the poet. Whereas the critical apparatus of the NYU Press edition is difficult to use, the *WWA* has fostered a new understanding of the text by showing the visual evidence. A Whitman scholar we interviewed said, "It is eye-opening to me to see original editions and the integration of images. . . . To have total editions there is tremendously valuable." Previously, Whitman scholarship focused on just a few editions, but the *WWA* has shifted attention to a more detailed analysis of other editions of Whitman's work. A Whitman scholar we interviewed noted,

> Whitman scholarship used to valorize the bookmaking of the 1855 and deathbed editions, but ignored others on the way—but that's completely broken down now. Many more people are moving to things like talking about the design of the 1867 volume. . . . Now you no longer need a fellowship to a research library to do that kind of work. . . . Now you can look at different images and books and can chart how a poem has evolved from edition to edition, how the table of contents evolved from edition to edition.

By allowing scholars to trace the evolution of Whitman's work, the *WWA* supports deeper understanding not only of the history of the book but also of Whitman's relationship to American culture, what a Whitman scholar we interviewed calls "the big story of Whitman: how the book changed with changes in the nation and his life."

The *WWA* is also advancing the study of contexts surrounding Whitman, including periodical literature, the works of his disciples, and visual culture. Recently, the *WWA* released Susan Belasco's edition of Whitman's periodical poems, allowing readers to understand Whitman's engagement with journalism and to trace the development of a poem from notebook to manuscript to periodical to book. As one scholar we interviewed commented, "The periodical poems section of the site is making it possible to study the print culture environment that Whitman worked in, which is unprecedented." Through another recent addition, researchers can more easily study Horace Traubel's massive *With Walt Whitman in Camden,* which collects Traubel's extensive notes on his conversations with Whitman near the end of the poet's life. Because the nine-volume *With Walt Whitman in Camden* is so poorly indexed, finding information is quite difficult. Edited by Matt Cohen, the electronic edition (which currently makes available six volumes) aims to make the text more accessible, to reveal the contexts surrounding it through interlinking, and to enable search and retrieval. As one Whitman scholar we interviewed said, "*With Walt Whitman in Camden* is a great resource for factual historical research that wasn't getting fully exploited before it was available in electronic form. It seems like more Whitman scholars are citing Traubel as a result of its being more readily available through the *Walt Whitman Archive.*"

Whitman scholars see a few potential limitations of the *WWA.* One scholar we interviewed put forward the remote possibility that its emphasis on individual editions might push aside scholarship that focuses on larger issues in Whitman's life and work: "If in 20 years panels at the ALA [American Literature Association] all focused on different editions of *Leaves*, if we have a situation where the people who work on the 1867 edition are one group, and the 1872 edition are another group, that would be too bad." In addition, the ease of access may mean that scholars will miss the contexts surrounding works, such as articles near a poem that Whitman published in a magazine. As one Whitman scholar we interviewed said, "I do think there is still some value in looking at the reviews of Whitman brought together from various sources—but there is still value in looking at the original to see the context in which it's placed." Likewise, an interviewee worried that the serendipity of discovery would be lost if researchers work in digital archives instead of physical ones: "Sometimes if you look in a physical archive, you might open up an envelope and something falls out. With a digitized archive, you're not going to have that."

Whitman scholars appreciate the breadth of materials available through the *WWA* but want even more. The most common request for improvement was for the site to make more material available, such as recordings of Whitman's poetry and music inspired by it, the complete issues of magazines in which his poetry appeared, and more contemporary critical essays. As Folsom and Price argue, the Web "is the perfect medium for an author who was always revising and reordering and rethinking his work."[13]

The Impact of the *Dickinson Electronic Archives* on Scholarship

The *DEA* is acknowledged for fostering a new awareness of Dickinson's poetic practices and of the potential of digital collections. In her overview of scholarship on nineteenth-century American women's literature, Sharon M. Harris credits the *DEA* editors with "challenging almost every facet of what we thought we knew about Emily Dickinson's poetry." She adds that "they are educating us to ways in which electronic sites such as *Dickinson Electronic Archives* can become vehicles for collective scholarly exchange."[14] As a resource for research, the *DEA* received an average ranking of 4.18 (out of 5) from scholars who cited it and 3.44 from scholars who did not. In survey comments on the impact of the *DEA* on Dickinson scholarship, respondents described it as "major" and "outstanding" and suggested that the collection is a "great model for future creators of online archives."

Initially, Martha Nell Smith and her colleagues intended for the *Dickinson Electronic Archives* to be comprehensive and offer access to all documents related to Dickinson. However, copyright restrictions limited what the *DEA* could make available online, since Harvard and Amherst College own the copyright to Dickinson's poetry and tightly control access to it. According to Smith, copyright limitations prompted the editors to be creative in exploring other means of contributing to the ongoing conversation about Dickinson.[15] Thus the *DEA* brought out a series of interpretive digital articles about topics such as Dickinson's letter poem and her "writing workshop" with Susan Dickinson, as well as the *Titanic Operas,* which contains readings and reflections on Dickinson by contemporary female poets, including Gwendolyn Brooks, Maxine Kumin, and Adrienne Rich.

With the publication of Smith's *Rowing in Eden* and other works, attention has been focused on the friendship between Dickinson and her sister-in-law Susan Dickinson, an intimate relationship that helped to shape Dickinson's poetry. To make available otherwise inaccessible materials and to enable further research on Susan Dickinson, the *DEA* includes a section entitled "Writings of Susan Dickinson," which collects her poems, reviews, essays, stories, and correspondence. Scholars who discuss Susan Dickinson's relationship with Emily Dickinson often cite the *DEA,* but reactions to the *DEA*'s emphasis on Susan Dickinson seem mixed. In responses to our survey, one scholar acknowledged "direct[ing] students toward writings of Susan Dickinson" in the *DEA,* while another criticized "Professor Smith's fascination with the (to me) unfascinating Susan Dickinson."

Even though most Dickinson scholars understand the copyright conundrum the *DEA* faces, they suggest that it would become more valuable for research by providing access to more of Dickinson's works. One survey respondent noted, "The last time I looked at the archives there was very little by Emily Dickinson. This profoundly limits their value." In interviews and survey responses about the *DEA*'s impact on scholarship, the word *potential* recurred. As one scholar observed in survey comments, "The potential is tremendous, particularly once it is possible to examine all versions of each Dickinson poem." In any case, scholars working outside the United States or at universities with small libraries value the *DEA* for providing access to unique materials, as a survey respondent suggests: "It offers the opportunity for scholars, especially those not based in the USA, to access, read, and search Dickinson's manuscripts online."

Whereas Whitman scholars seem to have embraced the *WWA* for providing access to digital facsimiles of the poet's manuscripts, the *DEA* is frequently cited by scholars debating the significance of Dickinson's manuscripts, reflecting what Betsy Erkkila calls the "Dickinson Wars."[16] Critics such as Ellen Hart, Jerome McGann, Susan Howe, and others argue that the manuscript gives the best witness to Dickinson's work as a poet and that Dickinson's lineation, punctuation, and other aspects of her material text cannot be adequately represented in transcription. This emphasis on manuscripts and on textual transmission guides the *DEA*, which aims to make available high-quality digital facsimiles of Dickinson's manuscripts and to empower readers to make their own editorial judgments. Yet critics such as Domhnall Mitchell argue that the significance of the manuscript has been exaggerated.[17] Some responses to our survey reflected this scholarly debate; one interviewee observed that critics such as Mitchell are making a "useful intervention."

The *DEA*'s willingness to experiment with new analytical tools distinguishes it. As part of the digital article "Emily Dickinson Writing a Poem," Martha Nell Smith and Lara Vetter include a section called "Interactive Explorations," where they invite readers to experiment with "dynamic, hands-on exercises that exploit digital tools recently developed at the Maryland Institute for Technology in the Humanities (MITH)."[18] Using the Virtual Lightbox, readers can manipulate digital images of different versions of Dickinson's "Safe in Their Alabaster Chambers." Through the Versioning Machine, readers can compare and contrast the different versions of the poem. The *DEA* also participated in efforts to develop even more sophisticated software by collaborating with Nora (http://www.noraproject.org/) and its successor, MONK (http://monkproject.org/), to build text-mining and visualization tools that enable literary scholars to detect patterns and develop insights. To determine if a Dickinson poem is erotic, for instance, the scholar "trains" the Nora software by first classifying a small sample as "hot or not," then runs the software to automatically detect eroticism in a larger set of texts. According to Smith, using Nora brought new insights about Dickinson's poetry. She reported in an e-mail to the Nora team, "The data mining has made me plumb much more deeply into little four- and five-letter words, the function of which I thought I was already sure, and has also enabled me to expand and deepen some critical connections I've been making for the last 20 years."[19] Rather than replacing human intelligence, applications such as Nora enable scholars to test—and see past—assumptions, revealing previously unrecognized patterns and opening up new ways of approaching texts. Tools for zooming and comparing images are included in *Emily Dickinson's Correspondences: A Born Digital Inquiry*, a critical edition edited by Martha Nell Smith and Lara Vetter that was published by the University of Virginia Press's Rotunda electronic imprint in December 2008.[20]

Despite the controversies over editorial approaches to Dickinson, most Dickinson scholars seem to see advantages to building a digital collection of her works. Jonathan Morse compares the fixity of print to the fluidity of the digital: "The Dickinson of the variorum, old or new, is a poet of eternity who has been locked into time. It seems all but certain that twenty-first-century publishing technologies are massing now to liberate her."[21]

The Impact of *Uncle Tom's Cabin & American Culture* on Scholarship

Although there is less awareness of *UTCAC* in the scholarly community, this digital collection sets itself apart by providing access to a broad range of multimedia materials. *UTCAC* is most often cited by works on the media history of *Uncle Tom's Cabin*, general research guides, and histories of the Civil War. Scholars who cite *UTCAC* use laudatory language when mentioning it in their footnotes, describing it as "superb"[22] and "comprehensive."[23] In evaluating *UTCAC*'s usefulness for research, scholars who cited it rated it as 5 out of 5, while the average score by scholars who did not cite it was 4. In response to our survey question about its impact on research, scholars said that *UTCAC* "makes rare materials easily available; expands boundaries of textual criticism" and is "a crucial collection that may well become a definitive source for research on the book, gathering as it does so much information on the novel."

For scholars, *UTCAC*'s primary value seems to come from providing a single point of access to the rich contexts surrounding the novel. Our interviewee said that *UTCAC*'s greatest contribution is aggregating "the material that frames *Uncle Tom's Cabin*—ephemera, pamphlets, advertising cards, playbills, sheet music. It's giving scholars immediate access to surrounding materials that get at responses to *Uncle Tom's Cabin*." In *The Annotated Uncle Tom's Cabin*, editors Henry Louis Gates and Hollis Robbins write, "See Stephen Railton's excellent website, '*Uncle Tom's Cabin and American Culture*,' for film clips."[24] In *The Publishing History of Uncle Tom's Cabin*

(2007), Claire Parfait cites *UTCAC* so frequently that she includes it in the list of abbreviations, along with the American Antiquarian Society and Huntington Library. Just as with the *WWA* and *DEA,* the most significant recommendation for improvement from scholars is for *UTCAC* to provide more content, such as more films and new sections about the novel in an international context and about American reform culture.

UTCAC collaborates with archives to make *UTC* resources available online and collaborates with scholars to provide critical essays about the novel. In the summer of 2007, *UTCAC* partnered with the Harriet Beecher Stowe Center to host an NEH-sponsored conference called "*Uncle Tom's Cabin* in the Web of Culture: A Multi-Disciplinary Conference." This conference brought together 12 nationally known scholars in fields such as women's studies, African American studies, children's literature, art history, and film studies to discuss the cultural impact of the novel. Not only did the conference raise the profile of *UTCAC,* but it also produced several multimedia essays that incorporate digital objects from *UTCAC.* For example, Michael Winship's essay on *Uncle Tom's Cabin* and the history of the book contains links to 35 digital objects from *UTCAC.*[25]

Recommendations

On the whole, scholars are beginning to embrace digital resources as important to their research, but they call for the following:

Access to more comprehensive, high-quality digital collections. More than anything else, scholars want access to more digital resources. Scholars responding to our general survey asked for more material to be made available electronically, particularly noncanonical works. If works are not digitized, they may be ignored as scholarship increasingly moves online. When we asked Whitman, Dickinson, and *UTC* scholars what enhancements to the digital collections they would recommend, the most desired features were more works by the author (84 percent) and more recent criticism (64 percent). Yet comprehensiveness presents its own challenges in making the digital collection usable, securing access to materials, and establishing selection criteria. Martha Nell Smith argues that comprehensiveness is an illusion, since editors must always leave something out: "The very idea that an archive can be comprehensive doesn't ask the question about how materials got in the library, why they're there, and why the archives are comprehensive."[26]

Vetting mechanisms so that good scholarship is rewarded and so that scholars can quickly evaluate the quality of a resource. When we asked Whitman, Dickinson, and *UTC* scholars what would increase and enhance their usage of digital resources overall, the most common response (55 percent) was recognition of these resources by scholarly societies and communities. Such a response indicates that scholars see a need for a cultural shift in how digital resources are regarded by their scholarly communities before they will feel comfortable citing them. One Whitman scholar recommended that digital archives follow the lead of the *William Blake Archive* and seek the imprimatur of the MLA critical editions.[27]

Better institutional support for digital scholarship. Forty-one percent of Dickinson, Whitman, and *UTC* scholars called for increased institutional funding for using digital resources in research.

Enhanced tools, particularly search tools. In the last few years, the digital humanities community has shifted its attention from building digital collections to developing tools that support inquiry and collaboration, particularly text-mining tools. Yet the humanities community has been slow in adopting such tools. Nevertheless, "traditional" scholars do want tools that help them do their research more efficiently. Respondents to our general survey ranked "search tools that go across multiple scholarly web sites" (88 percent) and "search tools that are powerful and easy to use" (88 percent) most highly; tools to help them collect (62 percent), annotate (63 percent), and cite (66 percent) digital information also scored well. However, few respondents ranked text visualization (29 percent), dynamic mapping (13 percent), or timeline tools (28 percent) as being desired features.

Just because fewer scholars viewed sophisticated tools as a priority does not mean that they are hostile to them. Rather, as our follow-up interviews indicated, many "traditional" scholars lack awareness of what these tools can do and how to use them. As one Dickinson scholar observed, "I don't know enough about what would be possible to envision what tools would look like."

Training in using digital collections. Although only 24 percent of Whitman, Dickinson, and *UTC* scholars selected training as a means of increasing the use of digital resources, several survey respondents and interviewees did emphasize how useful it would be: "The institutional funding that would help most . . . would be great attention to training researchers how to use electronic resources." Likewise, a Dickinson scholar suggested that the developers of digital collections run workshops at conferences such as the American Literature Association so that their colleagues would know about such resources and how to use them.

Better publicity for digital collections. Awareness of digital collections remains an important issue: 38 percent of all the scholars we surveyed suggested that usage of digital resources would increase with better publicity efforts by archive developers. To address the lack of awareness, developers of digital archives can promote them through announcements on discussion networks, blogs, and other means of electronic communication, but the most effective method seems to be old-fashioned word of mouth and existing scholarly channels, such as citations in publications. Among the survey respondents who cited the *WWA,* 71.4 percent said they learned about the archive through personal contact with a project developer, and 63.6 percent of those who cited the *DEA* said this, while 66.7 percent of scholars citing *UTCAC* said that they learned about it through a colleague and through citations in other publications. Whether by consulting the bibliographies of trusted scholars or trading information at conferences, scholars often come to find and rely on resources by evaluating the reputation of the scholars with which they are associated. As a Whitman interviewee stated, "Given the stature of Ed Folsom and Ken Price, it contributes untold value to the Web site. They're very established, have strong records at the top of Whitman field, and bring scholars of their own stature to this. It helps tremendously to legitimize, and opens up electronic archives as a field that has value to expand to other areas."

Open access to digital resources. As our Cultural Commonwealth acknowledges, open access to digital collections supports inquiry, collaboration, and the core academic value of promoting the growth of knowledge. The *WWA,* the *DEA* (many sections), and *UTCAC* all provide free and open access to their collections, a scholarly good embraced by several survey respondents. Independent scholars and those at less wealthy institutions often have difficulty accessing subscription-based online resources, since journal collections such as JSTOR do not provide a pricing structure for individual users.

Along with open access, scholars wanted assurances that these digital collections would remain available for the long term. For a Whitman scholar, the only negative to digital collections like the *WWA* is the potential instability of the electronic medium as opposed to the relative permanence of the print: "The problem with sites like the WWA is that the future is uncertain. What if funding gets pulled, or editors retire, or sites are not maintained—will they be reliable and authoritative sources indefinitely?" Price acknowledges that sustainability is the most significant weakness for digital collections such as the *WWA,* but he argues that the library community and scholars are too invested in these projects to allow them to disappear.[28]

A shift in the culture of scholarly citation. To overcome scholars' reluctance to cite online resources, interviewees suggested raising the awareness of the conventions for citing an online resource. One Whitman scholar recommended that the *WWA* post a notice on the home page asking researchers to cite the archive and reminding them that having more citations raises its profile and supports its fund-raising efforts. It might also be useful to include as part of the Web site information on how to cite the resource.

Conclusion

Our study suggests that research practices in American literature are beginning to change as more material becomes available online. Scholars use whatever resources advance their research, as long as they are of high quality and easy to access. They see important advantages to having research materials in electronic formats, such as the ability to rapidly search across databases, access rare collections, and draw in materials from multiple fields. However, many remain reluctant to cite digital resources, since they are not yet regarded as being as credible as print. While the *WWA,* the *DEA,* and *UTCAC* still are not cited very frequently in the scholarly literature, all three have made substantial contributions to their fields. As scholars turn their attention to resources previously neglected because of problems of access, such as manuscripts of *Leaves of Grass,* the works of Susan Dickinson, or film versions of *Uncle Tom's Cabin,* the scope of research is changing.

Yet even as scholars embrace the efficiencies and access provided by electronic resources, traditional research practices remain in play; researchers still find sources by consulting bibliographies or colleagues, view peer-reviewed resources as being most credible, and give most value to tools that make it easier to find information rather than those that enable new modes of inquiry, such as text visualization. Nevertheless, in the last 15 years, tools once foreign to many humanities scholars—including e-mail, word-processing applications, and research databases—have become essential to their daily work. We expect humanities scholarship to continue transforming as research tools become easier to use and serve particular research problems, as more and more resources become available online, and as institutional barriers to digital scholarship recede.

Notes

1. This essay is based on a presentation that was part of the Digital Americanists panel at the 2007 American Literature Association conference in Boston. The authors would like to thank the scholars who took our surveys and participated in follow-up interviews, as well as Ken Price, Martha Nell Smith, Steve Railton, Andy Jewell, Amy Earhart, Pamela Francis, Caroline Levander, and Geneva Henry. Quotations from scholars have been lightly edited for spelling, capitalization, and punctuation and may not be exact transcriptions. For more survey results and other information about our study, see http://library.rice.edu/services/dmc/about/projects/the-impact-of-digital-resources-on-humanities-research.

2. Patrick Leary, "Googling the Victorians," *Journal of Victorian Culture* 10, no. 1 (2005): 72–86, http://victorianresearch.org/googling.pdf.

3. Matthew G. Kirschenbaum, "The Remaking of Reading: Data Mining and the Digital Humanities," in *The National Science Foundation Symposium on Next Generation of Data Mining and Cyber-Enabled Discovery for Innovation, Baltimore, MD, October 11, 2007*, http://www.cs.umbc.edu/~hillol/NGDM07/abstracts/talks/MKirschenbaum.pdf.

4. Anthony Grafton, "Future Reading," *New Yorker*, November 12, 2007, http://www.newyorker.com/reporting/2007/11/05/071105fa_fact_grafton.

5. William S. Brockman, Laura Neumann, Carole L. Palmer, and Tonyia J. Tidline, *Scholarly Work in the Humanities and the Evolving Information Environment* (Washington, DC: Digital Library Federation, Council on Library and Information Resources, 2001), http://www.clir.org/pubs/reports/pub104/pub104.pdf.

6. Martha L. Brogan and Daphnée Rentfrow, *A Kaleidoscope of Digital American Literature* (Washington, DC: Digital Library Federation, Council on Library and Information Resources, 2005), http://www.clir.org/pubs/reports/pub132/pub132.pdf.

7. Jerome McGann, "Information Technology and the Troubled Humanities," *Text Technology* 14, no. 2 (2005): 112, http://texttechnology.mcmaster.ca/pdf/vol14_2/mcgann14-2.pdf.

8. In the interest of full disclosure, we note that Lisa Spiro did some text encoding for *UTCAC* and that its director, Steve Railton, was her dissertation advisor. At the time

that the University of Virginia's Institute for Advanced Technology in the Humanities (IATH) was helping to develop the *WWA* and *DEA*, Spiro worked for IATH as a managing editor of the online journal *Postmodern Culture*.

9. Dickinson Editing Collective, "Proposal for Dickinson Electronic Archives," *Dickinson Electronic Archives*, http://www.emilydickinson.org/archive_description.html (accessed 15 November 2007).

10. The 2008 MLA Bibliography did not appear to be complete at the time of our research.

11. Although we did not ask the project directors of the digital archives to take our survey, we did invite the participation of scholars who had worked on the digital archive and published in the field. To protect participants' confidentiality, we are not referring to them by name. Since we were able to speak to many more Whitman scholars than Dickinson or *UTC* scholars, our discussion of scholars' perception of the *WWA*'s impact is more detailed.

12. The third edition of the *MLA Style Manual and Guide to Scholarly Publishing* no longer requires URLs to be included in citations, regarding them as too unstable. In addition, the MLA no longer treats print as being "the default medium of publication." See Tim Johnson, "MLA Changes Course on Web Citations," *University Affairs*, 6 October 2008, http://www.universityaffairs.ca/mla-changes-course-on-web-citations.aspx.

13. Ed Folsom and Kenneth M. Price, *Re-Scripting Walt Whitman: An Introduction to His Life and Work* (Malden, MA: Blackwell, 2005), 145.

14. Sharon Harris, "'A New Era in Female History': Nineteenth-Century U.S. Women Writers," *American Literature* 74, no. 3 (2002): 617, http://muse.jhu.edu/journals/american_literature/v074/74.3harris.html.

15. Interview with Martha Nell Smith, 23 May 2007.

16. At the 2001 Emily Dickinson International Conference in Trondheim, Norway, Smith gave a presentation entitled "Give Peace a Chance: A Proposal to End the 'Dickinson Wars,'" suggesting that the Dickinson community avoid using violent language to describe scholarly debate.

17. Domhnall Mitchell, "The Grammar of Ornament: Emily Dickinson's Manuscripts and Their Meanings," *Nineteenth-Century Literature* 55, no. 4 (2001): 497.

18. Martha Nell Smith and Lara Vetter, "Emily Dickinson Writing a Poem," *Dickinson Electronic Archives*, http://www.emilydickinson.org/safe/ (accessed 16 November 2007).

19. Quoted by John M. Unsworth, "New Methods for Humanities Research" (Lyman Award Lecture, National Humanities Center, Research Triangle Park, NC, 2005), http://www3.isrl.uiuc.edu/~unsworth/lyman.htm (accessed 8 November 2007).

20. See http://rotunda.upress.virginia.edu:8080/edc/.

21. Jonathan Morse, "Bibliographical Essay," in *A Historical Guide to Emily Dickinson*, ed. Vivian R. Pollak (Oxford: Oxford University Press, 2004), 268.

22. Joy Jordan-Lake, *Whitewashing "Uncle Tom's Cabin": Nineteenth-Century Women Novelists Respond to Stowe* (Nashville: Vanderbilt University Press, 2005), xvii.

23. Cindy Weinstein, *Family, Kinship, and Sympathy in Nineteenth-Century American Literature* (New York: Cambridge University Press, 2004), 212.

24. Harriet Beecher Stowe, *The Annotated Uncle Tom's Cabin,* ed. Henry Louis Gates and Hollis Robbins (New York: W. W. Norton, 2007).

25. Michael Winship, "*Uncle Tom's Cabin:* History of the Book in the 19th-Century United States," *Uncle Tom's Cabin & American Culture,* http://www.iath.virginia.edu/utc/interpret/exhibits/winship/winship.html (accessed 7 November 2007).

26. Martha Nell Smith, "Computing: What's American Literary Study Got to Do with IT?" *American Literature* 74, no. 4 (2002), http://muse.jhu.edu/journals/american_literature/v074/74.4smith.html.

27. The MLA recently revised its *Guidelines for Editors of Scholarly Editions* to include electronic editions (http://www.mla.org/cse_guidelines).

28. Kenneth M. Price, "The Walt Whitman Archive at Ten: Some Backward Glances and Vistas Ahead," *Mickle Street Review* nos. 17–18 (2005). http://micklestreet.rutgers.edu/archives/Issue%201718/pages/Scholarship/Price.htm.

PART 2

Markup and Tools: New Models and Methods for Humanistic Inquiry

A Case for Heavy Editing: The Example of *Race and Children's Literature in the Gilded Age*

AMANDA GAILEY

Historically, the verb *search* comes from words meaning "to seek," "to surround," and "to go round," and indeed, for centuries, the usage of *search* echoed these origins. Typical uses since the fourteenth century have involved thoroughness, examination, and, importantly, exploration. Whether one searched a place, one's self, or a stack of books, the searching required the searcher to thoroughly explore what she or he searched, which left open the possibility of finding something that the searcher had not particularly been seeking. In the 1990s, *search* took on new meaning, as Internet access became widespread. People began employing computers to search data in very specific ways—usually checking for specified text strings in indexed files, especially Web pages. While some aspects of the original meaning of *search* are reflected in computerized searching—verifying the presence or absence of something—other aspects are lost. The human involved in the searching need not look at the texts at all, only determine the query and view the results. Exploration, at least by humans, is not required or is kept at arm's length, and many critics have noted the loss of the kind of serendipity that can accompany a thorough, personally performed search.

Search now is a contronym: just as *dust* means to remove dust (dusting the shelves) or to add it (dusting with sugar), and as *fast* means moving quickly or stuck in one place, *search* can mean either to thoroughly explore something, to scrutinize it, or to simply ask a computer whether something contains a piece of information, without ever looking at it at all. Today, when a student announces that she or he has "searched *Leaves of Grass* for references to slavery," the student could mean that she or he reread the book, keeping an eye out for passages that treat or allude to the topic, or simply that she or he plugged words like *slavery* and *enslave* into a find-on-page function of a browser. In fact, *search* has become a contronym very similar to *scan,* which can mean both to examine closely and to look over quickly and has similarly been influenced by technology: the *Oxford English Dictionary* finds most early uses of the "looking over quickly" sense in computing contexts.

Literary scholars are now actively engaged in computer-based searching, looking over huge numbers of digitized texts quickly. Close reading is an exercise in searching in the older sense: such scrutiny and exploration can result in discovery. So it is fitting that new modes of literary scholarship, implementing computerized searches and other processes to expose patterns in literature, have sometimes been called "distant reading."[1] Distant reading and other query-based modes of scholarship have become popular in digital literary scholarship; in the minds of some policy makers, such modes have even become definitive of the field. Recently, a representative from the National Endowment for the Humanities gave a talk about the agency's new digital initiative, which earmarks funds for humanities research projects that make use of or develop digital tools. He explained that this initiative is exciting because, as he put it, "we can solve a lot of humanities problems now through digital technologies." This comment may give some digital humanists pause. Certainly, computing has made great strides in the collection, dissemination, and analysis of humanities materials. But there is a tacit assumption in his comment: digital technologies in the humanities are primarily used to solve problems, rather than to expose problems or allow for unexpected discovery. The "problem solving" model of humanities research assumes a specific methodology, one almost certainly influenced by the prevalence of searching—in its newer sense—as a mode of research: that a scholar begins with a question, poses a query through a digital tool, and receives useful results. It assumes that digital scholarship is algorithmic, that it is procedurally predefined and not exploratory.

Certainly, query-based and statistical analyses are at work in humanities computing and have resulted in some fascinating scholarship. For example, WordHoard,[2] a project directed by Martin Mueller of Northwestern University, "applies to highly canonical literary texts the insights and techniques of corpus linguistics, that is to say, the empirical and computer-assisted study of large bodies of written texts or transcribed speech."[3] The encoding provided by WordHoard allows users to derive sophisticated concordances from works by Homer, Chaucer, Spenser, and Shakespeare, among others. The concordances can be customized to different contexts, such as the gender of the speaker, genre, and so on. The concordances are fascinating and are only realistically retrievable using digital tools. WordHoard shows that the most commonly used nouns in Homer's corpus are *man, ship, god, spirit,* and *hand.* In Shakespeare, they are *lord, man, sir, love,* and *king.* In both cases, the queries return results that fit well with our expectations and give us five-word summaries that capture, to our minds, the zeitgeists of ancient Greece and Renaissance England. The Nora project,[4] which has since joined with WordHoard and become the interinstitutional MONK project,[5] set out to "produce software for discovering, visualizing, and exploring significant patterns across large collections of full-text humanities resources in existing digital libraries."[6] When the project worked with scholars to find markers of the erotic in Emily Dickinson's poems, several words surfaced that were wholly unpredicted by Dickinson scholars, including *mine, must, Bud, Woman,* and Dickinson's sister's name, *Vinnie.* This kind of challenge to the intuitions of practiced readers is clearly a strength of humanities computing. Despite such inspiring work, it is important for us to consider aspects of humanities scholarship that humanities computing is weaker at addressing and to reflect on how digital editors can help alleviate these problems.

A great irony of humanities computing is the disparity between the kind of work required to produce scholarly archives and the kind of work that these resources currently enable for their users. To illustrate, I will offer some examples from my experience at the *Walt Whitman Archive,* a vast and mature "research and teaching tool," as the editors put it, "that sets out to make Whitman's vast work, for the first time, easily and conveniently accessible to scholars, students, and general readers."[7] The *Whitman Archive* requires several people to scrutinize the smallest details of a Whitman manuscript as it is digitized for online display: first a tagger, who applies XML encoding, or "tags," to interesting features of a manuscript, usually while transcribing it; then a proofreader, who enforces basic quality control and notes any genuine anomalies in the markup; then an editor, who makes final decisions about questionable markup and transcriptions and supplies needed annotations; and finally a technical editor, who "blesses" the XML file after ensuring that it can be properly processed and displayed through the project's technical infrastructure. This level of scrutiny leads to all sorts of exciting discoveries—a famous example within *Whitman Archive* lore is when Andrew Jewell, having spent far too much time looking at manuscript scans, noticed that a glue stain on a manuscript at the University of Virginia matched one on a manuscript at Dartmouth, thus proving that, at some point, Whitman had fastened the two manuscripts together as one. The discovery was enabled by digitization—he was unlikely to have compared distributed manuscripts otherwise—but directly resulted from searching in the old sense: a thorough, explorative scrutiny. While preparing a Whitman manuscript in the Trent Collection at Duke University, we used Adobe Photoshop to discover that where Whitman wrote the word *comrade* in ink, he later thought about using the word *lover,* which he wrote in pencil before erasing it and settling on the safer original word (figs. 1 and 2). All of this shows that the labor behind such an archive primarily consists of old-fashioned, meticulous close reading, so close, in fact, that it often becomes forensic.

Users of resources like the *Whitman Archive* or other literary projects involving large or extremely large corpora, however, are poised for a very different kind of scholarly research. The size of these resources, together with the technological underpinnings of XML-based transcriptions, encourage not close reading but directed querying or searching in the newer sense and, for those so inclined, statistical analysis. Certainly, the results of such research can be illuminating: Brian Pytlik Zillig has developed a tool called TokenX that analyzes word frequencies across corpora, such as the six editions of *Leaves of Grass,* allowing scholars to track, for example, whether Whitman's use of the word *America* grew or shrank after the Civil War and, eventually, whether his use of the word was more or less frequent than that of other poets writing in the United States at the time.[8] While such findings are indisputably useful and exciting, it is important for us to take note of the kinds of inquiry that digital archives and common tools do not actively promote, so that valuable aspects of literary study do not become neglected as we increasingly move to digital scholarship.

The Text Encoding Initiative (or TEI) is the implementation of XML

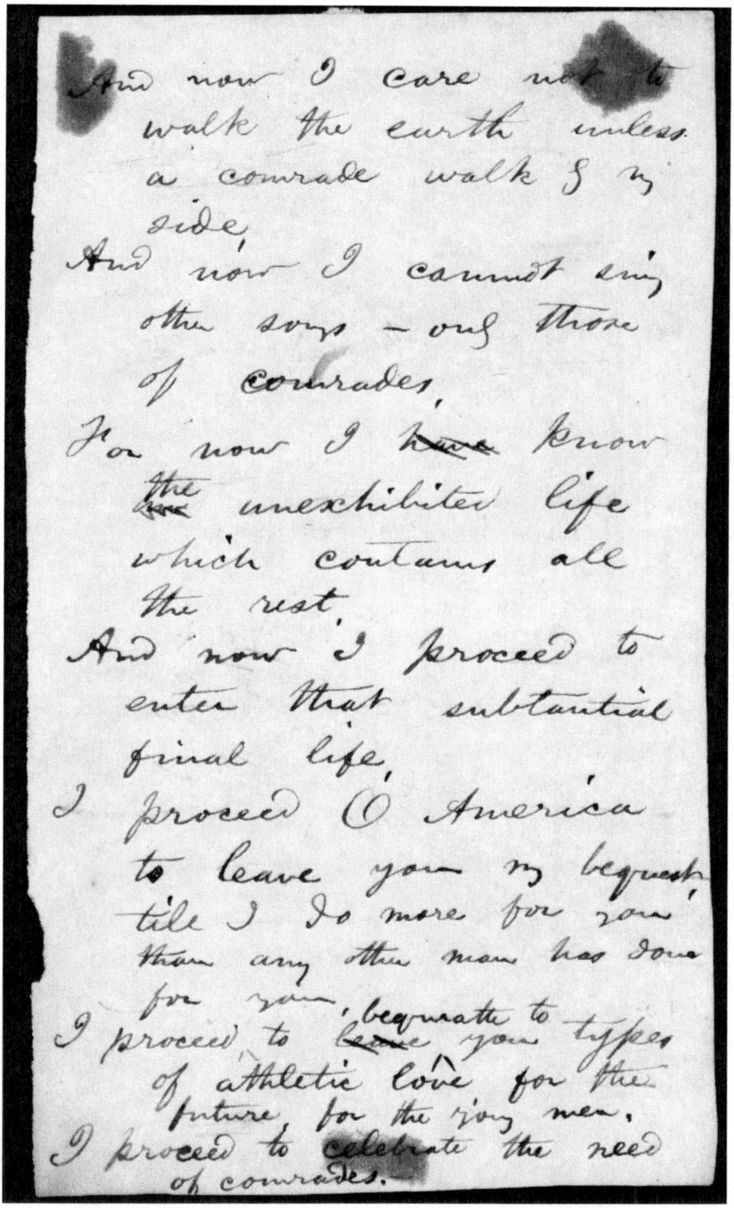

And now I care not to
walk the earth unless
a comrade walk by my
side,
And now I cannot sing
other songs — only those
of comrades,
For now I ~~have~~ know
the ~~[illegible]~~ unexhibited life
which contains all
the rest,
And now I proceed to
enter that substantial
final life,
I proceed O America
to leave you my bequest,
till I do more for you
than any other man has done
for you,
I proceed to ~~leave~~ bequeath to you types
of athletic love for the
future, for the young men,
I proceed to celebrate the need
of comrades.

Fig. 1. "[And now I care not to]" (later "In Paths Untrodden"). (Trent Collection of Whitmaniana, Duke University; available online through the *Walt Whitman Archive.* See the finding aid for Duke University's collection at www.whitmanarchive.org/manuscripts/index.html.)

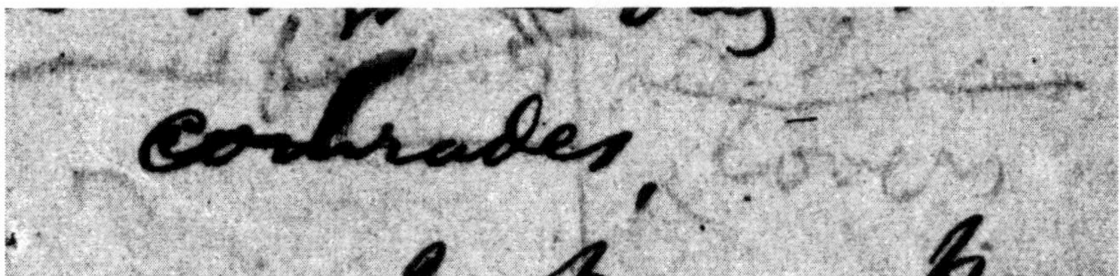

Fig. 2. Digitally enhanced detail of "[And now I care not to]." (Trent Collection of Whitmaniana, Duke University.)

(Extensible Markup Language) that is the lingua franca of digital projects in the humanities. XML provides a general syntax for labeling, or "tagging," data using terms that the tagger sees fit, whether the data is a store's inventory, phone listings, or literary texts. XML provides the general rules for structuring tags: for example, that an opened tag must be properly closed and that a tag opened inside another tag must "nest" within the tag that contains it. Any XML file that violates these rules is not considered well formed and will not be processed properly by programs using the XML file. TEI is a socially agreed on set of guidelines directing humanities scholars on which tags to use in which types of contexts. Generally speaking, XML provides the syntax, and TEI provides the semantics. For example, a simple XML version of a literary scholar's tagging of Whitman's "O Captain!" may look something like the following:

```
<lg type="stanza">
    <l>O Captain! my Captain! our fearful trip is done,</l>
    <l>The ship has weather'd every rack, the prize we sought is won,</l>
    <l>The port is near, the bells I hear, the people all exulting,</l>
    <l>While follow eyes the steady keel, the vessel grim and daring;</l>
    <l>But O heart! heart! heart!</l>
    <l>O the bleeding drops of red,</l>
    <l>Where on the deck my Captain lies,</l>
    <l>Fallen cold and dead.</l>
</lg>
```

XML syntax enforces certain conventions on this markup: the tags (the bracketed information) that open must close, and individual elements must "nest" properly (i.e., close before their parent tag closes). However, XML makes no demands about what we call poems and poetic lines. The example would still be well formed even if we substituted <monkeys> for <lg> or <potato-chips> for <l>, as long as the terms are in brackets and we close and nest them properly. This is what makes XML so flexible—it can accommodate the particular vocabularies of the zookeeper, the vending machine franchiser, and the digital humanist. It is up to the people using XML to ensure that the tags they use make sense to whomever will use the file and that the same types of things are consistently referred to by the same labels: if we call something <potato-chips> in one place, we must make sure not to call it <crunchy-snacks> somewhere else.

This is where the TEI steps in. The TEI is an organization that vets suggestions from participating digital projects in order to publish a recommended vocabulary for the treatment of humanities texts.[9] The TEI tells us that projects seeking TEI compliance should refer to poetic lines with the <l> tag. Further, it places some sensible constraints on the vocabulary: it tells us, for example, that lines (<l>) can fall within line groups (<lg>) but that line groups cannot occur within lines. The most recent publication of the TEI guidelines, P5 (for "Publication 5"), documents over 500 allowable tags for conformant projects. Projects that discover textual features that seem not to be addressed by these guidelines can ask for assistance from the TEI community—mostly comprised of humanities scholars, librarians, and digital publishers— who will either guide them in how to use existing tagging or suggest that the guidelines be modified to accommodate the textual feature. The iterative development of the guidelines has caused the number of tags to almost triple since the first version, P1, was released in 1990.[10] The TEI has been so widely adopted that any digital project seeking funding from major humanities grant agencies in the United States today must claim TEI conformance or explain why they should not use the TEI.

TEI is descriptive markup—that is, it is primarily focused on noting the structural or formal features of a text. While marking such features is always interpretive to some degree (sometimes notably so), descriptive markup is generally less controversial than overtly interpretive or critical claims: an editor can reasonably assume that fewer people will contest her or his labeling of a poetic line than her or his labeling of the homoerotic. There is nothing about XML that precludes using it to make interpretive claims about texts, but such markup is seldom used, for several reasons. First, most editors of digital projects have the same concerns that editors of print scholarly editions do, and they are primarily interested in setting a reliable text, not in offering criticism. Second, a fundamental limitation of XML is that it cannot gracefully accommodate claims about a text that compete hierarchically; that is, XML requires tags to nest within each other, which would cause technical errors if critics tried to make claims about overlapping segments of text, and surely this would happen more often than not. In other words, XML can easily allow for interpretive claims about a text but would almost certainly fail to accommodate several different interpretations of the text coexisting in the same file. Because most editors know this from the outset, they choose to avoid putting any clearly contentious claims about the text in the markup. This tendency is even stronger among mass digitization projects, which are likely to be led by professionals who are not necessarily scholars of the texts and so are more wary of inserting controversial claims. Further, deep, critical markup is time-consuming—a factor influencing any digital project—and so is less likely to be a priority for projects hoping to turn out as many texts as efficiently as possible. For all these reasons, most projects adopt a Muzak approach that is as unlikely to offend as it is to enthrall. If the technology did not rule out the inclusion of conflicting interests in the text, though, contestable tagging would not severely limit the usability of the document and might seem a more viable possibility for projects directed by literary scholars.

Some scholars and teachers have begun to see TEI as a theory of the text, one that requires a tagger to assert an interpretation through the markup. Because of the vocabulary of TEI and the structure of XML, these interpretations tend to be primarily formalistic and heavily concerned with ontology—the tagger must ask herself or himself, what constitutes a poem, a stanza, or even a word? How about a work? What makes the 1855 *Leaves of Grass* different than the 1892 edition? How can we rigorously express their relationship to each other and to the manuscript drafts that trace their compositional histories? These questions are provocative and can be surprisingly engaging even to novice taggers. Some teachers have expressed interest in requiring students to tag a poem using TEI in classes where a digital project is not the goal, for the act of tagging a text is pedagogically useful in itself.

However—crucially—the kind of engagement required to mark up a text is not required or even suggested to the user of the digital file. Regardless of its pedagogical and scholarly value to the tagger, markup for a digital edition is almost always inserted in a transcription to facilitate searching (in the new sense), not a reader's extended engagement with the text. The searchability of a TEI document consists of the markup—usually limited to formal features—and text indexing, or the contents of the transcription. Editors of digital editions typically add markup to a text in order to make features of a text explicit, conformant to a controlled vocabulary, and so available for searching. So a user would find "O Captain, My Captain" after searching for the word *captain,* because it is in the transcription already, but a user could also search for poetic lines or stanzas, because the markup notes them as such. The markup, in effect, though human-written, is meant to be machine-readable.[11]

But what about the stuff that is in neither the transcription nor the markup of a text? Some texts are at least as interesting for what they *do not* do as they are for what they do. "O Captain" is such a text. Anyone who had to study the poem in high school learned that it was Whitman's homage to Abraham Lincoln. Yet Lincoln's name appears nowhere in this poem. If a user were interested in all Whitman manuscripts that talk about Abraham Lincoln, searching for the name *Lincoln* would not call up this one or even "When Lilacs Last in the Dooryard Bloom'd." In order for a search to return what are arguably the most salient results for a search on Lincoln in Whitman's corpus, the markup might look like the following, noting that Lincoln is the referent of the metaphor (note that the following is not TEI compliant):

```
<lg type="stanza">
    <l>O
    <metaphor referent="Abraham Lincoln">Captain</metaphor>!
    my
    <metaphor referent="Abraham Lincoln">Captain</metaphor>!
    our fearful trip is done,</l>
    <l>The ship has weather'd every rack, the prize we sought is won,</l>
    [. . .]
</lg>
```

Things get slipperier from there: to more fully do justice to the metaphor, we would also need to note that "fearful trip" refers to the Civil War. Even riskier, what do we do with "the prize we sought"? Should it be tagged as the abolition of slavery or as the reconciliation of the Union? To avoid these time-consuming and contestable decisions, the *Whitman Archive* opts to not tag the metaphor, or at least to defer such tagging, and at the same time limits the potential of *search*-based research. In his discussion of text searching, Jeffrey Garrett has speculated that the humanities have turned a blind eye to the shortcomings of new technologies in teaching and research, because, as he puts it, "the prospect of finding anything, anytime, anywhere, is so exciting, so intoxicating." As the example of "O Captain" shows, though, we are not always finding what we are looking for.

These issues have become keenly apparent for a project I coedit with Gerald Early and D. B. Dowd, *Race and Children's Literature of the Gilded Age,* or *RCLGA.* As the title suggests, our interest in the texts is more thesis-driven than most digital projects. We are in the early phases of work on the archive, but eventually it will include scans and transcriptions of children's literature published in the United States between 1867, the beginning of Reconstruction, and 1913, the foundation of the NAACP. We have started with the works of Joel Chandler Harris, and as we work, we are finding that some authors, such as Harris, have been so neglected in recent scholarship—digital and print—that we want to create subarchives of now minor authors whose works have fallen into disregard. For instance, we have now digitized about 25 of Harris's books, including several that were not meant for a juvenile audience. We believe that Harris, an author who, when he died in 1908, was second in popularity only to Mark Twain, is in need of a digital archive and that such a context will help scholars who are interested in the impact of his children's books on conceptions of racial difference to understand these books in the context of his larger career.

Many of Harris's books, especially the well-known Uncle Remus stories, are as powerful for what they do not say as they are for their literal content. Critics have variously read some of these stories—problematically filtered through narrative layers and phonetically rendered dialect—as fables that emerged among slaves and that allegorically represent interactions among slaves and whites. This allegorical reading cannot be properly accessed through data-mining tools that rely on text indexing, because, as fables, their allegorical meanings are not rendered literally. Further, if a user were interested in searching for occurrences of a particular word, it is likely that if the word were spoken by an African American character in Harris's work, as with the majority of the Uncle Remus books, the phonetic spelling would prevent the search engine from picking it up. For example, consider the following excerpts:

> . . . de'yll take on dat slonchidickler grin . . .

> . . . ole Brer Wolf want ter eat de little Rabs all der time . . .

Regularizing the spelling is problematic for a few reasons.[12] The standard written English equivalents of many of the words are obscure, such as *slonchidickler* for *slantendicular* or even *want* in the second excerpt: it is already spelled like a standard written English word, but is it meant to stand in for *wants* or *wanted*? Also, some might argue that it does too much violence to the text to regularize it in this way. "Translating" these passages into standard written English, one might argue, fundamentally undermines Harris's artistic project. Further, it may seem distasteful to treat the speech of African American characters as so alien that it requires translation, though in response to that concern, I would point out that we are reading the speech of African Americans as imagined and spun by a white author.

These problems are real, and even the project's staff are not unanimously supportive of any single treatment of the texts. But if we are to accept some of these stories as distorted records of a largely neglected tradition, we must somehow take on these problems so that we do not render an important source of folktales unusable by data harvesters and search engines. Further, regardless of their fidelity to actual oral traditions, these problematic stories defined African American folklore to enormous numbers of American readers in the early twentieth century. As Leonard Diepeveen points out, in the 40 years following the publication of Harris's *Uncle Remus: His Songs and Sayings* (1880), half a million copies sold, and by the 1920s, polls of English instructors ranked it as the fifth most important work of American literature.[13] The Uncle Remus tales became so definitive of black folklore, in fact, that when—27 years after Harris's death—Zora Neale Hurston published one of the few volumes of black folktales written by an African American (*Mules and Men,* 1935), critics seemed to only understand the work by how it did or did not resemble Harris's tales. Providing some sort of regularized text is the only way to ensure that this vastly influential body of literature is available to a dominant mode of literary research, the search.

Currently, our plan is to embed a normalization of the text into the encoding, paragraph by paragraph, so that when users search for the word *rabbits,* they will retrieve Uncle Remus's use of the word, but the normalization will not be automatically displayed. For example, our tagging may look something like the following:

```
<lg type=“poem”>
    <l>
    <choice>
        <orig type=“eye-dialect”>
        Dar once wuz a time when most er de creeturs
        </orig>
        <reg>
        There once was a time when most of the creatures
        </reg>
    </choice>
    </l>
    [. . .]
</lg>
```

The <choice> tag yokes together two competing readings. The <orig> tag indicates the original text, while the <reg> tag indicates the material in regularized form. Providing and labeling both forms will eventually allow users to turn on or off views of the text, so that they can suppress our heavy-handed regularization if they wish or invoke it when they perform a search. Taking advantage of an important nuance in TEI, we will use the <orig> and <reg> combination instead of the <sic> and <cor> combination (meaning *sic* and “correction”), as the former pair makes no claim about the rightness or wrongness of the readings, only how standardized their spellings are. Without this regularization—possible only through extended, close editorial supervision of the kind mass digitization projects cannot provide—large quantities of the texts would be unavailable to search-based scholarship.

Without editorial intervention, search would fail this literature in other ways as well. In my work on *Race and Children's Literature* so far, I have been struck by just how frequently omissions and gaps seem integral to a thorough study of these texts. One example arises in Harris's 1892 *On the*

"He des sot dar, he did, an' look at um."

Fig. 3. "He des sot dar, he did, an' look at um." (Illustration from *On the Plantation* [1892] by E. W. Kemble.)

Plantation, which includes a fable about why owls say "Hoo." An illustration by E. W. Kemble, the first illustrator of *Huckleberry Finn,* shows two angry birds reprimanding an owl for falling asleep at his post (fig. 3). The crow and owl are wearing suits, while the third bird is naked. Unsurprisingly, the story explains that the third bird is a jaybird. The story itself makes no mention of his nakedness, however, so it seems that this was a bit of visual humor inserted by Kemble. Interestingly, though, this illustration was published one year *before* the first usage in print of the phrase "naked as a jaybird."[14] The most plausible explanation for this is that the idiom was already in common usage and just had not made its way into print yet. Arguably, then, this illustration is the first published use of the idiom, even though the phrase "naked as a jaybird" appears nowhere in the story. If you were researching idioms, a search engine would not help you discover this.

Another more striking example of meaningful omission is in Harris's 1899 children's book, *Plantation Pageants,* which chronicles the adventures of three children: Sweetest Susan and Buster John, the children of former slaveholders, and Drusilla, the recently freed daughter of recently freed slaves. Throughout the book, Drusilla serves as a clownish sidekick to her dignified white playmates. The book is full of innumerable subtle and not-so-subtle debasements of Drusilla's character, as shown in E. Boyd Smith's illustration titled "Drusilla turned and ran, and the children after her" (fig. 4). The illustration engages a minstrel-style depiction of Drusilla, and the moment in the plot that it corresponds to involves Drusilla's stereotyped, comic cowardice. But perhaps the most telling denigration here is in an omission, the failure of the caption to include the word *other* before the word *children.* Quite plausibly, it is just this kind of distancing, the unconscious and subtle implication that Drusilla is something other than a child, that would have worked most profoundly on the book's intended audience. This is the kind of textual nuance that searching with a computer will not retrieve.

Searching also risks neglecting uncanonical or unpopular works. Works widely held as cultural treasures are more likely to be digitized than acutely problematic material. Currently, most of the well-known, freely accessible digital American literature projects on the Web (excluding amateur or aficionado sites) fall largely into three categories: useful but technologically lagging Web sites, such as Steven Railton's dazzlingly encyclopedic *Mark Twain in His Times;* digital library projects that offer sometimes dizzyingly vast numbers of texts with very light markup, such as *Wright American Fiction;* and rigorously edited, usually well-funded digital scholarly editions, such as the *Walt Whitman Archive,* the *Dickinson Electronic Archives,* and the *Willa Cather Archive.*[15] In rigor, funding sources, and general approach, projects in the latter category resemble British literature projects, such as the *William Blake Archive* and the *Rossetti Archive.*[16] Unsurprisingly, almost all of the best funded, most meticulously constructed archives focus on figures who have gained popularity or maintained popularity since their deaths; certainly Whitman, Dickinson, and Blake would have never received such expensive and focused editorial attention during their lives. But what of authors such as Harris, whose reputation has consistently shrunk after his death? Many authors enjoy the transformation "from outlaw to classic," as Alan Golding has put it, but others—such as Harris, whose troubling depictions of African Americans no longer jibe comfortably with most readers' sensibilities—have fallen from classic to outlaw.[17] Disney's decision to indefinitely withhold *Song of the South,* the controversial film from 1946 based on Harris's Uncle Remus stories, powerfully comments on Harris's

DRUSILLA TURNED AND RAN, AND THE CHILDREN AFTER HER

Fig. 4. "Drusilla turned and ran, and the children after her." (Illustration from *Plantation Pageants* [1899] by Joel Chandler Harris.)

decline. The absence of such figures from the pantheon of authors receiving prime digital treatment is conspicuous. It suggests that American literature is moving into a stratified digital environment, in which authors who represent troubling aspects of our past are relegated to a less thorough scholarly treatment than those whose sensibilities better correspond to our own, regardless of how anachronistic this disparity may be. When individual users or data-mining tools delve into these resources, then, they may be looking at underdeveloped or optimistically skewed visions of our past.

The blind spots of search-based inquiry show us that the humanities computing community should encourage close reading; that is, we should ask ourselves how close reading can emerge because of and not despite the new tools available to literary scholars. Reducing the limitations of search-based literary scholarship will involve several factors. First, scholarly editions will eventually need to tag literature so as to make as much nonliteral and nonstandard content as possible available to searching. This is as much a social problem as a technological one: it requires funding agencies and others to not view the editing of a text as complete simply because it is available in a mass digitization environment, which will almost certainly only provide light structural markup. Glenn Most has written, "An edition can be thought of as a mechanism intended to bring people texts from out of an archive in to a market."[18] Mass digitization projects are much closer to archives than they are to editions. They are open and available, unlike many archives, but they do little beyond what an archive would do as far as providing guidance to the searcher, human or computer.

Second, editions such as *RCLGA* should develop strategies both to elicit reader annotations and to support what is currently viewed as a heavy editorial presence—including commentary, normalization, and synopses. In an essay that predates digital literary editions, Ian Small addresses many practical and conceptual difficulties faced by editors looking to provide such annotations. One looming challenge that the annotator faces is determining which two bodies of readers to bridge. The job of the editor/annotator is to make the contemporaneous meaning of a text clear to modern readers by explaining references, semantic shifts, and so on. But, as Small points out, this is a very complicated task, requiring the annotator first to determine the original audience and their likely understanding of the text, then to determine the modern audience and their likely understanding of the text, and then to inform the latter group on the points where they differ from the former. This is difficult, if not impossible, even among homogenous reading groups, and it is even more difficult when—as must always be the case—the text has been read by heterogenous groups of readers.[19] A sampling of likely readers of Harris at the turn of the century illustrates the problem well: how can we assume a common interpretation of Uncle Remus stories among Northern and Southern blacks and whites, children and adults, or even among individuals in any one of these groups? Within the Harlem Renaissance alone, critics were of mixed opinion about Harris's stories. Some, such as Arthur Huff Fauset, saw them as primarily responsible for opening a valuable folk tradition to the white reading public while also perpetuating a comic caricature of African Americans.[20] Moreover, for whom are we translating these readerly perspectives—contemporary academics, high school students, or readers who retain fond memories of growing up with Harris's tales and who are likely to view most editorial information as politically correct polemicizing? To be sure, these issues should be carefully considered by editors formulating annotations. But the digital environment does provide some assistance in such matters. A few projects are starting to develop tools to allow user annotations, and a few more are working on standoff markup systems, which, by keeping markup in separate files from transcriptions, may circumvent XML's problems with conflicting hierarchies. These developments will soon allow editors and even readers to suggest different annotations, even categorizing them so that a contemporary high school student interested in Northern nineteenth-century responses to Harris's work can "turn on" and "turn off" various commentaries on the texts.

For projects such as *RCLGA,* heavy editing—deep markup and conspicuous editorial guidance—is arguably necessary for many readers to make even basic use of the resource. As Gerald Early has recently noted, "Without annotation and contextualization, the importance of the dialect and also the problematic nature of the dialect would never be fully understood or appreciated by today's readers, who would simply see the dialect as offensive or impenetrable."[21] Indeed, the public outcry over *Song of the South* suggests how loaded this material is. Today, most mentions of Harris in print or online are either sweepingly condemnatory or disturbingly nostalgic. The simple act of publishing the works online can be viewed as an affront to both camps: the first worries about perpetuating racially troublesome texts; the second resents any treatment of the texts that acknowledges their problems. Consequently, the editors of *RCLGA* must be keenly aware of our responsibility to couch the texts in proper and very visible editorial contexts, including commentary, synopses, and directed points of access to the site. In our opinion, requiring readers to move through some degree of editorial mediation—perhaps as little as a disclaimer—before gaining unfettered access to these books is the only responsible way, both educationally and ethically, to present the materials.

Jeffrey Garret has argued that "searching [is] our generation's answer to the problem of information glut."[22] I would like to suggest, though, that we think of heavy editing as another answer. The shortcomings of full-text searching can be reduced by attaching deep markup and commentary, both interpretive and explanatory, to the text. We can encourage close reading not only by alerting readers to the limitations of query-based research but also by gracefully integrating our critical apparatus, commentary, and even regularizations into the reading interface. We can also invite readers to contribute annotations and guide them to places to begin studying the texts, rather than offering up a vast corpus whose presentation primarily encourages arm's-length analysis.

Literary scholars are faced with at once intimidating and captivating quantities of textual information. *Wright American Fiction* has digitized almost 3,000 books from the mid-nineteenth century. *Making of America* currently boasts almost 10,000 books and 50,000 journal articles. To a scholar approaching such resources, searching and automated data mining seems not only an exciting new way to glean statistical information that was not possible with print scholarship but the only sane way to take on such overwhelming quantities of text. In such a context, close reading is almost maddening—the sheer quantity of texts can make a close reader of any one of them feel that she or he has chosen to document the dimensions of one grain of sand on the beach. However, it is important not to let dominant technologies unnecessarily dictate our inquiries. The quantity of sand on the beach may be intimidating, but we need a microscope as much as a bird's eye if we are to fully describe what the sand is.

Notes

1. Franco Moretti, *Graphs, Maps, Trees: Abstract Models for a Literary Theory* (London: Verso, 2005).

2. See http://wordhoard.northwestern.edu.

3. "What is WordHoard?" http://wordhoard.northwestern.edu/userman/whatiswordhoard.html.

4. See http://www.noraproject.org.

5. See http://monkproject.org.

6. "Project Descriptions (Long)," http://monkproject.org/?page_id=13.

7. See http://www.whitmanarchive.org/about/over.html.

8. See http://tokenx.unl.edu.

9. See http://www.tei-c.org.

10. Fotis Jannidis, "TEI in a Crystal Ball" (talk delivered at the annual TEI members meeting, University Park, MD, 2 November 2007).

11. Journals such as *Digital Humanities Quarterly* (http://digitalhumanities.org) and *Literary and Linguistic Computing* (http://llc.oxfordjournals.org/) have published several articles detailing how disparate humanities projects have used deep encoding to address textual complexities. See, e.g., Malte Rehbein, "Reconstructing the Textual Evolution of a Medieval Manuscript," *Literary and Linguistic Computing* 24, no. 3 (2009): 319–27; Linda Patrik, "Encoding for Endangered Tibetan Texts," *Digital Humanities Quarterly* 1, no. 1 (2007).

12. Regularizing orthography to enable better searching is controversial but not unprecedented. Some projects, such as WordHoard, tag each word with its lemma, or the form that would be used as a dictionary heading, in order to enable accurate concordances. Other projects, with a predictable, limited set of anomalous spellings, have built the alternate spellings into a dictionary that works with their search engines, so that when a user searches for the word *tomorrow,* for example, instances of *to-morrow* will be included in the results, even though the spelling is not regularized in the source document. Recently, a German digital project team has even developed an algorithm that describes the patterns of common morphological and phonological differences between the German of their source texts and contemporary German, so that when a user inputs a query, it is adjusted according to these patterns in order to pick up the older spellings. See Thomas Pilz et al., "Rule-based Search in Text Databases with Nonstandard Orthography," *Literary and Linguistic Computing* 21, no. 2 (2006): 179–86.

13. Leonard Diepeveen, "Folktales in the Harlem Renaissance," *American Literature* 58, no. 1 (1986): 70.

14. The first known usage of the phrase in print was in 1893, according to J. E. Lighter, *Random House Historical Dictionary of American Slang,* vol. 2 (New York: Random House, 1997).

15. See http://etext.virginia.edu/railton/index2.html, http://www.letrs.indiana.edu/web/w/wright2, http://www.emilydickinson.org, and http://cather.unl.edu. Some new projects in American literature, which are neither author-centered nor mass digitization projects, are offering new possibilities for organizing literary materials. See Amy Earhart's *19th-Century Concord Digital Archive* (http://www.digitalconcord.org) and

The Vault at Pfaff's, a collection of materials related to bohemianism in mid-nineteenth-century New York, directed by Edward Whitley (http://digital.lib.lehigh.edu/pfaffs).

16. See http://www.blakearchive.org and http://www.rossettiarchive.org.

17. Alan Golding, *From Outlaw to Classic: Canons in American Poetry* (Madison: University of Wisconsin Press, 1995).

18. *Editing Texts = Texte Edieren,* ed. Glen W. Most (Göttingen: Vandenhoeck und Ruprecht, 1998), v.

19. Ian Small, "The Editor as Annotator as Ideal Reader," in *The Theory and Practice of Text Editing,* ed. Ian Small (Cambridge University Press, 1992), 197–204.

20. Diepeveen, "Folktales," 69–73.

21. *Cross Currents: Newsletter of the Center for Programs* (Washington University, St. Louis), Spring 2007, 5.

22. Jeffrey Garrett, "KWIC and Dirty? Human Cognition and the Claims of Full-Text Searching," *Journal of Electronic Publishing* 9, no. 1 (Winter 2006), available at hdl.handle.net/2027/spo.3336451.0009.106 (accessed 10 November 2008).

Where Is the Text of America? Witnessing Revision and the Online Critical Archive

JOHN BRYANT

In 2003, *Emerson Society Quarterly* (*ESQ*), flagship for the study of antebellum writing, devoted a special issue to "Reexamining the American Renaissance." All but one of the contributors affirmed the continuing critical utility of designating the period as a "Renaissance."[1] Some called for further expansions of the canon to include otherwise underexamined popular genres, writers, and texts. However, none took on the problem of what exactly constitutes the "text of the American Renaissance," a problem that is generally assigned to textual scholars. As one who has committed acts of scholarly editing, I am not surprised by the lack of interest in textuality among antebellum specialists. The apathy is endemic throughout the profession. They are no different from scholars and critics in other historicist fields: we take it for granted that the texts, canonical or noncanonical, that define our discipline arrive on our desks or screens as fixed, unitary, and "reliable." We forget that editors, publishers, even historical readers, as well as the writers themselves, have shaped those texts, that modern scholars reconstruct them and, in constructing their standardized texts out of numerous variants and alternative versions, shape the wording to conform to preexistent critical standards and effectively conceal other discourses. The question "What is the text of America?" becomes more compelling the more we recognize writing as a variable, revisionary, collaborative thing.

By and large, texts arrive as givens in our classrooms, libraries, and canons. They are called "definitive" or "authoritative" and are taken to be an immutable representation of the writer's intention. The material singularity of a literary work is seemingly a self-evident truth. But in fact, literary works in all periods exist in multiple versions, or what I call a "fluid text." Cooper revised *The Spy* in major ways at least twice in his lifetime; *Moby-Dick* first appeared in two versions, American and British, and became a third version in the hands of modern scholars; Whitman famously, inveterately revised, expanded, and contracted *Leaves of Grass*; similarly, Poe revised his poems, as Douglass revised his "life"; Dickinson, keeping most of her poems to herself in manuscript, also revised (by herself and with her sister-in-law), but she left it to subsequent editors to reinvent her in print, also famously and inveterately. In fact, the materiality of any literary work is not singular or fixed but strikingly variant. But these facts of variability in individual works are more than just a secondary concern; they indicate how the construction of texts is inflected by vectors of personal and social force and how the causes of revision have cultural relevance worthy of our study.

While *ESQ*'s reexamination of the American Renaissance might speak of Emerson, Thoreau, Hawthorne, Melville, Douglass, Stowe, Native American writers, and numerous female writers for adults and children, it gives no hint that these writers' works passed through rounds of aesthetically and culturally significant revision. The problem of textual fluidity is finally not so much a matter of *what* a text is and whether we choose one version over another or conflate them but, rather, *how* one version evolves into the next and how unseen processes of revision link one and the other. The crucial concern, then, is *where* is this invisible text of revision? Like America, this text is located in the dynamics of change and in spaces between versions.

Generally speaking, our profession and the publishing industry are insensitive to textual fluidity, and elsewhere I discuss how we might confront this syndrome in our editing practices.[2] Digital scholarship offers alternatives that can raise the consciousness of readers about the inherent fluidity of texts and the modes of revision that cause textual fluidity. Let me begin with the understanding that the "text of revision" of American literature is invisible because it has yet to be edited into existence. Editing revision involves new kinds of intervention and new forms of critical thinking that are best exercised along with a community of editors gathering at what I call an online "critical archive." Even so, while digital technology is the most effective means by which readers may gain access to multiple versions and revision texts, it is also our greatest obstacle. To address these matters, I would like first to consider our textual condition in light of Emerson.

Emerson's Coin: Textuality and Double Consciousness

"Every fact is related on one side to sensation, and on the other to morals. The game of thought is, on the appearance of one of these two sides, to find the other. . . . Life is the pitching of this penny,—heads or tails." With this opening to his essay on Montaigne, Emerson whistles the same tune that begins "The Transcendentalist," only the two sides of what he calls life's "double consciousness" are materialism and idealism.[3] The condition of life, he argues, is that our focus on materiality (this river, this stone) is interrupted by brief Zen-like moments of ideality in which we apperceive matter as symbol (not river but flux, not stone but inertia). We are forever pitched between the "all buzz and din" of the actual world and the "all infinitude and paradise" of transcendent reality.

Texts possess a similar Emersonian duality, recognized through our capacity for double consciousness, except that with textuality, things are reversed. Our relation to texts generally begins in ideality and is only awakened to a fuller awareness when we are made aware of a text's materiality. Let me explain.

As representations, words exist as a conveyance of things, thought, and emotion. When we write "this river" or "this stone," we imagine the thing the word represents and feel associated thoughts and emotions. When we read "this river" or "this stone," we experience additional associations shaped in new ways by our separate readerly reality. But in such instances, our mind is focused not on the word as letters but on what the mind feels it represents: "Mind," Emerson intones, "is the only reality" (194), and to the extent that textuality involves a writer-reader process, it operates as a mode of ideality (or "abstraction," to use an Emersonian alternative). But if we were to witness, in manuscript, that "this river" has been crossed out and "this stone" placed above, or if we were to discover, through the comparison of different editions, that "this stone" appears instead of "this river," we are suddenly pitched into a different kind of Zen, or what I call a "fluid text moment." Someone—author, editor, printer—has changed the wording. Somehow the text exists in two versions; suddenly we are aware that texts are objects, not just representations. This awareness launches our reversed

Emersonian double consciousness, allowing us to comprehend the simultaneous ideality and materiality of texts. Thus, textuality inverts Emerson's pattern of transcendence. Instead of escaping everyday life in unexpected bursts of enlightenment, we see more deeply into textuality when we escape our idealized assumptions about texts and wonder at the material causes of textual variation and then the forces of creation behind these causes. Thus, in knowing textuality, readers are shaken out of the perfect ideality of their reading experience and into the muddy yet fuller reality of the processes of creation and revision.

This muddy materiality of revision involves its own kind of reading experience even for us to perceive the revision as revision. We know how to read one text, but how do we read two versions of a text—*river* and *stone*—at the same time? Are we not reading the revisionary events represented by the time separating the two words as well as the semantics of the words themselves? But is the reading of revision as revision meaningful, and if so, how do editors edit fluid texts to facilitate such reading? Surely, an academic response to the relevance of revision in literary studies would assert that, like anything, revision is worth studying, to a certain degree. The *river-stone* transformation, invented for demonstration purposes only, might seem more compelling if an actual writer acting under actual pressures made this actual change. But similar kinds of change abound: in speaking of awakening to Beauty in his journals, Emerson first imagines a "selfish Capitalist" but then revises to a "selfish sensualist."[4] Why the depoliticization? We find similar patterns of revision in *Typee,* too. In manuscript, Melville first designated his Polynesian hosts as "savages," but he routinely altered his wording to refer to them as "natives" or "islanders"; yet, in certain places, he also reversed the direction of revision, changing the word *native* to *savage.* What is the personal and cultural meaning of the liberalizing *savage-native* revision; what is the rhetorical strategy of the *native-savage* inversion; what, too, is the social relevance of these oscillating terms in light of today's multiculturalism?[5]

Finding interpretive potential in "revision texts" is easy enough, once you locate a fluid text that strikes your fancy. In the occasional critical study, we might find reference to an isolated revision, but criticism generally discourages sustained aesthetic or historicist interpretation of textual fluidity. By and large, our profession resorts to—in fact, insists on—an idealized notion of the textuality in literary works and remains unawakened to the reality that the material (not just semantic) instability of texts has a meaningfulness worth pursuing.

Of course, this Emersonian critique of contemporary criticism is not entirely fair. Textual editors have labored throughout most of the last century to create shelves full of "critical editions" that record a work's textual variants (most revealing important revisions). But this modern editorial genre (established by Walter Greg, promoted by Fredson Bowers among Americanists, and modified by G. Thomas Tanselle) adheres to its own brand of textual ideality achieved through editorial eclecticism. An eclectic critical edition's "reading text" mixes texts from different versions in order to represent the editors' conception of the author's final intentions. Generally devoid of on-the-page annotation, it is designed to standardize (I would say, "singularize") a work to facilitate reprinting, and its evidence of textual fluidity is consigned to a coded textual apparatus invariably parked in an appendix, which publishers are happy to omit—and do omit—when they reprint the reading text only. In the past two decades, textual scholars, who have been reclaiming a fuller role in current critical practice, have objected to this eclectic genre of the critical edition. In recent years, editors in print and online have offered editorial alternatives that make textual fluidity not only more accessible but witnessable. What I mean by "witness and access" is best explained by relating my own experiences in bringing out an electronic edition of Melville's *Typee* manuscript and in initiating a "critical archive" called the *Melville Electronic Library* (*MEL*).

Witnessing the Text of Revision: The Example of *Typee*

In *Melville Unfolding,* I tell the story of how, upon examining, in 1984, the just-discovered *Typee* manuscript, I was "seduced" into becoming a textual scholar.[6] A continuation of that story includes the slower seduction into digital scholarship. These two textual seductions actually happened simultaneously but at different rates.

The peculiar materiality of Melville's manuscript first caught me up. Although this text object comprises only three (however central) chapters from Melville's first published book, this sizable working draft displays over 500 sites of revision and enough to give us a fair sampling of Melville's creative process at the debut of his writing career. Moreover, when I compared the manuscript's final reading (with Melville's changes made) to the first edition's print version, I found an additional 500 or so revision sites, indicating further revisions by Melville, his brother, and his editors, revealing that Melville's writing process also was collaborative. I felt in 1984 and feel now that this manuscript is a gold mine. These messy pages not only record Melville's nascent artistic growth but also provide more insight into the interpenetration of writer and culture than one could ever adduce from reading a modernized print edition alone. I was also baffled that no one was mining this gold mine.

One reason for this striking critical apathy for something I found so seductive is that the manuscript is a unique and hidden object. Located in a vault inside the New York Public Library (NYPL), this fragile object is available only to scholars who can make a persuasive argument for having to see it. No wonder critics were not mining the manuscript; it was nearly impossible to access directly, or indirectly, in the sullen, whizzing microfilm made available by the library. My own need to handle the pages and eventually publish them helped induce NYPL to create high-resolution photographs and then digital images of the document. But having access to the text object in even high-quality reproductions is not the same as witnessing Melville's revisions. The object of critical desire here is not so much the reproduced or even the original document but the elusive "text of revision" on it. How does one "see" a revision text?

My first step was to make a diplomatic transcription of the manuscript's 34 pages in order to make that desired text witnessable at the fundamental level of inscription. This step took several years of on-and-off work. I purchased a microfilm copy, from which I made enlarged xerographs and transcribed what I saw or thought I saw. From time to time, I was allowed to compare my transcription against the actual manuscript itself. Using the layout software called PageMaker, I fashioned the diplomatic transcription, which reproduces all deletions and insertions and simulates the exact placement of all words on the page.

I soon enough recognized that my transcription was only marginally more witnessable than the manuscript itself. While readers might be able to "read" my typing far more readily than Melville's notoriously bad handwriting, they had virtually no guidance in discerning Melville's process or the sequencing of his revisions. They could now access a readable simulation of the manuscript page but could not comprehend it. They really would not be able to witness revision at all.

This problem raises the question of what I mean by "witnessing" a text.[7] I suppose that in today's political climate, as inflected by Christian fundamentalism, the idea of "witnessing," which for evangelists means testifying to the personal, salvific nature of God, might suggest that I presume witnessing to be a direct connection to the "truth" of the text. Not too far removed from this religious connotation of witnessing is the venerable scholarly notion that a medieval scribe's fair copy of a work stands as a more or less de-formed "witness" to an "urtext," the now-lost original and closest representation of a writer's intention. But putting aside religious and scribal notions, I am bending "witness" into a critical dimension. One can have access to a unique, locked-up working-draft manuscript; one can even "read" it, in the sense of viewing the inscriptions on the page. But in order to witness Melville's process of revision, we must first comprehend what Melville's "revision codes"—that is, the manuscript's deletions and insertions—actually represent: one has to decode the codes.

The previously mentioned shiftings from *river* to *stone* or from *savage* to *native* are encoded textual fluidities that must be translated (i.e., edited) in order to be witnessed. When the word *Capitalist* is overlaid with the word *sensualist,* the result is not merely the sum of the meanings of these two words. Emerson's sequential inscriptions mean something more like "Emerson initially inscribed *Capitalist,* but for some reason at some later time, perhaps immediately, perhaps days later, he changed his mind or perhaps corrected himself and inscribed *sensualist* instead, thus giving the wording at this point a history and politics beyond what any dictionary can convey." More focused editors will supply more facts and insight in their necessarily interpretive decoding, converting certain perhapses into near certainties and speculating more freely, so that we begin to recognize that in "reading" this *Capitalist-sensualist* revision code, one is in effect "witnessing"—that is, seeing and interpreting—what the codes must or might mean. Witnessing revision is first an editorial act that is, by necessity (and problematically so), an interpretive act. It comprises detective work grounded in grammar and syntax, supposition and speculation based on context, and critical judgment based on what critical judgment is generally based on: ideology, a growing thesis, and desire.

What I found most seductive with the witnessing of revision is the way in which one's reading is dependent on the interpretive "seeing" one performs in attempting to unpack the revisions themselves. The eye, Emerson reminds us, creates. The idea that one interprets a revision before one "sees" it is unnerving and raises important questions. Perhaps the editor should stop at the diplomatic transcription, be content with the simulation of the text object, and surrender responsibility for further acts of witnessing to whoever might wrestle with the transcription. But should the editor stop short of categorizing revision sites for what they are or seem to be, enumerating the steps of revision encoded in the revision site, and drawing connections between one site and another? A cherished misconception about editing is that it is or should be objective, that it should leave interpretation to critics, that the reliable editor stops short of criticism. But once you admit to the editorial obligation of decoding revision codes, you are necessarily drawn to editorial interventions that are both necessary and speculative. The obvious dilemma is that if editors of revision must interpret, they run the risk of creating a master revision narrative that preempts further interpretation by others. What editorial protocols are needed, then, that will induce readers to participate in the construction of their own revision narratives? How might we seduce them into textual studies?

Revision Site, Revision Sequence, and Revision Narrative

In developing protocols for editing Melville's revision text, I recognized the necessity and yet inadequacy of diplomatic transcription, which only simulates coded text on the documentary page. A "genetic transcription" inserts a running translation of the revision codes within the regularly inscribed text so that we may read a writer's sequential revisions while attempting to read the final text itself. In fact, such transcriptions—festooned with editorial symbols representing compositional actions, such as insertion above or below the line, with or without an insertion device—are notoriously hard to read because these arbitrary codes compound, rather than elucidate, the author's already recondite revision codes. In my edition of the *Typee* manuscript, I let access and witness occupy separate spheres. I place diplomatic transcriptions next to each manuscript page so that readers may discern Melville's hard to decipher wordings. But I have also developed a separate protocol whereby readers might locate and witness over 1,000 revision sites.

My first step was to generate a "final reading" of the *Typee* manuscript as the edition's "base version" (fig. 1). To create this version, I simply followed the revision instructions Melville supplied in his working draft. I

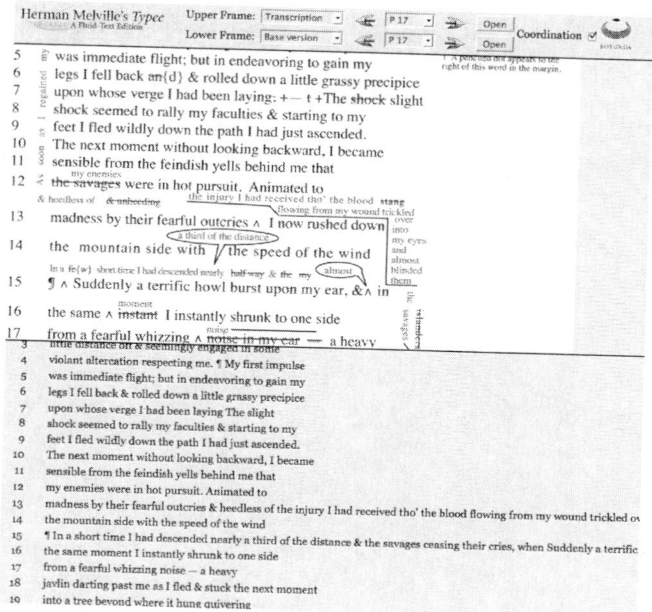

Fig. 1. In the University of Virginia Press's Rotunda electronic edition *Herman Melville's Typee,* users can view versions of the document in two frames, which can be scrolled synchronously. Here, the diplomatic transcription (above) appears with the corresponding portion of the "base version" (below) with revision sites mapped onto it. Note in line 12 an instance of the *savage* revision pattern in which Melville has changed "savages" to "my enemies."

dutifully deleted what he signaled should be deleted and inserted what he inserted. The result is the final wording Melville intended when he submitted the document for fair copying. (That fair copy has not been found.) In my edition, this readable base version serves as a textual terrain on which I map the various "revision sites" evident in the manuscript and diplomatic transcription.

Defining revision sites is itself an interpretive act. If you begin with the idea that the selection of a blank sheet of paper is itself an act of composition, then I suppose you could take any kind of inscription on that page as a revision of the page. That is, all writing is a site of revision. But this is an idea I am only beginning to entertain, one in some ways compelled by my later seduction into and deployment of digital scholarship. Initially, however, I distinguished regular composition—what appears to be an even flow of uninterrupted inscription, either freshly invented at the time of inscription or copied from earlier, unlocated manuscript pages—from distinct areas of revision involving deletions and insertions, either on the baseline or in some proximity to it (above or below the line, or in the margin). I gave a unique number to each revision site but quickly noted that the elements of a revision are not always contiguous. For instance, at one point, Melville interchanged the words *companion, comrade, he/him,* and *Toby* throughout several paragraphs down a page, and it is clear that this set of substitutions happened at one time (and equally clear, in my witnessing of this revision, that Melville was modifying his ambivalent relation to his shipmate). But rather than numbering the various revisions related to this one revision event with a single number, I decided to number each word change individually, adhering to a principle of spatial (rather than revisional or temporal) relation. Each revision site was numbered according to its position on a line and down the page, leaving the sequencing of noncontiguous but related revision sites to a further editorial process.

Other critical judgments occur in this deceptively simple numbering process. Surely, an isolated deletion or insertion constitutes a single site; other times, an insertion accompanies a deletion, and that substitution would be a site. More complicated revision sites might involve several deletions, each involving several words marked over with a single pen stroke. Multiple sets of multiword deletions over several consecutive manuscript lines might have happened in quick succession, to which might be added secondary insertions either at the time of the deletions or well afterward or tertiary polishings definitely happening after the initial deletions. One might designate such mare's nests as single revision sites; or one might hew to a principle of finer granularity, giving each deletion stroke, insertion, and tinkering a separate revision site number. Further discourse is needed, especially in light of digital applications, as to the identification of revision sites.

Discerning revision sites is not a mechanical matter. As the primary, secondary, and tertiary episodes of revision previously mentioned suggest, acts of revision occur in a particular sequence, either during one "moment" or involving several visits to the site over time. For instance, at one point in his narrative, Melville describes how several islanders claim their preference

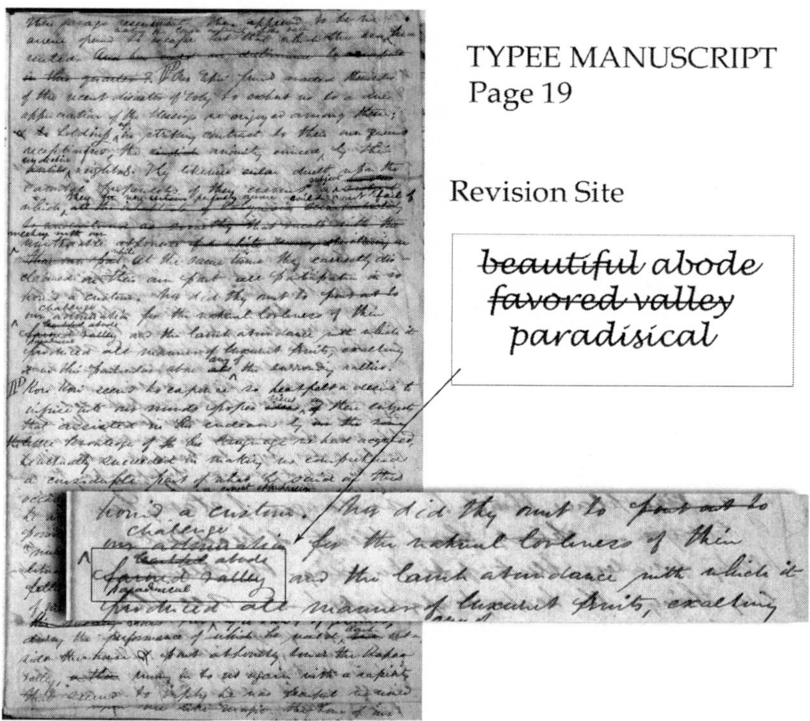

Fig. 2. The *favored valley* revision site on page 19 of the *Typee* manuscript

for their "favored valley" over their rival tribe's home. Sometime after completing his sentence or page, Melville altered his wording at this site from "favored valley" to "beautiful abode" to "paradisical abode" (fig. 2). Later, in print, the wording became simply "their own abode." Two observations can be made of this typical site. One is that while we may debate the order of revisions, we know that, independent of our speculation and like any historical event, Melville revised in one particular way only and that revision sequence has meaning. Second, regardless of how we speculate on the order of the steps in this sequence, each step represents a "wording" that Melville adopted but never fully inscribed. His inscribed revisions appear on the page as abbreviations of the full text he had in mind as he revised. Melville did not actually inscribe "paradisical abode" in the formulation seen here: he indicated the phrasing with added words inscribed above and below

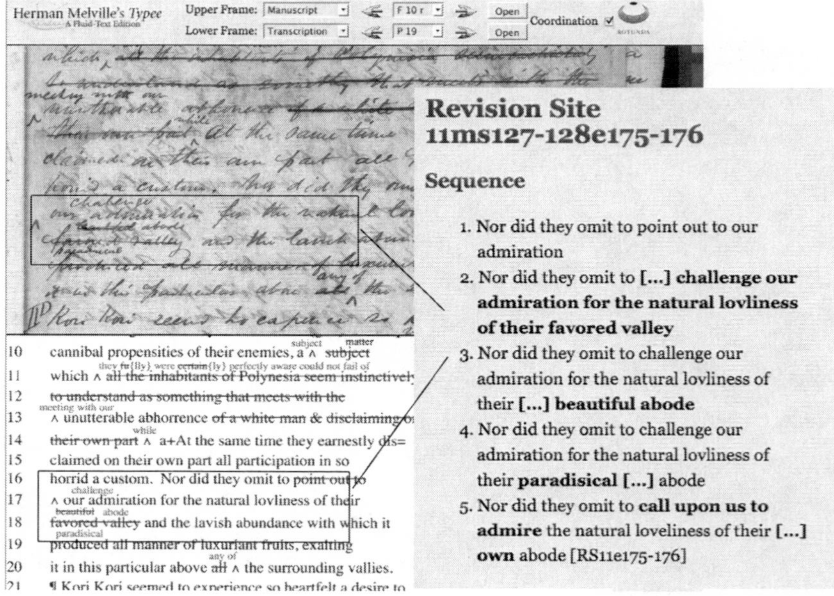

Fig. 3. The *favored valley* revision site (in boxes), with the manuscript and diplomatic transcription in the upper and lower frames, respectively, and the site's numbered revision sequence in the pop-up box

other deleted words. Taken together, the deleted and surviving wordings encode a sequence of revision texts that are otherwise invisible (because encoded), which the editor makes visible by decoding. In short, each revision site conceals texts we cannot begin to witness until the editor creates a revision sequence (fig. 3).

Some argue that because revision texts (or *avant texte*) are seemingly discarded, they do not represent a final intention and have little relevance. Presumably, publication confers the status of "text." But this shortsighted view discounts the meaning we may construct out of Melville's writing process, his shifting intentions, and his struggle with words. We assume that revision is a writer's attempt to find the "right word" and that this right word is the one appearing in the final step of a revision sequence. However, in my experience, Melville's revision sites reveal the oscillation of equally valid words representing variant psychological and social forces, each struggling for presence, so that the temporal sequencing of word

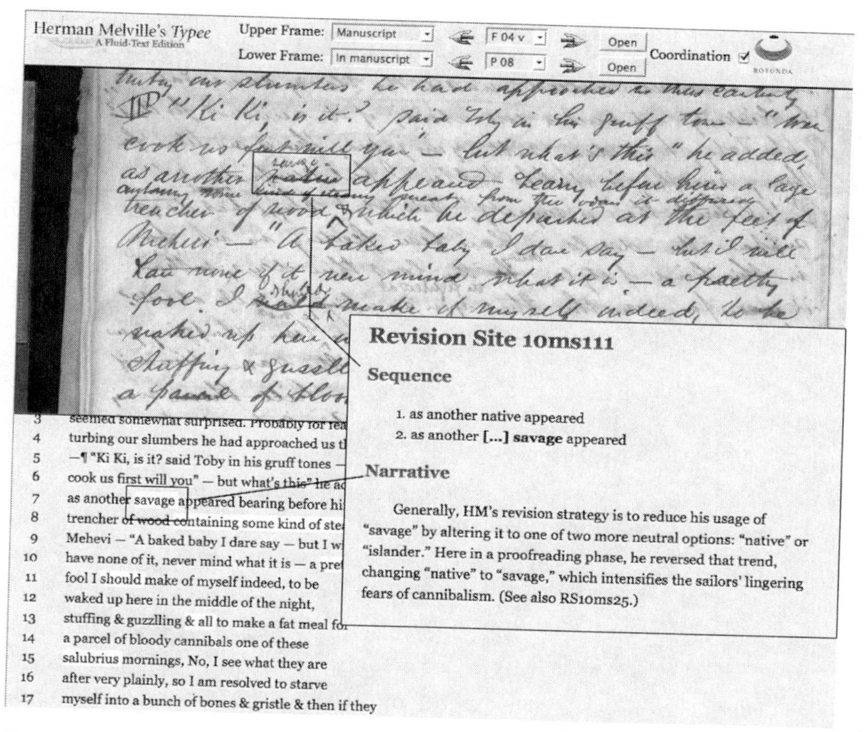

Fig. 4. The revision narrative and accompanying sequence (in pop-up) for one instance (in boxes) of the *savage* revision pattern appearing on page 8, line 7, of the *Typee* manuscript

options reifies a personal or cultural debate. If this nonteleological and, I think, deeper view of revision obtains, then there is all the more reason for an editor to generate one or several competing revision sequences for a given revision site.

But the act of creating a sequence entails the telling of a story. If a given site lends itself to multiple hypothetical sequences, the editor must expose his or her reasoning behind any and all sequencings. As noted, unpacking a revision site is both an editorial obligation and an act of interpretation. Therefore, in addition to creating revision sequences for the 1,000 or so revision sites in the *Typee* manuscript, I crafted a "revision narrative" for each site, with the revision sequence itself as a plotline (fig. 4). Written in plain English, each narrative explains the who, what, when, and possible why behind each revision and the site's sequentialized revision texts. The edition's revision narratives are not merely editorial annotation; they convey the arguments for the articulation and ordering of the now-visible revision texts and thereby validate the editorial process. More important, exposing the interpretations that ground the editor's construction of revision texts implicitly invites readers to offer variant sequences and narratives of their own.

Print or Digital? Print and Digital

No scientific or technical experimentation proceeds without trial and error, and the same truism holds for humanistic enterprise, in which words, text, data, something called "fact," and interpretation commingle to create argument. Accordingly, at any time and in various modalities, the critic, digital humanist, and, to be sure, the digital editor of fluid texts will make what goes for "mistakes" and experience moments of regret, despair, and what Americans call "failure." Some will argue that because they deal with interpretation only, humanists and critics are immune from failure. They fail only if their arguments do not "work," and the measure for any argument "working" is broad and itself a matter of interpretation, persuasion, or point of view. However, in digital humanities scholarship, the notion of failure takes on new dimensions that allow us to rethink the nature of failure in any humanistic enterprise.

Ostensibly, a digital project will proceed through a range of failures related to the inadequacy of one technical approach in light of a better one that follows. No project exists without technical failures, and just as scientific experiments require failure in order for a project eventually to "work," humanists and digital humanists alike will invariably embrace failure as a necessary "shock of recognition."[8] As Melville put it, "Failure is the true test of greatness." But failure has no practical values unless it either promotes a deeper understanding of theory or engenders a consideration of whether one's theory is the one to pursue. Technicians will tell you that anything can be done digitally—with "Time, Strength, Cash, and Patience" (as Melville also once put it)—but once achieved, a technical solution (elegant or not) is worthless unless it sufficiently and coherently embodies a critical vision. In my view, failure in the textual editing of revision would be the inability for a digital apparatus to seduce readers into deeper reading, of texts, texts in revision, and America.

I began editing the *Typee* manuscript in the mid-1980s when the only prospect for electronic editing was something called HyperCard and when the CD was all the rage. Even before I had developed my protocol for revision sites, sequences, and narrative in the early 1990s, I had imagined a program that would provide a visual reenactment of Melville's writing process, in which revision texts would fill up blank pages on a screen. Call it naive—I certainly do now—but it was compelling, then, to think that one might watch the simulation of a creative event: such is the ultimate fantasy of those wishing to catch a glimpse of the artist's workshop or to look over the artist's shoulder. As a critic, I did not have those particular fantasies to begin with, though I was willing to entertain them. Even so, certain realities intervened to dissuade me—or anyone, I should think—from attempting to put on such a show.

First of all, Melville's working-draft document exhibits various phases of revision. Melville made changes on the baseline as he wrote, inscribing one word or part of a word or even half an initial letter and then deleting it and inscribing a new word. Having completed a burst of writing—a sentence, paragraph, page, or episode—he proofread what he had just written, deleting and inserting words. He also made changes much later after subsequent bursts of writing inspired him to revisit older passages elsewhere in the manuscript. Given the kind of hopping about Melville did in performing these kinds of revision, any attempt to show Melville's revision process flowing evenly one line at a time on a computer screen would require a revision narrative so simplistic—and flatly wrong—as to be merely arbitrary and, finally, more for show than critical utility.

Secondly, the more critical the editor might attempt to make the show—that is, the more realistic in terms of the layerings of the phases of revisions and the writer's revisiting of sites for continued revision—the more leaping about from one screen page to another would have to be shown, with the result that the viewer's head would be spinning. The challenge of making revision accessible and witnessable—which is also the challenge of editing revision—is offering critical tools that reduce the head spinning, enhance analytical focus, and facilitate critical thinking about revision. Once I determined my protocols for editing revision (the diplomatic transcription, base version map, revision site, sequence, and narrative), I was ready for—in fact, seduced (once again) by—digital scholarship. The problem was that in the mid-1990s, digital scholarship was not ready for the study of revision.

In anticipation of a day when image and text programs, database, and markup might become more fully developed, and in hopes of external funding and more advanced infrastructure at my institution, I set about editing the *Typee* manuscript for print, keeping in mind the idea of converting to digital. More adventurously, I argued in *The Fluid Text* that future scholarly editions of texts in revision should be built on a synergy of print and digital technologies. In practical terms, I spent my time generating the editorial apparatus: I designed the transcription, designated revision sites, mapped them onto the base version, and began the laborious job of recording revision sequences and narratives. When this work was done, I had a massive amount of well-organized material that no print publisher would ever publish. I also created a "storyboard" for an electronic archive that would hyperlink sites, sequences, and narratives. At the same time, I composed a critical study of *Typee* based on the manuscript, which included a "selected edition" of those revision sequences and narratives I had used in the analysis. My idea was that users of the online archive, if mounted, would be able to generate their own study of the manuscript, based on their own selection of revision sites, just as I had done in print; any reader of my print study of *Typee,* if published with its appended selected edition, would be encouraged to visit the online archive in search of fuller details. I felt that this synergistic arrangement of online and print materials would demonstrate how textual scholarship and critical interpretation might and perhaps should be integrated.

By 2006, the University of Virginia Press adapted my storyboard into *Herman Melville's Typee: A Fluid-Text Edition* for Rotunda, its new online imprint.[9] In 2008, the University of Michigan Press issued the companion study of *Typee,* titled *Melville Unfolding: Sexuality, Politics, and the Versions of* Typee; *A Fluid-Text Analysis, with an Edition of the* Typee *Manuscript.* This innovative arrangement—the combined efforts of several inventive and resourceful helpmates at two university presses in all stages of editing and production—is an enormously satisfying manifestation of a critical and editorial integration, but it is something I knew from the get-go had to be a "failure" because the digital aspect of my project is a static display of my scholarship and not an online site where colleagues, students, and general readers can come together to perform critical and editorial acts. My understanding of how one might conduct online editing of revision has grown, as has digital technology, over the past decade.

Editing Revision: Collaboration, Technology, and the Critical Archive

The advantage of the electronic edition of the *Typee* manuscript over a print edition is that the user can place the sequential versions of the text together on the screen and, using the revision sequences and narratives, track the shifting texts from early draft and manuscript revisions to first edition and even to subsequent revisions found in print. Scholars and critics can also focus on selected lines of revision to offer arguments about the creative process and interpretations about the culture. In effect, one can access the otherwise invisible revision texts of this particular literary work and witness the meanings one might construct out of them. But one limitation—one bemoaned from the start—is that users have no direct means of interacting with the site itself. Indeed, all of the edition's content derives from my own scholarship and therefore necessarily reflects my editorial perspective. While users are encouraged to examine and reconfigure revision sites as well as devise revision sequences and narratives of their own, the online edition has no feature that would allow them to perform these critical acts in the site itself.

Some argue that this "limitation" is no limitation at all. Editors establish their work (and reputations) through print publication. Editorial work is reliable to the degree that it conforms to announced principles and procedures and because it is built to last. If conflict over the text arises, disputatious readers—and the more disputatious the better—are free to edit the same text and build their own edition, either from scratch or off of the current edition's spadework. But allowing readers to interact with editors while the edition is being built—which is a goal of Web 2.0 editing—would only blur the lines separating editor, edition, and reader. Indeed, or so the argument goes, the barrier against user intervention into the content of the site is no limitation at all; it is, in fact, a safeguard against the generation of unreliable, "bad" texts. While there may be some validity to such arguments, especially as we contemplate what some might call "too much democracy" in electronic editing, I am inclined to argue differently, especially with respect to the project before us of making the invisible text of revision in American literary works visible.

Whether one is editing a single text or multiple, revised versions requiring the devising of revision sites, sequences, and narratives, an editor cannot avoid making decisions based on critical and interpretive arguments. As postmodern textual scholars have noted for decades now, the problem of editorial judgment is necessarily one of hierarchy and power: whoever constructs the texts of revision controls the construction of meaning. Given the necessity of editing and therefore editors—texts do not exist without editorial interventions—this power relation is inevitable, but it is also manageable.

Our response to this problem depends on the degree to which we recognize it as a problem. Editors will always exercise power over a text, but the stakes are augmented with the editing of a fluid text because the fluid-text editor not only edits multiple versions but also defines the versions as versions and determines how and what revision acts shall be inscribed.[10] Editing involves too much textual power (it seems to me) for one individual to possess alone, and generally speaking, most editorial projects involve a team of editors discussing each step of the process. Since the generating of revision sequences and narratives is interpretive and since interpretation is enhanced but also managed and legitimized through debate, collaborative editing achieved through digital means does not have to produce "bad" texts but can in fact engage more people in the discourse editors use to distinguish "good" from "bad." Keeping the problem of textual power in mind, I included in the storyboard for my online edition of the *Typee* manuscript a feature called TextLab that would enable users to identify revision sites, derive sequences, craft narratives, and discuss their variant editorial interventions online. To facilitate editorial discourse, users of TextLab could also create editions, full or selected, of the manuscript. The discourse field established within TextLab would serve as a control over what might be feared: random, thoughtless creation and dissemination of "bad" texts.

Needless to say, TextLab does not appear in *Herman Melville's Typee,* and it remains an imagined thing for a couple of reasons. To begin with, it did not become part of our work on the Rotunda electronic edition because there seemed little reason to make it so: the site was not "born digital"; instead, it mounted my already assembled scholarship online. To be sure, the site is a model for an online fluid-text edition: it offers powerful innovative features allowing users to compare various texts in multiple frames that scroll synchronously, and it provides links from my base version map to my revision sequences and narratives. But for the most part, the edition itself was the product of conventional scholarship and not something that could be generated online by me, others, or a team. If something called TextLab had been appended to the site, it would have simply been a place (or blog) where users could respond to a preestablished edition rather than help construct it. But a second reason for the nonappearance of TextLab was that the technology needed to create it had not been developed.

Structuring TextLab depends on how we might structure the "critical archive" that contains it. For all intents and purposes, *critical archive* is another name for one type of site that digital scholars and editors have in mind when they create the sites they create. Recently, Whitman archive codirector Kenneth Price has engaged the problem of how we name digital projects, noting that none of our present terms adequately conveys the fullness of what we find in a digital site.[11] According to Price, sites may be called databases, editions, archives, "knowledge sites," or, his preference, "thematic research collections." The latter expression seems to move away from the dusty, static implications of "archive," and is intended to suggest a place where more kinds of material—not just texts, textual versions, and images but also data concerning biography, census, voting, and economy, or, let's say, travel routes keyed to journal entries and so on—can be brought together. Although the emphasis on thematics may seem restrictive—"topical" might be a more useful description—a thematic research collection that assembles texts and images regarding the life, work, and associations of a writer sounds like a good name for the *Melville Electronic Library,* which, when realized, will "contain multitudes." But more: my conception of *MEL* is that it will also include programs, like TextLab, that enable users to build more knowledge out of the available content stored in the edition, archive, knowledge site, or research collection. For the time being, I would like to offer the term *critical archive* as a name for this kind of digital site.

The term is a conscious echoing of the "critical edition," itself a storehouse of materials, though, once again, highly abbreviated and encoded. This modern scholarly genre showcases the edition's reading text but also includes a remarkable array of biographical, bibliographical, and textual data, generally located in an introduction, appendix, or related documents. The critical edition-*cum*-storehouse approaches the fullness of an archive that might contain other supplementary materials but is, of course, highly restricted by the limits of print technology. Whereas a print critical edition might allude to or quote from a source, a critical archive can summon up the entire source, with links to parallel passages and verbal echoes. Obviously, an online critical archive can contain a much fuller range of texts and images. The eight "rooms" that constitute the current conception of *MEL* are

1. Published Works: reading texts and variant texts
2. Manuscripts: working drafts and fair copies
3. Melville's Reading: bibliography and annotations
4. Sources: texts of source works
5. Adaptations: versions of Melville's works in print, on stage, in film, and on radio
6. Gallery: photos of Melville, Melville's print collection, and Melville in fine art
7. Biography: Melville's letters, journals, family texts, and a time line
8. Bibliography: lists of secondary and critical works

It is a truism that "navigating" such an archive is a crucial concern, but a "critical archive" must provide more than the expected, powerful search engine. To be "critical," an archive must enable users to generate scholarship not simply out of the site but also in the site itself.

I have already mentioned how the imagined TextLab, currently under development at Hofstra's Faculty Computing Services, might work to facilitate the collaborative editing of manuscript revisions, but other digital tools might also be imagined. The consortium called Networked Infrastructure for Nineteenth-Century Electronic Scholarship (NINES) is not, strictly speaking, a critical archive but, rather, a research index for accessing nineteenth-century materials, which also offers an open source toolkit that will be a blessing for digital scholars.[12] For instance, with the NINES collation program Juxta, adapted to a Melville critical archive, users would be able to compare the texts of variant versions of Melville works instantaneously, thus providing the groundwork for any fluid text analysis. With Collex, users can pull appropriately coded text objects and images from the archive and compose annotations, class presentations, or full-length essays, suitable for mounting in a special "play space" or publishing in a digital journal located in the critical archive or anywhere else online. With the role-playing program called Ivanhoe, one can bring students and colleagues into a forum to discuss the consequences of variant texts. With these NINES programs in mind, we can imagine broader conceptions. Could a version of Juxta be built that would allow one to compare the text of scenes or episodes from adaptations of Melville's works, such as certain passages or chapters from *Moby-Dick* and their textual and visual counterparts in, for example, Ray Bradbury's 1953 screenplay *Moby Dick* and John Huston's 1956 film of that screenplay? Yet another program might link Melville's travel journal entries to maps and GPS tracking software to visualize Melville's itinerary on his trips to London, Europe, and the Near East. A similar kind of program might enable users to link up references in a Melville text to images in the gallery of his own fine arts collection. Already in the works is Melville's Marginalia Online, a site that displays the marginal annotations in the books Melville owned (http://www.boisestate.edu/melville/); might a program be invented that allows a reader to link Melville's marginalia and the passages he lifted from his source books to the texts he inscribed on manuscripts and printed in books? While these imagined tools will require time and labor to be brought into existence, they cannot exist unless they are first imagined.

Putting aside time, labor, and imagination, we notice, too, that in order to generate knowledge or "mount" anything online, one must also "edit" that piece of knowledge or thing; thus, no matter what kind of critical or interpretive act users of an archive engage in or what tool they might employ, they inevitably find themselves morphing into editors. The critical tools mentioned here not only convert users into editors; they convert the static archive itself into a critical archive: a site for the generation of interpretation. To return to our earlier observation, the critical archive, perhaps unexpectedly, models the announced intentions of the seemingly antique genre of the critical edition. The larger purpose of a critical edition's textual apparatus is to provide the focal work's textual variants so that readers may then construct on their own a different, critically derived reading text of that focal work, one independent of and at variance with the critical edition's own reading text.[13] For various reasons, readers rarely take up this challenge. But because an online critical archive provides the tools that facilitate the "unediting" and "reediting" of a text, the submerged critical intentions of the critical edition are more likely to be realized in the environment of a critical archive.

Thus far, TextLab remains in the neap tide of febrile conception and invention, and it can only exist once certain digital obstacles are overcome. With a National Endowment for the Humanities Digital Humanities Start-Up grant, a team of Hofstra programmers and I developed a proof-of-concept for creating an online forum that allows people to interact in order to link chunks of text and associated areas of interest on images of manuscripts and to preserve their collaborative revision sequences and narratives. Users would pull down an image of a Melville manuscript—for example, a leaf from the *Billy Budd* manuscript—define a particular revision site, click on it and construct a revision sequence and narrative, share both with other users, modify both, and display them as part of a fluid-text edition.

At the moment, we are in the first year of a subsequent NEH Scholarly Editions grant to construct MEL and have long since abandoned plans to use the complex version control program Subversion (used by programmers to track changes in their development of software). We have also abandoned, but might reconsider, the idea of using Scalable Vector Graphics (SVG) technology that allows users to mark areas of interest on an image and encode its text in XML. These abandonments might be called "failures." Instead, we are making headway with a MySQL database, Google Tools, and the newly developed forum space called XWiki. These technologies should allow us to store chunks of revision text and assemble them into revision sequences. But call me when you finish reading this essay to find out if we have not moved on to something else. Our team technicians have no doubt that we can build a program that can perform the tasks we want, and we are proceeding from one failure to the next. Or, rather, we prefer to say we are revising our approach as we move along, for as with any creative endeavor—the writing of *Billy Budd* or the writing of a TextLab program—the text is invariably revised, and revision simply transcends failure.

Regardless of the technological approach, we have settled on a two-stage strategy for dividing up the process of editing a working-draft manuscript. The endeavor requires, first, a team of "primary editors" (in a managerial role) to identify revision sites on the manuscript image and categorize or encode its unrevised and revised texts. With this markup in place, "secondary editors" (i.e., visitors to the site) will, in a reasonably felicitous interface, use a simplified version of TEI's "timeline" feature to piece the categorized chunks of text in a given revision site into a revision sequence stored in XWiki. Attaching revision narratives to these sequences should be relatively easy.

Conclusion

Where is the text of American literature? Teachers tell us to read between the lines, which is to say that we should discover the hinted meaning through acts of interpretation. But the assumption has always been that we together are looking always at one agreed-on standard set of lines. However, a deeper understanding of the textual condition urges us away from the notion of texts as single objects and to witness the different sequential versions of a work together as a representation of an invisible process of writing. Our task, therefore, is to read between the versions. In those in-between spaces, we find a new kind of text of America, a revision text that, when edited into existence, can provide concrete evidence of the ways in which writers and cultures evolve. Much is to be found—or, rather, constructed—once we have access to the versions of American literary works and the tools for sequencing the revisions that constitute those versions. An online critical archive, like the projected *Melville Electronic Library,* is the most likely place for this kind of research and interpretation to occur. So the final question is not so much what the text of America is or even where it is located but when will scholars, critics, instructors, students, and readers in general have access to the necessary critical archive itself. When will it appear? When will readers be ready for it? What will it allow us to do, and in what manner? More important, how shall the makers of the archive facilitate and delimit our ability to construct texts, editions, and knowledge? As digital scholars invent and experiment with programs and tools, as they edit and consider their obligation to engage others in editing, as they consider strategies and interfaces, Ishmael's oft-quoted invocation about the completion of any "grand erection"—he meant a cathedral—comes to mind: "Oh, Time, Strength, Cash, and Patience!" With no apologies for revising Melville, let us add, "Oh, Power, Word, Diligence, and Collaboration!"

Notes

1. Only Russ Castronovo asks that the term be retired, arguing that historicism (i.e., locating texts in their periods) precludes the "invest[ing] of these texts with new relevance" ("The Death of the American Renaissance: History, Heidegger, Poe," *ESQ: A Journal of the American Renaissance* 49, nos. 1–3 [2003]: 179–92, at 190).

2. See *The Fluid Text: A Theory of Revision and Editing for Book and Screen* (Ann Arbor: University of Michigan Press, 2002), chap. 7.

3. *Selections from Ralph Waldo Emerson,* ed. Stephen E. Whicher (Boston: Houghton Mifflin, 1957), 284, 193, subsequently cited in text by page number in parentheses.

4. Quoted in Robert Milder, "A Literature for the Times," *ESQ: A Journal of the American Renaissance* 49, nos. 1–3 (2003): 193–205, at 199.

5. See my *Melville Unfolding: Sexuality, Politics, and the Versions of "Typee"; A Fluid-Text Analysis, with an Edition of the "Typee" Manuscript* (Ann Arbor: University of Michigan Press, 2008), chap. 10.

6. See *Melville Unfolding,* chap. 2.

7. I offer a fuller discussion of the interpretive nature of witnessing in "Witness and Access: The Uses of the Fluid Text," *Textual Cultures* 2, no. 1 (Spring 2007): 16–42.

8. Herman Melville, "Hawthorne and His Mosses," in *Piazza Tales, and Other Writings, 1839–1860,* ed. Harrison Hayford, Hershel Parker, and G. Thomas Tanselle (Evanston and Chicago: Northwestern University Press and The Newberry Library, 1987), 249.

9. The *Typee* edition can be accessed through Rotunda's home page, at http://rotunda.upress.virginia.edu/index.php?page_id=Home.

10. Readers might assume that a single version is "affixed" to a single physical object, such as a fair copy or print edition of a work. This one-to-one association is familiar enough, as in the case of *Typee*'s first British edition text and its revised American text: these two textual versions are coterminous with their respective book editions. However, in a working-draft manuscript, the textual condition is far more complicated, and we might find evidence of different modes of revision, constituting a set of "inferred versions" overlapping each other on a single manuscript document. In *The Fluid Text,* I discuss these complexities. In *Melville Unfolding* I focus on three inferred versions in *Typee:* transcription, transformation, and translation.

11. Kenneth M. Price, "Edition, Project, Database, Archive, Thematic Research Collection: What's in a Name?" *Digital Humanities Quarterly* 3, no. 3 (Summer 2009), http://www.digitalhumanities.org/dhq/vol/3/3/000053/000053.html.

12. NINES (http://www.nines.org/) was organized and created at the University of Virginia under the leadership of Jerome J. McGann and is currently maintained by Andrew Stauffer at the university and by the NINES Executive Council. It provides access to hundreds of thousands of image and text objects related to British and American literature from 1775 to 1914, as well as tools for comparing texts, collecting materials, and exhibiting critical treatments.

13. For instance, in preparing the text for the Longman critical edition of *Moby-Dick,* I began with the textual apparatus of the Northwestern-Newberry edition of that work but also compared my text to the first American and British editions.

"Counted Out at Last": Text Analysis on the *Willa Cather Archive*

ANDREW JEWELL AND BRIAN L. PYTLIK ZILLIG

I am dying, Egypt, dying,
Ebbs the crimson life-tide fast;
And the dark Plutonian shadows
Gather on the evening blast;
Ah I counted, Queen, and counted,
And rows of figures massed
Till e'en my days are numbered,
And I'm counted out at last.

—Willa Cather, "He Took Analytics" (1893)

In December 1893, when Willa Cather published "He Took Analytics"—unsigned—in the *Hesperian,* the University of Nebraska's student literary magazine, her audience knew the target of her mocking verse. Playing on the popular poem "Antony and Cleopatra" by writer and Civil War officer William Haines Lytle, Cather made mock-heroic the suffering of students forced to take Analytics at the university with English professor Lucius A. Sherman.[1] In his courses on British literature, Sherman asked his students to join him in sentence counting and quantitative analyses as a way to build data for his research computing words-per-sentence ratios, "force-ratios," and other such concerns.[2] That year, Sherman had published his *Analytics of Literature,* subtitled *A Manual for the Objective Study of English Prose and Poetry* and dedicated to a pseudoscientific method of literary analysis. A book filled with charts, tables, numbers, and graphs following (among other things) the climbs and dips of the "force-curve" of Robert Browning's *Count Gismond,* it was a "curious combination of excruciatingly tedious analytical exercises and philosophical treatises on the nature of literary imagination and the relationship necessarily fostered between artist and audience."[3] Representative of the philologically driven, seemingly scientific school of literary analysis, Sherman's work sought to find objective tools for approaching literature, replicable experiments that all students could execute.

Willa Cather, Sherman's precocious student in the early 1890s, would have none of it. Solidly in the aesthetic school of criticism (which was battling with the philological school in the late nineteenth century), Cather found literature's power in the emotional response of the reader: the "scientific manner" of "the critics" may "take a microscope and see all the beauty of the cell organization, a field which men of the emotional school never enter. They say, 'This caused life,' or 'This resulted from life,' but life they never find. . . . [T]hey never feel the hot blood riot in the pulses, nor hear the great heart-beat."[4] In her Shakespeare classes, Cather mocked, she "was busy trying to find the least common multiple of Hamlet and the greatest common divisor of Macbeth."[5] I think most people currently engaged in the professional study of literature would, on looking into Sherman's book, agree with Cather's assessment. Contemporary literary critical minds, influenced by postmodern suspicions of measurable meaning, are bound to be skeptical of statements like "In the prose passage from Carlyle there is more than seventy per cent of emphasis, but the force-ratio of the present paragraph and the next is 25:45, or only fifty-five per cent."[6] This approach runs against much of how we have learned to read and to criticize that which we read; how can the "force-ratio," a mere number, tell us anything about literary art?

Oh, how Lucius A. Sherman would love the digital humanities! Though no digital humanities scholars I know would dare speak seriously of "objective" study of literature, *numbers* abound in digital literary analysis. The power of the computer—a dumb machine that is absolutely without subjective judgment—has been harnessed to get numbers, fascinating numbers, about enormous corpora of digital texts. Sure, Sherman and his students counted all 41,579 sentences in T. B. Macaulay's *History of England,* but computers have counted every paragraph, sentence, word, letter, and punctuation mark across all the English-language novels of the nineteenth century.[7] And, ironically, a computer allows users of the *Willa Cather Archive* (http://cather.unl.edu) to analyze the entire body of Cather's fiction—from her first published story ("Peter," 1892) to her last ("The Best Years," 1948)—to detect language patterns, trace changes in word usage, visualize her texts in new and pedagogically useful ways, alter methods of textual interaction in order to facilitate new ways of reading, and more. Perhaps one could even find the least common multiple of *Death Comes for the Archbishop.*

Though Cather herself might squirm at this analysis of her work, I believe one can both "analyze" and "feel the hot blood riot in the pulses"; such things are not mutually exclusive, no matter what the teenage Cather thought. Her mockery of Sherman's analytic methods fails to recognize that his purpose was to improve the teaching of literature, to make recognizable literary qualities important to the criticism of his day, to "render somewhat the higher interpretation of literature possible to such as have little normal bent towards letters" and to help "the better gifted to understand more definitely and confidently their own processes."[8] Sherman's stated purpose to improve the study of literature through distinctive analytical techniques resonates with the purposes we regularly articulate for digital humanities projects. We seek to make the materials we study—American literature and culture—more discernible and more accessible, to encourage better research, and to provide new ways of seeing and understanding.

This essay considers an unresolved question suggested by the Cather-Sherman conflict: can astute literary criticism benefit from quantitative data about works of literature? Do numbers about words help us better understand the words? As the editor of the *Willa Cather Archive,* I try to balance two motivations: I want the *Cather Archive* to be obviously useful to its audience, and I want it to offer potentially powerful approaches that are otherwise unfamiliar to its audience, approaches that hopefully encourage meaningful innovations in literary criticism. In this second category is text analysis, which separates the nearly 1.2 million words of Cather's fiction into countable parts and renders her complex prose as quantified data. Textual analysis of Cather's work does not, by itself, tell us anything new about Cather's work. In fact, on the surface, the analysis dismantles Cather's work, separating carefully constructed sentences and paragraphs into artificially detached individualized units of words or phrases. Discovering Cather's work through text analysis is fundamentally unlike discovering Cather as a reader: there is no dialogue, no narrative, no character—only statistical data.

But perhaps the notion of being "a reader" is changing, as the preponderance of digital technology is forcing us to redefine what we mean by "reading." That shift in readerly experiences is easy to see if we consider how different it is "to read a newspaper" in the twenty-first century; readers of newspapers past never received headlines from the *New York Times* in their RSS feed reader or witnessed a continually updated digest of news stories mined from sources around the world. But is "reading Willa Cather" different in the digital age? For most people who experience her fiction for the first time on paper in the bound pages of a commercially produced book, it might not seem so. Digital tools and thematic research collections like the *Willa Cather Archive,* however, are increasingly becoming part of readers' library of resources. As readers become more comfortable with digital resources, they may conclude that "reading Willa Cather" very much involves computational manipulations of Cather's texts—user-generated alterations of the text that, at least on the surface, feel and look very different from reading a printed book. These manipulations, however, are only successful if they stimulate us to a new and productive understanding of the literature Cather produced; new ways of reading literary texts ought to help us better understand and experience the old ways of reading literary texts. It is in this spirit that we introduced text analysis to the *Willa Cather Archive* in the summer of 2007.

Tools for text analysis have long been a focus of many digital humanities scholars, yet the results produced by those tools are rarely utilized in typical scholarly criticism. Though the reasons for this disconnect are varied, two primary hurdles are visibility and intelligibility. Specifically, most text analysis tools and research are not found on the sites that traditional literary scholars use most, and most text analysis tools are not designed for average humanities scholars but are meant for those with more technical sophistication. To put it another way, scholars who are not specialists in linguistics or digital humanities are not typically encountering the tools, and when they are, they are confronted with something designed for specialists in linguistics or digital humanities.

Existing and developing tools—like those associated with TAPoR, WordHoard, and the MONK project[9]—are doing amazing things: allowing scholars to perform sophisticated analyses across ranges of texts, gathering textual data from enormous corpora, and generally enabling innovative and rich textual research. These ambitious projects are wonderful as an aid to thinking through enormously complicated and wide-ranging problems, including language usage within a specific literary culture, such as the United States in the nineteenth century or classical Greece. In supporting such research, it is possible that these projects will alter the way we think about the use of language and our approach to humanities study. However, these large-scope projects are challenging a tradition—in the humanities in general and in literary study in particular—to focus critical arguments quite closely on a limited set of textual sources. It is, of course, not uncommon for a scholarly monograph or article to focus intensely on a confined set of texts, sometimes even just one.

Since the vast majority of literary scholars make arguments about a narrow topic, such as a work or works by a single author, there is a place for textual analysis within a different parameter, one based on a logically defined set of texts. Textual analysis tools could be a part of the research of literary scholars who understand their work, at least partially, by close reading. Though tools that analyze an entire corpus—even if that corpus is just defined as the fictional writings of one reasonably prolific author—are rarely seen as an aid to close reading, more information about a text, including quantitative information, can offer evidence on which to build critical arguments. In a 1925 interview, Willa Cather offered a metaphor that helps illustrate the theory behind bringing text analysis to the *Cather Archive:* "[Schools] can only teach those patterns which have proved successful. If one is going to do new business the patterns cannot help. . . . *My Ántonia,* for instance, is just the other side of the rug, the pattern that is supposed not to count in a story."[10] Cather's metaphor for her innovative approach within her 1918 novel *My Ántonia* also works for what we seek to do, at this moment, for Cather scholarship: to make visible the patterns that are "supposed not to count" in a literary scholarship tradition that, justifiably, privileges the aesthetic, subjective human interaction with a human-created work of art.

What if, in addition to that human interaction, we could add a layer of computer-text interaction that would potentially supplement and alter the human's experience of the text? Of course, we do not expect any number derived from computational analysis to provide an "answer" to a literary problem or even a "reading" of that text in any typical understanding of that term. Instead, what we hope is that, by making patterns visible, we might be able to push along scholarship that is interested in the literary use of language. Along with a traditional, paragraph-by-paragraph reading of a text, a scholar is able to see new kinds of information about that text, information that would require sophisticated human engagement and interpretation before any new meaning was made from it. If a text's common words are, as John Burrows suggests, "a barely visible web that gives shape to whatever is being said,"[11] then it is the ambition of text analysis tools to expose the dimensions of that web for further inquiry.

When the *Willa Cather Archive* added TokenX (http://tokenx.unl.edu), a tool for text analysis, visualization, and play that was created by Brian L. Pytlik Zillig, the archive became, as far as I know, the first thematic research collection to integrate text analysis with access to original content. Installing TokenX on the *Willa Cather Archive* made sense not because Cather's work is particularly fit for textual analysis but because there was, in this specific thematic research collection, a known audience of traditional literary scholars, an editor who wanted to move the *Cather Archive* into innovative territory, and a desire to find a legal way to interact with Cather texts still protected by copyright law.[12] The application of TokenX on the *Cather Archive* is a prototypical one, a first step toward what, we hope, is a broader use of such tools on sites of all types that focus on defined humanistic, text-rich materials.

Specifically, TokenX can do a number of things with the texts that have been loaded into it (in the case of the *Cather Archive,* the texts are digital transcriptions of her complete fiction, including both novels and short stories). A user may select one text from the drop-down menu and then revisualize that text in a number of ways. For example, one can select certain words to visually highlight, can see a concordance of the chosen text, can get a list showing each time a selected term was used in the chosen text and the context in which it was used, and can even playfully swap words for other words or for images.[13] TokenX allows a user to generate quantified data about a text, visualize it in a number of different ways, and willfully distort the original text as a way to emphasize certain qualities of it (imagine replacing all the male-gendered pronouns in a story with female-gendered pronouns; might the shock of the changed text help students understand certain emphases that were otherwise invisible to them?).

In addition to TokenX's power with individual texts, it also has the capability to do cross-text analysis. This function allows users of TokenX to track word usage across all of Cather's fiction. TokenX can track usage of both individual words and sequences of words (commonly called "*n*-grams" among practitioners of text analysis) in the text collection. The results of the analyses are given in a large table that allows the user to see at a glance the number of times the chosen words were used in discrete texts. If a user is interested in a certain result, the number indicating frequency of use can be clicked on, and a new window opens. In that new window is a list of every time the chosen word appeared in the chosen text, and the list shows the word in its original context (i.e., it shows the word with the 20 words that surround it within the original text and provides the chapter and paragraph location of each use). Furthermore, if a user wishes to see the context more fully, he or she can click on "complete text" and go to a screen showing the full text, with the specific word in question highlighted each time it is used.

We make no claims that the data presented through TokenX on the *Willa Cather Archive* provides, by itself, critical insights into Willa Cather's fiction. Instead, it constitutes one of the many tools critics may draw on to form their own highly nuanced and subjective responses to Cather's work. In employing "algorithmic criticism," to use Stephen Ramsay's term, we hope to bring computational power to a large but well-defined group of texts in order to allow readers and critics to notice, confirm, or disturb theses they had already formed as they encountered the text as a work of art or to form new theses altogether. Ramsey explains,

> It is not that [critical] readings of texts can be arrived at algorithmically, but simply that algorithmic transformation can provide the alternative visions that give rise to such readings. The computer does this in a particularly useful way by carrying out transformations in a rigidly holistic manner. It is one thing to notice patterns of vocabulary, variations in line length, or images of darkness and light; it is another thing to employ a machine that can unerringly discover every instance of such features across a massive corpus of literary texts and then present those features in a visual format entirely foreign to the original organization in which these features appear. Or rather, it is the same thing at a different scale and with expanded powers of observation. It is in such results that the critic seeks not facts, but patterns. And from pattern, the critic may move to the grander rhetorical formations that constitute critical reading.[14]

As many have long observed, one can learn a great deal about a well-known object by disturbing the usual experience of it. If one encounters a text through computational analysis, it forces the mind to consider the material in an alien fashion, to have an "alternative vision." That unsettling of the reading experience can lead to questions, to curiosities, and, hopefully, to insights.

Knowledge of commonly occurring phrases can help critics locate motifs that perhaps would otherwise go unnoticed. For example, TokenX *n*-gram data shows that the phrase "when he was a little" occurs six times in Cather's 1922 Pulitzer Prize–winning novel, *One of Ours*. In five of these cases, the phrase is "when he was a little boy"; in the other case, the phrase is "when he was a little chap." In all cases, the boy or chap is the title character, Claude Wheeler. As a Cather reader, I was surprised by this, as I had never considered that novel to give special attention to retrospective glances of Claude's childhood. Of course, one of the first questions I must ask is, Does six repetitions merit special attention? TokenX allows me to compare phrase usage in other texts to help determine if repetition of a phrase in one text is distinctive. Since *My Ántonia* is told from the perspective of a man remembering his childhood, one might assume that the first-person singular version of this phrase, "when I was a little" (*I* replacing *he* to account for the first-person narrator), would appear at least somewhat frequently. In fact, it appears only two times in the novel, and one of the appearances is in the voice of a character other than the narrator, Jim Burden. Searching through Cather's complete corpus reveals that "when he/she/I was a little" occurs more than two times in only one other work, *O Pioneers!* In that work, the phrase occurs only four times, referring to the experiences of two different characters.

It does appear that "when he was a little" is used significantly more in the novel *One of Ours* than in other works. Before I could, as a literary critic, draw persuasive conclusions from this observance, I would need to thoroughly search for other versions of the phrase across Cather's corpus: "when I was little," "when he was younger," "as a child, she," and so on. I will not do that here, as a new reading of *One of Ours* is not the goal of this essay. Rather, the goal is to demonstrate that text analysis information makes the texts accessible in a new way. Though myriads of readers have experienced *One of Ours,* few, if any, are astute enough to recognize the six occurrences of "when he was a little" across all 126,258 words of the novel. Though this one example may feature a relatively small critical point, text analysis can provide evidence for dramatic readings of Cather's complete fiction, and it can influence interpretation of Cather as an author broadly. Ironically, the distant, objective, computational analysis of the text can help critics make close readings of specific moments in the text, for the analysis enhances the value of certain reoccurring strings of words; if one knows that "when he was a little" occurs significantly more in *One of Ours,* then one can draw more meaning out of each specific usage of the phrase.

As a glimpse into how text analysis might help draw new meanings from the complete work of an author, consider the following list of the four most frequently recurring four-word sequences (4-grams) in Cather's fiction (they appear 123, 118, 94, and 90 times, respectively):

as if he were
as if she were
the edge of the
the end of the

What conclusions about the content of Cather's fiction might I draw from this extraordinarily sparse representation of it? Is her body of work about characters ("he" and "she") strategically forming their personal identities in response to hoped-for characteristics? Who or what are "he" and "she" trying to be, or what do "he" and "she" have the audacity to compare themselves to, or what are other voices comparing "he" and "she" to? Does the recurrence of "edge" and "end" suggest that Cather's work is about anxious boundary lands or psychological moments of crisis? These questions cannot, of course, be sufficiently answered using only *n*-gram data, and these lists and numbers are not meant to provide any kind of conclusive insight. Instead, they are meant to provoke new questions, to provide one way into the text that is distinctive and potentially revealing.

As an experiment, I used text analysis to see if the final question just posed can be further explored through computational analysis of Cather's fiction and, especially, through the specific tool TokenX. Does Cather's work fixate on the "ends" and "edges" of things, both psychological and spatial? As a scholar of Cather's work, I am well aware of her interest in characters exiled from familiar landscapes and making their home, both literally and psychologically, in a new land: Ántonia Shimerda struggling as an immigrant to Nebraska (*My Ántonia*), Bishop LaTour trying to bring Roman Catholic tradition to the complex, arid New Mexico desert (*Death Comes for the Archbishop*), or Cécile Auclair trying to maintain a sense of French domestic tradition on the rock of colonial Quebec (*Shadows on the Rock*). But does her language generally reflect a fascination with the ends and edges of things?

First, I defined a list of individual words worth analyzing in TokenX. I began with the following ten synonymous nouns that reflect the "ends" and "edges" issue I am interested in (the list is not exhaustive but is used for example purposes only):

edge
end
border
boundary
margin
fringe
verge
brink
limit
periphery

For the analysis, I used both the singular and plural forms of the words, using the wildcard (*) to find the different endings. My initial search in TokenX, using the vertical line to divide different words, looked like this:

edge*|end*|border*|boundary|boundaries|margin*|fringe*
|verge*|brink*|limit*|periphery|peripheries

Unfortunately, this search found every word beginning with *end* and included many irrelevant terms, like *endeavor* and *endeared.* I altered the search immediately as follows:

to:edge*|end|ends|border*|boundary|boundaries|margin*
|fringe*|verge*|brink*|limit*|periphery|peripheries

WORD	TOTAL OCCURRENCES
border	10
bordered	11
bordering	1
borderland	2
borders	2
boundaries	5
boundary	3
brink	6
edge	180
edged	5
edges	16
end	511
ends	42
fringe	8
fringed	6
fringes	1
limit	9
limitation	2
limitations	7
limited	13
limits	4
margin	5
margins	3
verge	4
	856

Fig. 1. Results of one query from TokenX on the *Willa Cather Archive*

Figure 1 contains a list of terms that altogether occur 856 times in Cather's fiction. In this set, though, most of the words appear so infrequently that it can hardly be claimed that they constitute a pattern of usage. Only the following words from my list are used 10 or more times in Cather's complete fiction: *edge, edges, end, ends, border, bordered,* and *limited.*[15] Of these, by far the most commonly used word is, rather unsurprisingly, *end* (used 511 times), followed by *edge* (used 180 times). The novels *One of Ours* and *The Song of the Lark* use these words most of all: 88 and 82 times, respectively. However, those are also Cather's longest novels, so it makes sense that they would contain more of these words—and probably more of most common words—than do the other works.

With TokenX at my disposal, I can examine things a bit more closely to see if an interesting pattern does emerge. I decided to see whether *end* was significantly more common than, for example, one of its antonyms, *beginning,* in selected novels. For *The Song of the Lark,* the usage of the two words is comparable: *end* or *ends* is used 62 times; *begin, begins,* or *beginning* is used 64 times. The results for *One of Ours,* however, tell a different story. In that novel, which concerns Claude Wheeler's despondent years and bad marriage on the Nebraska prairie, his enlistment in the American Expeditionary Force, and his service and death in France, there is a distinct difference in beginnings and endings. *One of Ours* contains 58 occurrences of *end* or *ends* but only 35 occurrences of *begin, begins,* or *beginning.* That is a significant difference, especially when seen in light of *The Song of the Lark*'s numbers. Also reinforcing the point, the uses of *begin* and its derivatives in *One of Ours* are often paradoxically connected to endings, as in phrases like "beginning of the war," "beginning things and not getting very far with them," "beginning to grow dark," and "begin to destroy."

Of course, this analysis, by itself, does not reveal something completely new about *One of Ours.* One is not surprised that *The Song of the Lark,* a novel about the emergence of a great artist, contains more optimistic language than *One of Ours,* a novel about war and destruction. However, the attitude of *One of Ours* toward the war is hotly debated and has been since its publication in 1922. Some read the novel as naive and a glorification of war, for Claude Wheeler is transformed from a forlorn, insecure country boy into a heroic leader of men. Others see ample signs in the book that Cather is aware of the ironies and distortions in this perceived transformation, that she is actually filtering the novel through the highly subjective and ill-informed perspective of Claude. Could word analysis of *One of Ours* provide more evidence for one of these readings? One can imagine that a critic engaged in a more fully developed analysis than I intend here might carefully track usage of certain terms in *One of Ours,* compare it to usage patterns in other Cather texts, and formulate a convincing argument about the language in *One of Ours* and its relationship to overall themes and perspectives. Perhaps the predominance of "end" words suggests that a darker, more pessimistic language is at work in the novel.

The analysis that I have detailed here is only meant to be suggestive of the paths TokenX and other text analysis tools might lead us on. In the context of an article dedicated to intense literary analysis of a Cather novel, the queries would need to go much deeper, and the results would need to be traced back to the textual context with more regularity. Nevertheless, the data described here is sufficiently intriguing to encourage Cather scholars to consider how data on word usage might enhance or complicate their critical arguments.

As an editor of a thematic research collection, I know that my work chiefly benefits scholars, teachers, and students through the distinctive access it provides to important materials. In that way, it is immediately and obviously useful to a community that relies on access to texts and other objects in making sense of its subject of focus, and that usefulness is extremely satisfying to me. At the same time, though, I feel I must go beyond expected forms of access and offer tools and possibilities otherwise unknown to my audience; I desire to push scholarship on my subject into new and productive arenas. Naturally, things that are innovative are rarely, if ever, going to immediately seem useful. However, as Cather herself commented in a 1918 letter describing the response to her novel *My Ántonia,* no one ever consciously wants anything really new, as one must learn to appreciate innovative things.[16] Text analysis is something that, in the specific context of a thematic research collection built for literary scholars and critics, is quite new, and I believe its potential benefits to scholarship are significant enough that the audience will learn to love it and to depend on it.

Ultimately, though, we do not know which "new" things made possible by the digital environment will have real impact on the study of literature. Perhaps it will become customary for students of literature to sit in classrooms and remark, "Well, Professor, Cather's use of that word is distinctive in her corpus, and her choice to place it at the end of a sentence 35 percent of the time also suggests that it figures prominently in this text. Plus, you'll notice, Cather's use of this word was quite different from the way it was used by nineteenth-century novelists, though it is more consistent with twentieth-century writers. Maybe this word is more related to modernism than we previously thought." Perhaps such a conversation is possible, and perhaps scholars will publish wide-ranging articles on broad themes and close readings using textual analysis.[17] In fact, it is a real technical likelihood that such information will be readily available around the world. The question is, will such available information be used? I hope (as Lucius Sherman would, no doubt) that it will be used, not because it justifies the work we have accomplished on the *Willa Cather Archive,* but because it offers literary critics new evidence on which to build convincing arguments about the way literature works.

Notes

Readers of this chapter may wonder why, if there are two authors, they encounter first-person singular pronouns. Though the "I" of this chapter references Andrew Jewell, the content of it emerges from collaboration. Brian Pytlik Zillig is the sole author of the tool TokenX, which is the basis of the chapter. The two names under the title represent the collaboration that brought the intellectual content of the chapter into being. The authors would also like to thank Brett Barney for his extremely helpful comments during the preparation of this essay.

1. The opening stanza of Lytle's "Antony and Cleopatra," as it appeared in *The Poems of William Haines Lytle* (Cincinnati: Robert Clarke Company, 1894), follows:

I am dying, Egypt, dying!
Ebbs the crimson life-tide fast,
And the dark Plutonian shadows
Gather on the evening blast;
Let thine arm, oh Queen, enfold me,
Hush thy sobs and bow thine ear,
Listen to the great heart secrets
Thou, and thou alone, must hear.

Interestingly, some reprints of this poem (such as the version included in William Cullen Bryant's *A New Library of Poetry and Song* [New York: J. B. Ford, 1876]) included the subheading "Written in Hospital while Lying Mortally Wounded at Chicamauga [*sic*]." Though such a context may have added to the poem's melancholic tone, it is absolutely false. The poem was written and published in 1858, five years before Lytle died in battle at Chickamauga (Ruth C. Carter, ed., *For Honor, Glory, & Union: The Mexican and Civil War Letters of Brig. Gen. William Haines Lytle* [Lexington, KY: University Press of Kentucky, 1999], 105).

2. The "force-ratio" is Sherman's analysis of how many words of "force" are used in relation to total words. Sherman writes, "Force in poetry is the enthusiasm of the 'ego' called forth by some near approximation to one of its ideals, as on perception or contemplation of some moral or spiritual excellence" (Lucius A. Sherman, *Analytics of Literature* [Boston: Ginn, 1893], 18).

3. Evelyn I. Funda, "'With Scalpel and Microscope in Hand': The Influence of Professor Lucius Sherman's 19th-Century Literary Pedagogy on Willa Cather's Developing Aesthetic," *Prospects: An Annual of American Cultural Studies* 29 (2004): 289.

4. Willa Cather, "Shakespeare and Hamlet," *Nebraska State Journal,* 1 November 1891, 16, *Willa Cather Archive,* http://cather.unl.edu/j00090.html.

5. Willa Cather, "When I Knew Stephen Crane," reprinted in *The World and the Parish,* ed. William Curtin (Lincoln: University of Nebraska Press, 1970), 773.

6. Sherman, *Analytics of Literature,* 18.

7. Or, at least, they are trying to. See http://monkproject.org/.

8. Sherman, *Analytics of Literature,* x.

9. See http://tapor.ualberta.ca/, http://wordhoard.northwestern.edu/userman/index.html, and http://www.monkproject.org.

10. Flora Merrill, "A Short Story Course Can Only Delay, It Cannot Kill an Artist, Says Willa Cather," in *Willa Cather in Person,* ed. L. Brent Bohlke (Lincoln: University of Nebraska Press, 1986), *Willa Cather Archive,* http://cather.unl.edu/bohlke.i.21.html (accessed 28 January 2009).

11. John Burrows, "Textual Analysis," in *A Companion to Digital Humanities,* ed. Susan Schreibman, Ray Siemens, and John Unsworth (Oxford: Blackwell, 2004), http://www.digitalhumanities.org/companion/ (accessed 15 October 2008).

12. A good deal of Cather's major work was published after 1922, which means it is still protected by copyright and has not entered the public domain. At the *Cather Archive,* we wanted to find a way to give users some kind of legal access to these texts. Since text analysis results never display more than a small fraction of these protected texts, our use of them within TokenX falls within the fair use provision of American copyright law.

13. Some of these features are only possible on the texts not protected by copyright law. Though some access is provided to the complete corpus, those features that depend on reading the entirety of the text are restricted to works in the public domain.

14. Stephen Ramsay, "Algorithmic Criticism," in *A Companion to Digital Literary Studies,* ed. Susan Schreibman and Ray Siemens (Oxford: Blackwell, 2008), http://www.digitalhumanities.org/companionDLS/ (accessed 15 October 2008).

15. The rarity of terms across a corpus might also be revealing of insight. Is the use of a word more powerful if it is less common? In the case of *fringes,* a word from this list that appears only once, this is doubtful, as it refers to fringes on a shawl. However, the word *borderland* is also only used in one piece of fiction, the short story "The Sculptor's Funeral," and its usage is more intriguing: "There was only one boy ever raised in this borderland between ruffianism and civilization, who didn't come to grief." For a writer who often wrote about the rural or small-town Midwest, the setting of this particular story, it is interesting that Cather used this classic term to describe liminal space only the one time. "The Sculptor's Funeral" contains a dark and bitter view of village narrowness and was one of Cather's earlier pieces of fiction (published first in 1905). *O Pioneers!, Song of the Lark,* and *My Ántonia* (published in 1913, 1915, and 1918, respectively) represent Cather's more mature voice, and all explicitly deal with generally the same setting as "The Sculptor's Funeral." In these three novels, the words *border* and *bordered* are

used only eight times and describe national borders or other literal border markers, like creeks in a pasture or conch shells in a garden. The other variations on *border* in the list do not appear at all in the prairie novels. Cather's metaphorical use of a variation of *border* is unique to "The Sculptor's Funeral."

16. Willa Cather to Roscoe Cather, [November 28, 1918], Roscoe and Meta Cather Collection, Archives and Special Collections, University of Nebraska-Lincoln Libraries.

17. Currently, however, I am aware of only a handful of scholars who use text analysis in their literary criticism. See, e.g., Tanya Clement, "'A thing not beginning and not ending': Using Digital Tools to Distant-Read Gertrude Stein's *The Making of Americans,*" *Literary and Linguistic Computing* 23, no. 3 (2008): 362; the work of David L. Hoover, such as "The Future of Text Analysis" (keynote address, Canadian Symposium on Text Analysis, Saskatoon, Saskatchewan, Canada, 17 October 2008); or the dissertation work of Sarah Steger at the University of Georgia.

Visualizing the Archive

EDWARD WHITLEY

During the summer of 2008, *Time* magazine ran an article about the negative effects of digital media on human society. I have read a lot of articles like this over the years. Some of them have a profound effect on me, forcing me to rethink my reliance on word processors and contemplate a return to longhand composition. I am able to scoff at other such articles as the ill-founded fears of Luddites and technophobes. This particular article, however, left me feeling neither frightened nor smug but, instead, made me stop and reflect on what it is that the digital literary archives I have spent much of my professional life concerned with actually *do* that makes them better (or even different) than their print counterparts. The most arresting moment in this article was the suggestion that the centuries-old medium of the printed newspaper offers something that the digital revolution has struggled (if not outright failed) to provide, something that the article describes as an intellectual process of "serendipitous discovery and wide-angle perspective."[1]

I have read enough newspapers to think I know what this means: when you fold open a page of newsprint on your dining-room table, you have before you a series of hyperlinked texts in a visual arena much larger than even the biggest computer monitor, and as your eye is drawn from one article to the next, you find your perspective broadened through a series of unexpected discoveries. For as long as I have been working with electronic archives of American literature, though, I have thought that the real advantage that the digital medium has over print is that a rich archive of electronic texts can offer a "wide-angle perspective" on a large body of material,

material that is then searchable in ways that allow for the "serendipitous discovery" of new knowledge. Maybe it is naive of me to want the digital medium to be exponentially better, faster, and more sophisticated than its print predecessor, but if *Time* magazine is right that printed newspapers have already been providing "serendipitous discovery and wide-angle perspective" for centuries, then those of us who work with digital archives are not doing as much as we think we are to exploit the unique properties of the medium.

In this essay, I consider some of the opportunities that scholars working with digital archives have at their disposal for using the electronic medium to study literature in ways that would be difficult (if not impossible) to duplicate in print. Specifically, I look at digital text visualization tools, such as tools that display word patterns in graphical format and tools that rearrange the words of a text into playful and thought-provoking images. These visualization technologies not only have the potential to transform how we currently use digital literary archives, but they also challenge us to read texts differently than we otherwise would. At present, digital literary archives are rich, if somewhat static, repositories of information that give scholars and students more or less two methods for working with the documents they house: browse mode and search mode.[2] In browse mode, digital archives allow for a wide-angle perspective on their material by trusting to the wanderings of a curious mouse clicker. In search mode, the hope is that a search engine will serendipitously discover information that a browsing scholar or student might otherwise miss. Browse mode shows the patterns of the forest, while search mode pinpoints specific trees. The database structure that underlies many digital literary archives (either literally or figuratively) is designed to produce precisely this effect. As Stephen Ramsay writes, "To build a database one must be willing to move from the forest to the trees and back again. . . . [T]o use a database is to reap the benefits of enhanced vision from which the system affords."[3]

But the "enhanced vision" that Ramsay rightly attributes to the structure of many digital archives is still, at present, limited. By taking greater advantage of the visualization tools that scholars and professionals in the fields of computer science, graphic design, and information architecture have developed in recent years, those of us who work with digital archives will have the opportunity not only to enhance our vision but also to rethink some of our basic assumptions about how to read.[4] Most text visualization tools carry with them a number of methodological and theoretical implications about reading that run counter to what scholars and teachers of literature traditionally think of as the "proper way" to read a text. Rather than ask us to perform a close reading of a text (as we might ordinarily do), text visualization tools propose *distant reading* and *spatial reading* as complementary practices to the traditional method of close reading, practices that promise, among other things, wide-angle perspective on the large corpora of texts housed in digital archives and serendipitous discovery of the knowledge these archives contain.[5]

Distant Reading

Most of us are familiar with visual representations of numerical data. Pie charts, bar graphs, and scatter plots appear frequently in newspapers and textbooks and on the evening news. Such visualizations help us to perceive patterns in data that we might otherwise miss and to hear the stories that numbers alone might otherwise struggle to tell. Because numbers are quantitative, turning numerical data into a visual image is a relatively straightforward task. But words, which are more qualitative than quantitative, are another matter (and the words of literary texts, which I will get to in a moment, are yet another matter entirely). During election season, we are often surfeited with pie charts and bar graphs as news outlets present us with information graphics that attempt to reduce voter opinion to a single image that is then made to serve as a representative snapshot of the nation as a whole. But even though these ubiquitous campaign infographics are based on numerical data, those data were originally collected through verbal conversations between pollsters and voters, conversations that were rich in nuance and detail. As anyone who has ever fielded a phone call from a pollster knows, conversations that begin with open-ended questions like "Are you better off than you were four years ago?" invariably end with questions that attempt to turn your words into a quantifiable number, such as "On a scale of one to ten, are you better off than you were four years ago?" It is the job of pollsters to turn detailed conversations into raw numbers, and then those numbers—not the original words—determine the shape of the information graphic. For literature scholars, however, words *are* data, not static noise that needs to be winnowed away to get at the quantifiable information that can then be plotted on a visual graph.

Given that the entire profession of information visualization has grown up around quantifiable data, it comes as no surprise that literature scholars have been reluctant to turn to graphical representation as a methodology for interpreting literary texts. Literature scholars tend to value close reading—the subtlety of word choice, the nuance of phrasing—over the broad brush-strokes of information visualization. In many ways, the two fields seem to be at a methodological impasse: the virtue of information visualization is that it can make complex data sets more accessible than they might otherwise be, whereas literary close readings often reveal that apparently straightforward texts are more complex than they might otherwise seem. Information visualization seems better suited to analyzing the ups and downs of marketing trends or the changing patterns of crime in a big city than to interpreting the language of literary texts. Nevertheless, scholars working in the digital humanities have found ways to use the tools of information visualization to supplement traditional close readings of literary texts. Instead of parsing out the nuance of individual words and phrases, these scholars have used digital technology to search for patterns and to trace broad outlines, either in a single text or across a body of related texts.

A number of these scholars have cited Franco Moretti's concept of "distant reading" in an effort to differentiate between the traditional practice of close reading and the new ways that digital technologies are allowing literature scholars to read texts. Moretti has argued that close reading of individual texts is not the best way to keep track of the thousands of texts that make up literary history. Rather, he counsels scholars to step back and look at the broad patterns that emerge when you consider a wide swath of texts. He writes that "instead of concrete, individual works" serving as the building blocks of literary history, large-scale patterns of publication and reception provide "a sharper sense of [the] overall interconnection" of texts.[6] Moretti's 2005 book *Graphs, Maps, Trees: Abstract Models for a Literary History* is filled with information graphics that detail, for example, the rise of the British novel from 1700 to 1840 and the number of European book imports to India from 1850 to 1900. Moretti himself does not focus his work in the digital medium, but his insistence that literary texts can be productively read from a distance as well as up close has provided a critical vocabulary for scholarly projects that use digital visualization tools to wrestle with questions that close reading alone might otherwise be unable to answer.

One such visualization project involves the *Poetess Archive,* a digital archive of poetry from the eighteenth and nineteenth centuries belonging to what project director Laura Mandell refers to as "the 'poetess tradition,' the extraordinarily popular, but much criticized, flowery poetry written in Britain and America between 1750 and 1900."[7] Scholars have known for years that a massive amount of poetry was written and published during this period—a period that Mandell and her collaborators refer to as a "bull market" for poetry. Yet, given the tendency of literary scholarship to focus on a few exceptional poets rather than on an entire poetic scene, the landscape of the poetess tradition has yet to be sufficiently charted. In an effort to fill this gap, Mandell and her collaborators have proposed a visualization tool that will enable visitors to the *Poetess Archive* to import data gleaned from thousands of poetic documents into a program that "will allow users to try out various hypotheses about poetry production during the period," including topics "from metrical forms to semantics, publication venue to graphics on the page, images, book boards, slipcases, etc."[8] A scholar using this tool could generate a list of poems that share similar criteria—for example, poems published in periodicals where illustrations were used to accompany the poetry—and then have the information from this list plotted on a graph with coordinates for, say, date and place of publication. The visualization would then cluster together similar texts into patterns that might not otherwise be apparent, and these resulting patterns would in turn lead to hypotheses about the poetry of the period. Would poems by William Wordsworth, for example, appear anywhere near those of Letitia Elizabeth Landon on such a graph? If so, how might that encourage a scholar to rethink the relationship between High Romanticism and the popular poetry of the poetess tradition?

As the majority of scholars in the digital humanities concur, such visualizations are intended neither to stand as definitive interpretations of literary texts nor to provide direct answers to research questions. Rather, the goal in visualizing data from a literary text (or body of texts) is to spark inquiry. While we might be tempted to think of charts and graphs as the final piece of evidence to definitively nail down an argument (as the talking heads on a cable news show, for example, may use polling data to make claims about the electorate), these scholars in the digital humanities have encouraged us to see visualization tools as a component in a larger interpretative process. Johanna Drucker has referred to this paradigm shift as "a methodological reversal which makes visualization a procedure rather than a product and integrates interpretation into digitization in a concrete way."[9] Other scholars, such as those involved in the Nora and MONK projects, have similarly described visualization and related technologies as "instruments for provoking interpretation"—that is, tools that can provoke or inspire inquiry rather than merely answer a specific question—and have posited that a central goal of digital visualization should be, in Matthew Kirschenbaum's words, to "make visualizations function as interfaces in an iterative process that allows [scholars] to explore and tinker."[10] While data visualization may present itself as a scholarly problem-solving tool, these scholars have encouraged us to see visualization as a problem-*generating* tool.

To say that digital visualizations can "provoke" interpretative possibilities is to fulfill, in many ways, the challenge that Jerome McGann laid out for digital literary studies almost a decade ago. "The general field of humanities education and scholarship will not take the use of digital scholarship seriously," McGann wrote, "until one demonstrates how its tools improve the ways we explore and explain aesthetic works—until, that is, they expand our interpretational procedures."[11] The possibility that digital visualization will allow scholars to read and interpret texts differently—by reading them from a distance, for example, rather than up close—is a project that is still very much in its infancy. Nevertheless, there are early indications that visualization tools can help to produce revolutionary interpretations of literary texts. One recent example is Tanya Clement's use of a suite of digital tools developed under the auspices of the MONK project to distant-read Gertrude Stein's 1925 novel, *The Making of Americans.*[12] Twentieth-century critics of Stein's infamously difficult novel have had a love/hate relationship with the text, either dismissing it as "a disaster" whose "tireless and inert repetitiveness . . . amounts in the end to linguistic murder" or praising it as "a postmodern exercise in incomprehensibility that in itself poses a comment on the modernist desire for identity and truth" (Clement, 362). By distant reading *The Making of Americans* with the aid of textual analytics and digital visualization, however, Clement has made the compelling case that Stein's novel is, contrary to the critical commonplaces of the past century, "intricately and purposefully structured" (363).

Given that *The Making of Americans* eschews traditional narrative for a series of oft-repeated words and phrases that Stein seems to sprinkle at random throughout the more than 900 pages of the novel (as Clement notes, "there are 517,207 total words [in the novel] and only 5,329 unique words"), close reading the text has proven to be a frustrating experiences for critics (362). Clement's methodology, in contrast, is to visualize the most commonly repeated words and phrases of the novel—using the FeatureLens software developed in association with MONK as well as more traditional two- and three-dimensional scatter plots—and then to find in these visualizations evidence that Stein had structured her novel according to identifiable patterns of linguistic repetition.[13] Amid "the chaos of the more frequent repetitions," Clement argues, this difficult novel has a deep structure that "readers may have missed with close reading" (363). This structure, she contends, shows that *The Making of Americans* is neither a postmodern exercise in the process of meaning making nor a "disastrous" application of Stein's experimental poetics to the novel form but, instead, a deeply philosophical reflection on the life of an American family.

Aside from the contribution that Clement has made to scholarship on Stein's monumental novel, she has also offered some valuable insight into the challenges of working with digital literary archives. Clement observes that "the particular reading difficulties engendered by the complicated patterns of repetition in *The Making of Americans* mirror those a reader might face attempting to read a large collection of like texts all at once without getting lost" (361). This experience of getting lost among a large collection of texts should resonate with anyone whose initial kid-in-a-candy-store feeling at beginning to work with a rich digital archive of literary texts turned into a deer-in-the-headlights feeling at the prospect of making sense of so vast a repository of information. Matthew Kirschenbaum has noted that "literary scholars . . . traditionally do not contend with very large amounts of data in their research" ("Poetry"). Now that digital literary archives have made it possible for more scholars than ever to access such "very large amounts of data," it has become imperative that we reflect on the ways that we will have to work differently—and even *read* differently—given our access to this expanding body of textual data. Reading distantly is one option; reading spatially is another.

Spatial Reading

The field of information visualization was born, as Usama Fayyad and Georges G. Grinstein write, from "the explosive generation of massive data sets and our need to extract the data's inherent information."[14] A comparable "explosion" is taking place in the study of American literature as digital archives are becoming an increasingly important part of our teaching and scholarship. While digital visualization tools are poised to deal with a similar set of issues as those faced by our colleagues in the sciences and social sciences, some of the assumptions about reading expressed in the scholarship on information visualization tend not to sit well with scholars and teachers of literature. We might balk at many of these assumptions, but as professional readers—which, among other things, is what literature scholars are—it behooves us to be involved in the conversations that are taking place about the fate of reading in an era of digital visualization.

For example, a decade or so ago, a group of research scientists in the field of information visualization claimed that the realities of the digital age necessitated a fundamental change in the way that people read. "Modern information technologies," they argued, "have made so much text available that it overwhelms the traditional reading methods of inspection, sift and synthesis."[15] As a way to deal with this "overwhelming" proliferation of texts, they proposed that computer-generated visualizations of text patterns would be able to "reduce [readers'] mental workload" by extracting the valuable information from a text so that readers would not "hav[e] to read it in the manner that text normally requires" ("Visualizing," 442). Most teachers and scholars of literature—and I include myself in this group—have an immediate knee-jerk reaction to statements such as these. Given that we spend so much of our professional lives encouraging people to read more rather than less and to read slowly and carefully rather than in a quick and cursory manner, the prospect of developing technological means for reducing readers' "mental workload" and thereby freeing them from an intellectual process of "inspection, sift and synthesis" seems anathema to what we think the experience of reading should be. Similarly, when computer scientists and graphic designers argue that "human intuition can be more of a hindrance than a helpful factor" for finding the pertinent information in large amounts of text ("Introduction," 2) or when they prophesy that "the limitations of an Information Age will not be set by the speed with which a human mind can read" ("Visualizing," 449), it is hard not to cringe.

Granted, the kinds of text that scholars in the field of information visualization have traditionally been concerned with are not nuanced works of imaginative literature but information-rich documents filled with medical, scientific, and other types of quantifiable data. The fact that the information visualization community has already expressed interest in how to visualize literary texts, however, makes it all the more important for literature scholars to join this conversation. By joining it, not only will we be able to share what we have learned about the distinct properties of literary texts, but we will also, in the spirit of interdisciplinarity (if not humility), be in a position to learn something about the challenges involved in reading large amounts of texts. Specifically, literature scholars could do with a crash course in the cognition of reading, a topic that many scholars of information visualization have spent a good bit of time thinking about.

By and large, literature scholars are not only people of the book and people of the word but people of the-typeface-that-does-not-call-attention-to-itself. We tend to assume that knowledge is transmitted through those supposedly transparent carriers of thought: printed words. Many scholars in the field of information visualization, in comparison, have taken to studying the cognitive and perceptual dynamics that shape the reading process, pondering, for example, the ways in which visual stimuli such as shape, color, and texture affect the brain's ability to process information. Their effort to create visual abstractions of textual patterns is motivated not only by a desire to use technology to speed up the reading process but also by an eagerness to learn more about the workings of the human mind.

One of the main concepts driving the recent research on reading, cognition, and digital visualization is the notion that the mind is just as capable (if not more so) of extracting meaning from shapes and patterns as it is at processing written language. As one group of scholars has written, "Humans are quite adept at perceptual visual cues and recognizing subtle shape differences. In fact, it has been shown that humans can distinguish shape during the pre-attentive psychophysical process." Because, they continue, "humans are pre-wired for understanding and visualizing shape," digital tools that transform textual patterns into visual shapes will assist readers in "harnessing these skills of shape perception."[16] The idea that there is a preattentive information process, or (as another group puts it) "a preconscious visual form for information" whereby the mind intuitively recognizes and comprehends patterns of meaning, has led a number of scholars to speculate that digital visualizations will accelerate the reading process by allowing readers to access that portion of the mind that processes information spatially rather than sequentially ("Visualizing," 445).[17]

Along these lines, one group of research scientists has argued that "the bottleneck in the human processing and understanding of information in large amounts of text can be overcome if the text is spatialized in a manner that takes advantage of common powers of perception" ("Visualizing," 443). The motivation to create digital tools for "transforming the text information to a spatial representation which may then be accessed and explored by visual processes" emerges from a desire to privilege readers' capacity for spatial perception over their usual habit of sequential reading. In so doing, the thinking goes, readers will then be able to escape "the rather slow serial process of mentally encoding a text document" and "instead use their primarily preattentive, parallel processing powers of visual perception" ("Visualizing," 442). While literature scholars tend to assume that reading is a necessarily sequential act—for us, reading usually means following a string of words from beginning to end—a number of scholars and professionals in the field of information visualization have attempted to represent the meaningful patterns in a corpus of texts as "concept shapes" whose meaning can be quickly apprehended by the brain's natural propensity for spatial recognition.

Creating "concept shapes" out of texts is similar to graphically representing data patterns with more conventional visualizations, such as scatter plots. In a scatter plot, data are charted onto a graph so that an analyst can observe the patterns that emerge as data points cluster together relative to the axes *x*, *y*, and *z* that define the boundaries of the graph. Similarly, in an effort to help readers of large textual corpora "better understand document content and relationships," one group of scholars has devised a method for representing texts as semispherical objects in a virtually rendered three-dimensional space ("Shape," 1). When texts in a document corpus demonstrate patterns of similarity (based on such factors as, say, common word usage), these spherical objects blend together to create a variety of quasi-organic shapes referred to as "blobby models, meatballs, or soft objects" ("Shape," 2). As part of their experiment in visualizing text patterns as blobs of virtual goo, these scholars also took a crack at literary analysis. Figure 1, which I have taken from their published findings, "shows a detailed example of three documents. The two that are clustered together are Shakespeare's plays *Richard II* and *Richard III* while the solitary document within its own cluster is a document on information visualization (two vastly different concepts from vastly different ages)" ("Shape," 7). It is both

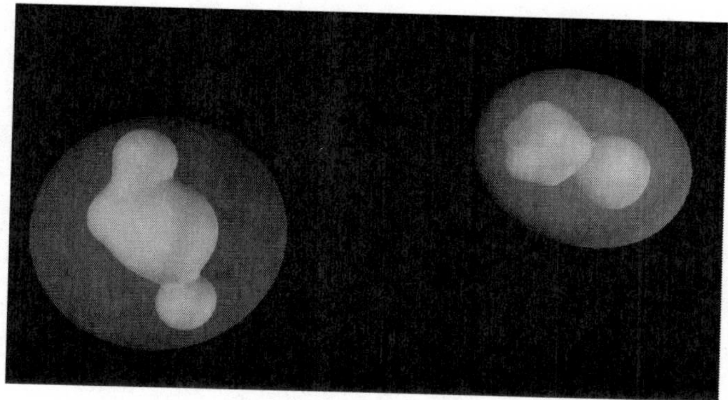

Fig. 1. Information visualization cluster and Shakespeare cluster (*Richard II, Richard III*). (From Randall M. Rohrer, David S. Ebert, and John L. Sibert, "The Shape of Shakespeare: Visualizing Text Using Implicit Surfaces," *Proceedings of the 1998 IEEE Symposium on Information Visualization* [Washington, DC: IEEE Computer Society, 1998], 3, http://ieeexplore.ieee.org/stamp/stamp.jsp?arnumber=0072 9568.)

thrilling and, to be honest, a little disturbing to watch Shakespeare's plays digitally morphed into a shape resembling nothing so much as a mutated chicken embryo. Nevertheless, I am reminded that such experiments in text visualization are motivated by the hope that physical shapes—more so than, say, the pinpoints on a scatter plot—will not only be able to trigger the mind's capacity for spatial recognition but will also allow readers to quickly and intuitively identify the patterns that might otherwise be overlooked when reading a large body of texts.

A related example comes from another group of research scientists, who, following a similar line of inquiry, have postulated that "spatializing text content for enhanced visual browsing and analysis" functions best when readers are given "an interaction with text that more nearly resembles perception and action with the natural world" ("Visualizing," 442). The resulting visualization tool that they have devised uses clusters of data points (again, similar to those in a scatter plot) as the basis for what they refer to as "galaxy visualizations." A galaxy visualization projects points of light, which represent information gleaned from a group of text documents, onto a black background, in a manner that is designed to "recapitulate experiences of viewing the night sky" ("Visualizing," 448–49). When meaningful patterns appear in the data, clustered points of light appear as constellations within the larger "galaxy." The conceit behind this visualization is that the same human capacity for finding meaning in the stars—the same capacity, that is, that anciently populated the night sky with gods and heroes—continues to function on a computer screen. Along the same lines, this group has also created a method for viewing data points as elements in a textured, three-dimensional wave—which they describe as a "visual metaphor" for "traversing landscapes"—that not only presents readers with an image reminiscent of the geographical contours of the earth's surface but also uses these data-driven peaks and valleys to evoke humans' innate ability to spatially process their physical environment ("Visualizing," 448–49). As with their galaxy visualization, the implication of the landscape visualization is that the "primitive" cognition of hunter-gatherers buried deep in the evolutionary recesses of the mind can be reawakened in the digital age as a way to find meaningful patterns in large bodies of textual data.

Despite the neo-Romantic organicism that permeates these attempts to represent text patterns as shapes from the natural world, there is also a tacit acknowledgment by these same practitioners of information visualization that there is something fundamentally *un*natural about efforts to render words as images. Computer scientists and graphic designers often refer to text visualizations as attempts to "visualize the nonvisual," a formulation that suggests the irony, if not the futility, of making visual perception an integral part of the reading process. "Since visualizing text requires mapping the abstract to the physical," writes the group of scholars behind the quasi-organic "blobby" text models, the primary challenge facing any project in text visualization lies in creating an "interface for providing [a] layer of abstraction" between the original text and the resulting visual image ("Shape," 2). While blobby models and virtual landscapes represent fascinating attempts at designing an interface between word and image, some of the most promising text visualization projects of recent years take as their starting point the idea that words *are* images and that the search for a "layer of abstraction" between word and image has created a false dichotomy between reading and seeing.[18] By experimenting with such elementary bibliographic signifiers as font size and the arrangement of words on the page (or screen), a new generation of text visualization projects have suggested possibilities for spatial reading that treat text as both words to be read and shapes to be viewed.

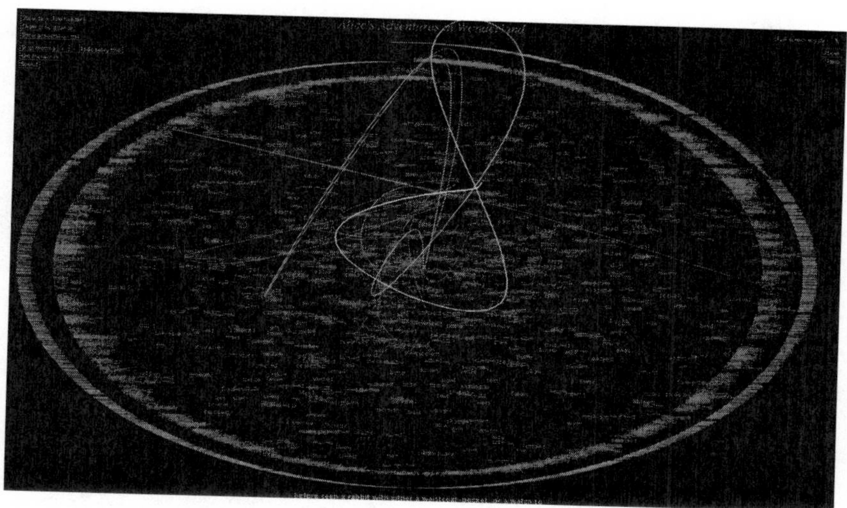

Fig. 2. W. Bradford Paley's TextArc rendition of Lewis Carroll's novel *Alice in Wonderland,* http://www.textarc.org/images/alice1.gif

One example of a text visualization process that retains the text *as* the visualization is W. Bradford Paley's 2002 TextArc project. Paley recites many of the same goals for visualizing text as do the scholars and professionals behind other projects. Writing, for example, that he wants "to help people discover patterns and concepts in any text by leveraging a powerful, underused resource: human visual processing," he claims that his project not only "taps into our pre-attentive ability to scan" for visual patterns of meaning but also facilitates a reader's "intuition [to] extract meaning from an unread text."[19] Despite these similarities, the visualizations produced by TextArc minimize (if not collapse) the need for a "layer of abstraction" between text and image found in other projects. A TextArc visualization, such as the one for Lewis Carroll's *Alice in Wonderland* in figure 2, is an image comprised entirely of words: the ellipse that frames the screen is a word-for-word reproduction of the complete text (in a one-pixel font), and the amorphous cloud that fills out the center of the ellipse is a color-coded array of the text's most commonly used words (oft-repeated words glow brighter than words that do not occur as frequently; and words that appear throughout the text migrate to the center of the cloud, while words that are specific to a given section of the text tend toward its peripheries). The visualization is also interactive. As the cursor floats over an individual word in the cloud, for example, rays of light connect that word to its occurrences throughout the text ellipse; and, if requested, a traditional concordance or keyword-in-context index can be generated alongside the visualization.

TextArc is, among other things, an experiment in spatial reading that is grounded in the belief that reading and seeing are complementary processes. Paley describes TextArc as a "balancing act" between reading and seeing, explaining that as readers experience the text visualization, "the eye and mind scan for ideas, then follow the ideas down to where and how they appear in the text" ("TextArc"). Such forms of digital textuality that blur the line between text and image are still very much in their infancy, and the interdisciplinary research into how, precisely, the eye and the mind process information in this format has yet to be fully conducted. While the academic community awaits the outcomes of this research, ambitious graphic designers and computer programmers have already begun populating the World Wide Web with text visualization tools that allow anyone with Internet access to upload the text of their choice and create a word cloud similar to the numinous field of text at the center of a TextArc. Around the middle of the 2000s, popular photo- and file-sharing sites began using tag clouds to indicate which descriptors (or "tags") were most frequently used to categorize files and photos, with larger-font tags indicating a higher frequency of usage than smaller-font tags. Since then, tag and word clouds have become ubiquitous on the Web.[20] Word clouds have proven to be quite popular with Internet users, both for their playful aesthetic quality and for their practical ability to visually identify the patterns of meaning in large and potentially unwieldy texts.[21]

Literature scholars have yet to fully theorize the ways in which spatially reading the text in a word cloud can lead to new and exciting interpretative possibilities.[22] As an informal experiment in spatial reading, I found a word cloud of Walt Whitman's "Song of Myself" on Wordle.net, a popular word-cloud generator, and attempted to compare my past experiences reading Whitman's monumental 1,300-line poem with the experience of reading it spatially as a digital cloud (see fig. 3). Reading/viewing "Song of Myself" as a cloud of words immediately refamiliarized me with a poem I have read many times before, but it also defamiliarized a poem that I thought I knew so well. I was not surprised at all to see words like *love, earth, see,* and *know* jump out of the cloud, but I was shocked to see the words *shall* and

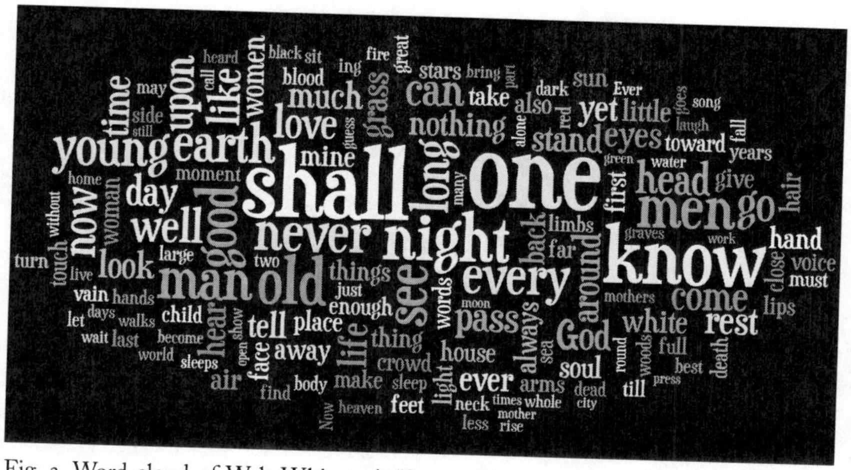

Fig. 3. Word cloud of Walt Whitman's "Song of Myself." (From Wordle.net, http://www.wordle.net/gallery/wrdl/180308/Song_of_Myself_-_Walt_Whitman.)

one emerge with such prominence. I tend to associate the word *shall* with the proscriptive language of the Bible, with its commandments of "Thou shall not" and "Thou shall." Whitman has always struck me as the poet of laissez-faire, content to observe rather than prescribe. But the word cloud reminded me that he is also a poet of the future, of possibility, of action—the poet, that is, of "shall." The word *one* had a similarly defamiliarizing effect on me. I had always thought of Whitman as a poet of diversity and expanse, of the many rather than the one. But reading "Song of Myself" in this format reminded me of the centripetal as well as centrifugal pull in Whitman's poetry, of his tendency to collapse all experience into the unity of the self. I often tell my students that Walt Whitman and Emily Dickinson teach us to read in very different ways: Dickinson requires us to drill down into the meaning of specific words if we are to make sense of the larger poem, whereas Whitman requires us to step back and get a sense of the entire landscape of the poem in order to grasp its meaning. I found, in this entirely unsystematic and wholly impressionistic exercise in spatial reading, that the word cloud of "Song of Myself" rekindled that sentiment for me in exciting and thought-provoking ways.[23]

At least two other scholars working in the digital humanities—Lisa Spiro and Sara Steger—have made similar attempts to read nineteenth-century literature as a cloud of digital text. Both Spiro and Steger have used word clouds generated with Wordle, along with other text analysis tools, to rethink the language of literary sentimentalism. Sentimentalism is a broad and often oversimplified term in literary studies, and Spiro and Steger make welcome additions to scholarship from the past two decades that has challenged preconceived notions about sentimental literature.[24] Steger's project involved running nearly four thousand mid-Victorian novels through digital text analysis tools available through MONK, sifting out the words and phrases most often identified as sentimental, and then using Wordle to visualize the patterns that emerged. Steger's preliminary findings were hardly controversial: she found, for example, that deathbed scenes in sentimental novels employ "vocabulary [that] emphasizes intimate relationships—'mamma,' 'papa,' 'darling,' and 'child.'" But Steger's greatest insights come not from the moments where the visualization highlights the most commonly appearing words but, rather, from those where it shows her "that which is absent." "What the word cloud does not include is almost as informative as what it does," she writes. "One of the most under-represented words is 'holy,' and it is followed by 'church,' 'saint,' 'faith,' 'believe' and 'truth.' It seems the Victorian deathbed scene is more concerned with relationships . . . than with personal convictions and declarations of faith."[25] For many readers, literary sentimentalism is inextricably connected to the larger religious worldview from which it is presumed to have emerged. Steger has found, in contrast, a much more complex relationship between sentimental discourse and nineteenth-century religious language.

Steger's use of word clouds to spatially read a large body of texts involves an interesting back-and-forth between close and distant reading: at one moment, her wide-angle perspective charts the broad contours of sentimental language across a vast array of texts, while at other moments, her intense focus on specific words feels like close reading on a microscopic scale. Lisa Spiro makes a similar move in her word-cloud analysis of the sentimental language in Donald Grant Mitchell's *Reveries of a Bachelor* (1850) and Herman Melville's *Pierre* (1852), a text that she argues is a "dark parody" of Mitchell's *Reveries.* Spiro's concern is with Melville's appropriation and transformation of sentimental language used in mainstream texts such as Mitchell's, and she uses word clouds to compare and contrast word frequency and usage between the two. Spiro comes to a number of thought-provoking conclusions in the course of her analysis—among them, that Melville often uses the same words as those employed in more traditional sentimental texts but derives from them a “different resonance,” taking, as she puts it, “some of the ingredients of sentimental literature and mak[ing] something entirely different with them.” But what most interests me about her methodology is the similar back-and-forth between close and distant reading that Steger also employs in her analysis of mid-Victorian literature (and, for that matter, that I use in my own informal spatial reading of the “Song of Myself” word cloud). Spiro writes that the spatialized text in the world cloud provided her with the “initial impression” that inspired her analysis of the two texts, but she then goes on to note that what made the most significant impact on her analysis was not the shape of the cloud itself but the quantitative values that determined which words would pop out of the cloud as larger and which would recede into the background as smaller. “Ultimately,” she writes, “I trusted the concreteness and specificity of numbers more than the more impressionistic imagery provided by the word cloud.” Despite granting this authority to quantitative analysis, however, she is quick to caveat that “the word cloud opened up my eyes so that I could see the stats more meaningfully.”[26]

There seems to be a push-and-pull involved in spatially reading a word cloud, as Spiro, Steger, and I all found ourselves alternating between observing the big picture and honing in on specific words. Spatial reading is a curious hybrid of close and distant reading, it seems, requiring both impressionistic reactions and quantitative analysis. This push toward the quantitative serves as a reminder that digital visualization often requires that we reduce language—that plastic, ambiguous, free-form media we scholars of literature love to play in—to the stable, albeit more dour, realm of numbers. By the same token, word clouds promise to keep the tension between words and numbers—not to mention images—at play in provocative and exciting ways. Whether or not the methods of reading and interpretative discovery provoked by word clouds (or by any digital visualization tool, for that matter) will become a part of our critical practice as scholars and teachers of literature remains to be seen. Again, such technologies are still in their infancy, but it bears noting that these infant technologies are growing up alongside our own still-young archives of digitized text. The forces of the digital era are rethinking the ways that we read at the same time that American literature scholars are rethinking the ways that we archive large bodies of texts. It would benefit both parties to pay closer attention to what the other is doing.

Notes

1. Samantha Power, "The Short Tail," *Time,* 2 June 2008, 34.

2. The digital archive *Uncle Tom's Cabin & American Culture* (http://www.iath.virginia.edu/utc/) uses the terms *search mode* and *browse mode* explicitly, while other archives implicitly structure the user experience in this way. There are notable exceptions, of course. The *Willa Cather Archive,* for example, has integrated TokenX, a text analysis and visualization tool, into the archive itself (see http://cather.unl.edu/tokenx.intro.html), as has the *Walt Whitman Archive* (see http://www.whitmanarchive.org/resources/tools/index.html).

3. Stephen Ramsay, "Databases," in *A Companion to Digital Humanities,* ed. Susan Schreibman, Ray Siemens, and John Unsworth (Malden, MA : Blackwell, 2004), 177–97, at 195. See the discussion of the database structure of archives—as both a literal and metaphorical structure—in *PMLA* 122, no. 5 (October 2007): Ed Folsom, "Database as Genre: The Epic Transformation of Archives," 1571–79; Jerome McGann's response, "Database, Interface, and Archival Fever," 1588–92; and Folsom's subsequent rejoinder, "Reply," 1608–12.

4. The literature on digital visualization has increased in both quantity and quality in recent years. For two particularly useful essays that overview innovation in the field, see John Risch et al., "Text Visualization for Visual Text Analytics," in *Visual Data Mining: Theory, Techniques, and Tools for Visual Analytics,* ed. Simeon Simoff, Michael Böhlen, and Arturas Mazeika (Berlin, Heidelberg, and New York: Springer, 2008), 154–71; Martyn Jessop, "Digital Visualization as a Scholarly Activity," *Literary and Linguistic Computing* 23, no. 3 (September 2008), 281–93. The essay by Risch et al. provides an overview of the technological and methodological innovations in text visualization in recent years, while Jessop's essay focuses on the applicability of digital visualization to humanities research.

5. In an effort to focus on the methodological and theoretical assumptions behind digital text visualization tools and how those assumptions affect the ways in which literature scholars tend to think about the reading process, I have dedicated the majority of this essay to a critical examination of these assumptions rather than to a survey of the text visualization projects that have been developed for the digital medium. Lisa Spiro has helpfully cataloged many of the most cutting-edge text visualization tools at http://www.diigo.com/user/lspiro/text_visualization.

6. Franco Moretti, *Graphs, Maps, Trees: Abstract Models for a Literary History* (New York: Verso, 2005), 1. Moretti first put forward this idea in the essay "Conjectures on World Literature," *New Left Review* 1 (January–February 2000), 54–68. Moretti was the keynote speaker at the 2007 meeting of the Association for Computers and the Humanities, where he spoke on the topic of distant reading and digital scholarship.

7. "Introduction to the Poetess Archive," *Poetess Archive,* http://unixgen.muohio.edu/~poetess/about/index.html (accessed 28 October 2008).

8. "Coming Soon: Visualization Tool for Poetic Elements, 1750–1850," *Poetess Archive*, http://unixgen.muohio.edu/~poetess/vmodel/vmodel.html (accessed 28 October 2008).

9. Johanna Drucker and Bethany Nowviskie, "Speculative Computing: Aesthetic Provocations in Humanities Computing," in Schreibman, Siemens, and Unsworth, *Companion to Digital Humanities*, 431–47, at 442.

10. Matthew Kirschenbaum, "Poetry, Patterns, and Provocation: The nora Project," *The Valve: A Literary Organ*, 12 January 2006, http://www.thevalve.org/go/valve/article/poetry_patterns_and_provocation_the_nora_project/ (accessed 10 August 2008) (hereafter cited in text as "Poetry"). For other research by scholars affiliated with the Nora and MONK projects, see Catherine Plaisant et al., "Exploring Erotics in Emily Dickinson's Correspondence with Text Mining and Visual Interfaces," in *Proceedings of the 6th ACM/IEEE-CS Joint Conference on Digital Libraries* (New York: ACM Press, 2006), 141–50, at 141.

11. Jerome McGann, *Radiant Textuality: Literature after the World Wide Web* (London: Palgrave Macmillan, 2001), xii.

12. Tanya Clement, "'A thing not beginning and not ending': Using Digital Tools to Distant-Read Gertrude Stein's *The Making of Americans*," *Literary and Linguistic Computing* 23, no. 3 (September 2008): 361–81 (hereafter cited in text as Clement).

13. For a description of the FeatureLens software, see Anthony Don et al., "Discovering Interesting Usage Patterns in Text Collections: Integrating Text Mining with Visualization," in *Proceedings of the Sixteenth ACM Conference on Information and Knowledge Management* (New York: ACM Press, 2007), 213–22.

14. Usama Fayyad and Georges G. Grinstein, introduction to *Information Visualization in Data Mining and Knowledge Discovery*, ed. Usama Fayyad, Georges G. Grinstein, and Andreas Wierse (San Francisco: Morgan Kaufmann, 2001), 1–17, at 1 (hereafter cited in text as "Introduction").

15. James A. Wise et al., "Visualizing the Non-visual: Spatial Analysis and Interaction with Information from Text Documents," in *Readings in Information Visualization: Using Vision to Think*, ed. Stuart K. Card, Jock D. Mackinlay, and Ben Shneiderman (San Francisco: Morgan Kaufmann, 1999), 442–49, at 442 (hereafter cited in text as "Visualizing").

16. Randall M. Rohrer, David S. Ebert, and John L. Sibert, "The Shape of Shakespeare: Visualizing Text Using Implicit Surfaces," in *Proceedings of the 1998 IEEE Symposium on Information Visualization* (Washington, DC: IEEE Computer Society, 1998), 3, http://ieeexplore.ieee.org/stamp/stamp.jsp?arnumber=00729568 (accessed 20 August 2008) (hereafter cited in text as "Shape").

17. See also Andrew J. Parker et al., "The Analysis of 3D Shape: Psychophysical Principles and Neural Mechanisms," in *Understanding Vision: An Interdisciplinary Perspective*, ed. Glyn Humphreys (Malden, MA: Blackwell, 1992).

18. For more on the word/image and reading/seeing dichotomy, see Matthew G. Kirschenbaum, "The Word as Image in an Age of Digital Reproduction," in *Eloquent*

Images: Word and Image in the Age of New Media (Cambridge, MA: MIT Press, 2003), 137–56; Johanna Drucker and Charles Bernstein, *Figuring the Word: Essays on Books, Writing, and Visual Poetics* (New York: Granary Books, 1998); Berjouli Bowler, *The Word as Image* (London: Studio Vista, 1970).

19. W. Bradford Paley, "TextArc: Revealing Word Associations, Distribution, and Frequency," 2002, http://www.textarc.org/TextArcOverview.pdf (accessed 20 August 2008) (hereafter cited as "TextArc"). The entire project is available online at http://www.textarc.org/. It bears noting that, as do other text visualization project directors, Paley relies on a set of organic metaphors to describe the cognitive processes involved in reading a TextArc: "A botanist learns visual strategies for distinguishing the type and health of a plant; likewise people looking at TextArcs have begun to develop visual strategies that help extract structural features in texts" ("TextArc").

20. For a scholarly overview of the phenomenon of tag clouds, see Martin Halvey and Mark T. Keane, "An Assessment of Tag Presentation Techniques," *Proceedings of the 16th International Conference on the World Wide Web* (New York: ACM Press, 2007), 1313–14; A. W. Rivadeneira et al., "Getting Our Head in the Clouds: Toward Evaluation Studies of Tagclouds," *Proceedings of the SIGCHI Conference on Human Factors in Computing Systems* (New York: ACM Press, 2007), 995–98.

21. As one Web developer recently commented, "Whether it's a campaign speech by a presidential contender, or a 300-page bestselling novel, large bodies of text are among the most requested topics for condensing into an infographic. The purpose can vary from highlighting specific relations to contrasting points or use of language, but all [such visualization tools] focus on distilling a volume of text down to a visualization" (Tim Showers, "Visualization Strategies: Text and Documents" August 2008, http://www.timshowers.com/2008/08/visualization-strategies-text-documents/ [accessed 31 October 2008]).

22. For an attempt to use word clouds for literary analysis, see Lisa Spiro, "Using Text Analysis Tools for Comparison: Mole & Chocolate Cake," 22 June 2008, http://digitalscholarship.wordpress.com/2008/06/22/using-text-analysis-tools-for-comparison-mole-chocolate-cake/ (accessed 10 August 2008).

23. Not only is reading a word cloud an admittedly subjective experience, but *creating* a word cloud is also highly subjective. The world cloud of "Song of Myself" I found on Wordle.net, for example, was designed such that commonly occurring words (e.g., *I, of, the, a, an*) were excluded. The choice of color, size, font, and arrangement of these words also no doubt influenced how I spatially read the poem. The fact that many different word-cloud versions of this same poem could be (and, indeed, have already been) created on such sites as Wordle.net does not, I believe, discredit the new interpretative possibilities that word clouds have to offer; it instead demands that readers of such clouds be self-reflexive as they read such texts spatially. I would argue that such human-computer interaction should be seen not as a limitation of digital visualization but, rather, as a productive site of possibility. For more on human-computer interac-

tion (HCI) and its relation to digital visualization, see Ben Shneiderman, "Inventing Discovery Tools: Combining Information Visualization with Data Mining," in *The Craft of Information Visualization: Readings and Reflections*, ed. Benjamin B. Bederson and Ben Shneiderman (New York: Morgan Kaufmann, 2003), 379–85.

24. For representative texts in this scholarship on sentimental literature, see Jane Tompkins, *Sensational Designs: The Cultural Work of American Fiction, 1790–1860* (New York: Oxford University Press, 1985); Joanne Dobson, "Reclaiming Sentimental Literature," *American Literature* 69 (June 1997): 263–88; and Elizabeth Maddock Dillon, "Sentimental Aesthetics," *American Literature* 76 (September 2004): 495–523.

25. Steger's work is described in a collaborative presentation by Tanya Clement, Sara Steger, John Unsworth, and Kirsten Uszkalo titled "How Not to Read a Million Books," presented originally at the Seminar in the History of the Book at Rutgers University, New Brunswick, NJ, 5 March 2009, and available online at http://www3.isrl.illinois.edu/~unsworth/hownot2read.html (accessed 31 August 2009). My thanks to Meredith McGill and Lisa Gitelman for bringing Steger's work to my attention.

26. Spiro, "Using Text Analysis Tools."

PART 3

Theoretical Challenges in Digital Americanist Scholarship

Digital Humanities and the Study of Race and Ethnicity

STEPHANIE P. BROWNER

The digital revolution has promised and delivered much to students of race and ethnicity. Manuscripts, photographs, diaries, court petitions, pamphlets, short stories, sermons, poems, audio recordings, video, and more, all related to race and ethnicity in America, can be found in just an hour of trawling on the Internet. There are comprehensive projects and small, well-formed sites; there are sites with frustratingly incomplete bibliographical information that have gems for the scholar willing to search; and there are sites that do not conform to best practices in digital editing but that teachers love because the wealth of materials and friendly interface draw in high school and college students. In short, there are exciting materials now available to anyone with Internet access, but scholars of race and ethnicity do not yet get online and find themselves in a deep, comprehensive, well-linked and indexed world of materials.

In a comprehensive survey, *Scholarship in the Digital Age: Information, Infrastructure, and the Internet,* Christine L. Borgman acknowledges the sense of possibility that attended the dawning of the digital age and the work yet to be done. In the early days of the Internet, we anticipated a deluge of primary sources freely available on the Web, materials previously accessible only to well-funded scholars who knew how to comb through special archives. We also anticipated that once peer-review processes were established, there would be a steady flow of monographs, essays, and scholarship in forms we could not yet imagine. But there has not been a flood. Before the Internet, we thought that it was the cost of publishing (paper, printing, shipping, advertising, and overhead) that was holding us back, but, as it turns out, it is us and the size of the task—the fact that our work takes time, money, training, and knowledge. As Borgman puts it, "Scholarly information is expensive to produce, requiring investments in expertise, instrumentation, fieldwork, laboratories, libraries, and archives." There are other costs as well, including investments in creating an infrastructure that ensures that information will be "permanently accessible." But, as Borgman rightly insists, the "real value in information infrastructure is in the information," and "building the content layer of that infrastructure is both the greatest challenge and the greatest payoff."[1]

Among humanities scholars who seek to understand race and ethnicity in America, building a deep "content layer" has long been recognized as a primary task, even before the birth of the Internet. Scholars have worked hard, often without institutional support, to find, preserve, edit, and republish neglected and forgotten texts. With the social movements of the 1960s, interest in noncanonical authors grew, and the work of text recovery began to garner financial support and institutional recognition. University presses and small independent presses found that texts by writers of color sold well, and in 1973, the Society for the Study of Multi-Ethnic Literature of the United States (MELUS) was founded at the annual MLA convention. Their mission was simple: "Locate the 'lost' texts. Publish the important ones, with English translations, if needed, by our own MELUS press."[2] What followed over the next 20 years was profound. Anthologies such as Berndt Peyer's *The Elders Wrote: An Anthology of Early Prose by North American Indians* (1982) introduced writers many students had never read, and critical studies such as William Andrews's *To Tell a Free Story: The First Century of Afro-American Autobiography, 1760–1865* (1986) provided careful analysis of texts previously ignored. In 1981, Jean Fagan Yellin verified Harriet Jacobs's authorship and published *Incidents in the Life of a Slave Girl,* a text now widely taught; in 1986, Dexter Fisher published an edition of Zitkala-Sa's *American Indian Short Stories;* and in 1990, Vintage brought out, in one volume, William Wells Brown's *Clotel,* Francis Harper's *Iola Leroy,* and Charles Chesnutt's *The Marrow of Tradition.* Contemporary writers of color also garnered increased attention, as Mary Jo Bona and Irma Maini have noted.[3] Between 1982 and 1988, Pulitzers were awarded to Alice Walker's *The Color Purple,* August Wilson's *Fences,* Rita Dove's *Thomas and Beulah,* and Toni Morrison's *Beloved.* Other awards went to

Louise Erdrich's *Love Medicine,* Bharati Mukherjee's *The Middleman, and Other Stories,* Amy Tan's *The Joy Luck Club,* and David Hwang's play *M. Butterfly.* The teaching canon took on a new shape in 1989 with the publication of *The Heath Anthology of American Literature,* and within a few years, the *Norton Anthology* offered a more diverse collection of writers. It may be easy, now, to forget what was at stake in the canon debates, but as Paul Lauter notes, canon debates are, in the end, about "who has power in determining priorities in American colleges" and "whose experiences and ideas become central to academic study."[4]

The Internet revolution, coming on the heels of the canon expansion, has the potential to help democratize the canon by leveling the publishing playing field, increasing access to texts, and perhaps challenging the very notion of center and margin. Patricia Keefe Durso suggests that the Web is particularly hospitable to the outsider paradigm of multiethnic literature and to features—such as fragmentation, multilinearity, and intertextuality—that Gloria Anzaldúa, Gerald Vizenor, Ramón Saldívar, and others identify as central to ethnic literatures. Durso also hypothesizes that the Internet's "nonhierarchical structure encourages and facilitates interaction with a text's history and politics."[5] Such interactions may be particularly important for texts whose social, political, and cultural contexts are not well known. Stephen Pulsford describes the new digital era as "post-Norton" and insists that the Internet "challenges the authority of the anthology" by replacing the canon with a town hall cacophony in which there is no privileged voice.[6] In short, the Internet has the potential to make a powerful contribution to the projects of recovery, canon expansion, and increased and enriched engagement with voices on the margins.

In 2005, when Durso sought to quantify the Internet's role in undoing the canon, she found that a Google search produced 32,000 hits for Zora Neale Hurston and 161,000 for Henry James, five times as many for James as for Hurston. In early 2009, a Google search yielded 653,000 hits for Hurston and 4 million for James, six times as many for James as for Hurston. But the loss in parity is less significant than the twentyfold increase in hits for Hurston, and the fact that the 2009 search results include the Library of Congress's digital collection of 10 mostly unpublished and unproduced plays by Hurston and 19 sound recordings of Hurston singing Florida folk songs, as well as sites with electronic versions of Hurston's works and commentary by fans and scholars. Thus, although the number of hits for William Wells

Brown (96,400), Harriet Jacobs (125,000), Zitkala-Sa (39,600), and Samson Occom (23,100) do not compare to those for Walt Whitman (7.4 million), Nathaniel Hawthorne (1.9 million), or Emily Dickinson (612,000), the fact that information about and texts by these writers are available to anyone with Internet access is worth celebrating.

In addition to contributing to the expansion and perhaps dismantling of the canon, the Internet also makes an important, though sometimes less visible, contribution to our understanding of ethnicity, because every Web site plays a part, explicitly or implicitly, in shaping how we preserve and transmit the nation's and the continent's cultural heritage in the digital age. All scholars working in the humanities have to decide what is collected, how it is preserved, what labels it receives, what commentary to offer, what texts and contexts are worthy of study and juxtaposition, what interface or apparatus is appropriate, and a host of other questions. Although scholars working in print have long grappled with these questions, digital scholars confront complex and distinctly unfamiliar technological questions, they engage audiences with more varied expectations, and they seek to disseminate their work via institutions and economic contexts that are rapidly changing. In short, the Internet offers the possibility of a radical break with the past, a chance to preserve and represent the cultural record in new ways, and an opportunity to think differently about race and ethnicity. The survey that follows identifies a handful of the many projects that are making good on this promise of recovery, increased access, innovative scholarship, and new frameworks for race and ethnicity studies. It also describes the fragile funding and institutional contexts that support much of this work.

North American Slave Narratives is an excellent example of what is possible in the work of recovering and increasing access to little-known texts with substantial institutional investment of time, money, and personnel over many years.[7] The site is a well-organized, well-designed scholarly site that welcomes all users, without charge. This collection is part of a larger digital publishing initiative, *Documenting the American South,* that offers 11 thematic collections and draws on the collections of the University of North Carolina and other academic libraries.[8] Edited by William Andrews, a pioneer in slave narrative studies, and supported by a project director, a project manager, a cataloger, a preservationist, nine contributing librarian staff, 15 contributing graduate students and librarians, and an editorial board of 25 scholars that oversees the entire *Documenting the American South* project, the *North American Slave Narratives* collection earned an early digitization grant from the NEH of $111,000. Not surprisingly, given the resources (people, expertise, and money) invested, the collection is excellent: it offers full-text searchable texts of "all known extant narratives written by fugitive and former slaves" (except a few of the earliest that cannot be found and the few that have only recently been published and thus are still under copyright). The collection includes materials from more than 70 repositories, and for each text, the site provides an HTML file, an XML-TEI source file, and an image of the title page and of all original illustrations. Some narratives are also accompanied by a summary and useful contextual and historical information.

Equally impressive is *The Church in the Southern Black Community,* a collection supported by a 1998 Library of Congress/Ameritech National Digital Library Competition grant for $74,500 and the expertise of 12 scholars and librarians.[9] The site offers about 100 works, "including autobiographies, sermons, church reports, religious periodicals, and denominational histories" relating to the church experience of Southern African Americans. The collection is supplemented by a carefully crafted index that identifies "descriptions written by slaves of religion and religious practice during the period of slavery" that are embedded within the wide range of texts in the collection. Both the slave narrative and the religion collection also include image indexes that direct the visitor to images of nineteenth-century African American writers and religious leaders. Given the paucity of images of nonwhite peoples in many versions of U.S. history and the objectification of the black body in U.S. culture, these images go a long way toward diversifying the visual record and putting faces to voices and experiences. More generally, the contributions made by these two digital collections are noteworthy: of the more than 500 texts available, fewer than half would typically be available in print at a major research university library, and as few as 10 or 20 are available to the general reading public via bookstores and public libraries. In 2002, upon the occasion of the thousandth text being added to *Documenting the American South,* Librarian Joe Hewitt noted that 60 percent of more than 1,500 comments over two and a half years came from the general public.[10]

Notably, both of these collections within *Documenting the American South* were completed eight years ago. Because they are well-built databases, more materials can be added, but they represent an early push, often with financial and technical help from the Library of Congress and the NEH, to spearhead precisely what is called for in the 2006 report *Our Cultural Commonwealth: The Report of the American Council of Learned Societies Commission on Cyberinfrastructure for Humanities and Social Sciences.* As the report notes,

> The emergence of the Internet has transformed the practice of the humanities and social sciences—more slowly than some might have hoped, but more profoundly than others may have expected. Digital cultural heritage resources have become a fundamental data-set for the humanities: these resources, combined with computer networks and software tools, now shape the way that scholars discover and make sense of the human record, while also shaping the way those understandings are communicated to students, colleagues, and the general public. But we will not see anything approaching complete digitization of the record of human culture, or the removal of legal and technical barriers to access, or the needed change in the academic reward system, unless the individuals, institutions, enterprises, organizations, and agencies, who are this generation's stewards of that record, make it their business to ensure that these things happen.[11]

Not surprisingly, well-funded libraries at research institutions have been able to make the greatest headway in moving us toward the goal of completeness.

The Library of Congress *American Memory* collection is a particularly useful example of what is achieved when public and private funds are dedicated to a comprehensive project aimed at making a significant contribution to the "complete digitization of the record of human culture" that the ACLS calls for, work that will take the commitment of "this generation's stewards." *American Memory* began as a pilot project in 1990. The Library of Congress "identified audiences for digital collections, established technical procedures, [and] wrestled with intellectual-property issues." In 1994, the Library of Congress turned from CD-ROMs to the Internet and launched the National Digital Library Program, drawing on $5 million from Congress and $45 million from private funding. The Library of Congress has also supported digital work at other libraries and hosted projects. *American Memory*'s mission is to systematically digitize "some of the foremost historical treasures in the Library and other major research archives" and to make these materials "readily available on the Web to Congress, scholars, educators, students, the general public, and the global Internet community."[12]

Through this commitment to digital preservation and access and to building the more than 100 collections now in *American Memory,* the Library of Congress has made a significant contribution to ensuring that scholars and the general public will be able to generate, for years to come, fresh and provocative understandings of race in America. For example, the *African-American Pamphlet Collection* provides access to the 351 titles collected for the "Exhibit of Negro Authorship" that W. E. B. DuBois curated for the 1900 Paris Exposition. *Slaves and the Courts, 1740–1860* provides page images of more than 100 pamphlets and books dealing with legal contests related to slavery. *The Frederick Douglass Papers at the Library of Congress* allows anyone with Internet access a chance to scour the more than 7,400 items that were in Douglass's personal library at his home in Anacostia, Washington, DC; and *Born in Slavery: Slave Narratives from the Federal Writers' Project, 1936–1938* offers images of the typescript pages for more than 2,300 narratives and more than 500 photographs of former slaves collected by the Federal Writers' Project.

American Memory also takes seriously what "access" means. As Adam Bank notes in *Race, Rhetoric, and Technology: Searching for Higher Ground,* owning a computer does not guarantee digital access; real access must be "material, functional, experiential, and critical."[13] Owning a computer and being able to click on a link is only the first and perhaps most easily addressed issue in assuring a real democracy of knowledge. Having intellectual access is much harder. *American Memory* extends a welcome to all visitors and seeks to facilitate access for the nonspecialist. The site works well, offering good searching capabilities (full text, keyword, subject, author, or title) as well as browsing by topic, time period, type of material, and place. In addition, secondary materials provide historical context, site overviews, and teaching materials. The "Learning Page" offers extensive help to teachers who want to use the more than seven million primary source documents available through *American Memory.* The chronological site map, lesson plans, and activities provide increased intellectual access to the collections, as they offer questions and ideas that lead the user into a collection or to specific materials and that indicate the kinds of questions that the archive might address.

Often, digital collections created by academic libraries have at their center an original print collection. Thus, the digital collection recapitulates the original rationale, whether that is the papers in Frederick Douglass's library at the time of his death, the pamphlets collected for the Paris Exposition, or the idiosyncratic habits of a particular collector, librarian, or library. Sites created by individual scholars typically claim a more comprehensive principle. For example, Loren Schweninge's *Race and Slavery Petitions Project* seeks to provide searchable abstracts for all legislative and county court petitions related to slavery. Similarly, *The Atlantic Slave Trade and Slave Life in the Americas: A Visual Record,* a handsome site recently published by Jerome S. Handler, Senior Scholar at the Virginia Foundation for the Humanities, and Michael Tuite of the Digital Media Lab at the University of Virginia, offers access to over 1,225 images associated with the Atlantic slave trade. Print copies of these images are not necessarily rare. For example, some come from periodical literature such as *Harper's Weekly,* which can be accessed at *Making of America,* or from slave narratives, travel accounts, and books commonly held by research libraries. But together, the clarity of the collection rationale, a good subject index that increases the possibility of targeted and meaningful access, the quality of the images, the commitment to including images from Africa and Europe, and the reach across a wide range of libraries ensure that the collection offers a comprehensive visual record that is compelling to view and a meaningful contribution to efforts to broaden and deepen our understanding of slavery.

What becomes evident with a close examination of sites such as the University of North Carolina's *North American Slave Narratives,* the Library of Congress's *African-American Pamphlet Collection,* or Handler and Tuite's *The Atlantic Slave Trade and Slave Life in the Americas* is the significant intellectual value-added that these digital archives provide, the very work that Borgman notes depends on time-consuming, expert scholarship. They have been created with careful attention to indexing, bibliographic accuracy, and a scholarly apparatus that provides information about the contents and the purpose of the archive and commentaries or essays that help a wide range of users engage the archive effectively. In addition, such sites have deep value-added if they are encoded well. At its simplest, encoding is the tagging of each document and the parts of each document so that the on-screen visual representation captures the information embedded in the original print design (layout, font, and spacing). However, more sophisticated tagging is now standard, and the Text Encoding Initiative, an international consortium, has developed a widely accepted and flexible "markup language for representing the structural, renditional, and conceptual features of texts."[14] In the process of tagging a document or an entire collection of documents in TEI-XML, digital scholars have to grapple with fundamental questions about the print materials and decide what should be tagged and how. Such decisions, it turns out, are not trivial or obvious. In creating *The Complete Writings and Pictures of Dante Gabriel Rossetti: A Hypermedia Archive,* for example, Jerome McGann and his colleagues discovered that they implemented their markup schema differently from one another and thus learned "what we didn't know about the project."[15]

The editors of *The Revised Dred Scott Case Collection* tell a similar story about learning more about the materials as they encoded documents related to Dred Scott's suit for freedom. In the courts for 11 years, *Dred Scott* took up critical questions about personhood, asking, "Who would count in the law of the land as a citizen, a political agent, an individual, a human being?"[16] The decision, written by Chief Justice Taney, swept away a large body of legal work that had made distinctions between the legal standing of various classes of people of color—slaves, former slaves, and free blacks—in diverse settings such as civil courts, criminal courts, state courts, federal courts, and other social, commercial, and legal venues. As a result, the Taney decision contributed to the reification and naturalization of both the Constitution and race, suggesting that law and racial categories were not open-ended discourses but, rather, closed systems with "logically deducible rules."[17]

The story of the creation of *The Dred Scott Case Collection* began with an appreciation for the significance of *Dred Scott* in U.S. history, and the project directors were eager to make accessible 85 documents that had been discovered in a civil courthouse in St. Louis, the site of the first petition filed by Scott in 1846. Published in 2000, the site was immediately popular and had more than 150,000 hits in a few weeks.[18] In 2006, recognizing that the site did not comply with newer standards and that its functionality was limited, the Digital Library Services at the University of Washington, the home of the site, proposed using TEI-XML encoding instead of HTML. In migrating to TEI encoding, the project staff discovered that the criteria they had used to encode document titles were inadequate and that even standard TEI was "limited in its ability to reflect the structure of legal documents."[19] But as an extensible markup scheme, TEI-XML allowed the editors to create a tag library that was more appropriate (allowing multiple dates and a range of authors—court, witness, notary, etc.). Significantly, in doing this work, the editors discovered that the 85 documents were, in fact, 78, since some were embedded in others and not appropriately considered separate documents. In addition, as the scholars tagged the documents in TEI, they acquired a deeper understanding of every line and abbreviation in each document, and they discovered that the documents pointed to an additional 25 texts, which they were able to locate. The site now offers 111 documents, all of which are full-text, searchable, and accompanied by high-resolution images of the originals. Given the importance of *Dred Scott,* having access to the earliest documents in the case allows scholars of race and U.S. law to hear a broader range of arguments that were adduced and challenged in the construction and deconstruction of such critical notions as legal standing, personhood, and state's rights.

As McGann notes, "when a book is produced it literally closes its covers on itself," and as a result, print editions are, inevitably, "instantiated arguments" about the various instances and the distinct authoritative value of each item in what is often "a vast, even bewildering array of documents." The digital archive, by contrast, is intended to be "open to alterations of its contents."[20] In fact, it was such openness that allowed the editors of *The Dred Scott Case Collection* to revisit the materials and revise their understanding of the very nature of some of the documents. For literary scholars, digital environments provide an appealing alternative to the single authoritative edition. As Daniel Ferrer, the director of the Institut des Textes et Manuscrits Modernes, suggests, the digital collection offers "an unlimited number of paths through the documents; it allows instant juxtaposition of facsimiles, transcriptions, and commentaries (which can be as long as necessary, in various depths of accessibility, so as not to stifle the manuscript themselves); and it welcomes dialogic readings, with unlimited possibilities of reordering, additions of new documents, and changes of reading."[21] For scholars of race and ethnicity, unbounded collections and increased opportunities to add and reorder texts should help with the work of upending canonical hierarchies. But as we become excited about the openness of digital archives and increased access to manuscripts and multiple versions of a text, we must also ask whose work will receive this kind of attention.

The texts and authors that get selected for this kind of intensive textual recovery in the digital world depend, as Rachel Blau DuPlessis reminds us, "upon extra-textual debates about value, canon, audience, and even sometimes market that cannot be ignored."[22]

Two important digital projects in African American literature—the *Digital Schomburg African American Women Writers of the Nineteenth Century* and Chris Mulvey's *Clotel: An Electronic Scholarly Edition*—offer useful examples of the role economic forces can play in the digital editing and publishing of writers of color. The Schomburg Center began as part of the Division of Negro Literature, History, and Prints of the 135th Street branch of the New York Public Library. It now has more than 10 million items, including remarkable holdings for many major African American writers, and the Center is aggressive in building its collection, even though it sometimes has had to pass on items that have attracted intense bidding from private collectors. In 1988, the Center published a 33-volume edition of 58 works by African American women first published between 1773 and 1920. Widely praised, *The Schomburg Library of Nineteenth-Century Black Women Writers* changed the landscape for scholars who study race, ethnicity, gender, and literary aesthetics. Although the *Schomburg Library* is now out of print, the Center has made the texts available at the *Digital Schomburg*. Creating the digital versions was an expensive undertaking, since it was essential to have each text double- or triple-keyed because dialect is common in many of the texts.[23] Completed in 1999, the digitization of the texts complied with TEI guidelines at that time. The searches work well, the texts are edited well, and the project makes texts available to those who may not have access to the print series, which was surely a purchase beyond the budgets of many small public libraries. Unfortunately, the corporation behind the software used for the project went out of business in 2002, and migrating to newer and better interfaces will require money and additional technical and literary expertise. As DuPlessis notes, "texts themselves—their creation and their subsequent publication—are part of social processes and bear the marks of those processes."[24] These works by African American women writers had limited runs and limited distribution in the nineteenth century, went out of print quickly, were recovered only with the concerted effort of dedicated scholars, and now exist in the digital environment in a fragile state. They may yet again disappear from view if, as the 2006 ACLS report previously cited says, we do not make it our business to ensure that our diverse cultural heritage is digitized and thus a part of how "scholars discover and make sense of the human record."

The costs and challenges of sustaining a site's interoperability with new platforms and software and also of designing an aesthetic and highly functional interface, including markup schema that conform to best practices, have led some scholars to turn to digital publishers. Those not affiliated with digital centers find valuable help with technical issues as well as marketing and long-term management services through such programs as the University of Virginia's Rotunda project, which is funded by the Andrew W. Mellon Foundation and the University of Virginia and dedicated to the "publication of original digital scholarship along with newly digitized critical and documentary editions in the humanities and social sciences."[25] It is true, of course, that such a choice typically means that the project is not freely available on the Web. But for some, this is an acceptable cost of getting what they hope is a guaranteed future for their digital scholarship.

This is the choice Chris Mulvey made in publishing *Clotel: An Electronic Scholarly Edition* with University of Virginia's Rotunda Press. William Wells Brown's *Clotel* has a complex publication history: Brown published four very different versions between 1853 and 1867. It also has a complex relationship with other texts, since Brown quotes, borrows, and some would say plagiarizes from a wide range of sources, including Lydia Maria Child's short story "The Quadroons," abolitionist tracts, newspaper articles, congressional debates, slave narratives, and poems.[26] Mulvey first approached the Electronic Text Center at the University of Virginia about creating an electronic edition of Brown's novel in 2001. The project, according to Matthew Gibson, posed a "sizeable challenge," since Mulvey wanted to "mark up regions of contextual similarity" across the different versions "without necessarily privileging any one version" and wanted to make it possible to use the site for "uninterrupted reading" without losing the option of comparing the texts side by side.[27] The result is a stable, well-functioning site that offers "the full extant texts of the novel's four versions," with full-text searching, parallel reading displays, and "line-by-line annotations and textual collation."[28] The price for access ranges from $420 for high schools and individuals to $845 for research universities, plus an annual maintenance fee. While this price limits access, the expectations of purchasers and the income may bolster the University of Virginia's commitment to maintaining and updating the site as technological changes require.

While this discussion of economic contexts underscores the role of the market in shaping what appears and disappears on the Internet, it is equally important for scholars to recognize the power they have to shape the questions, courses, syllabi, and research agendas that, in turn, can ensure that the digital revolution does not simply recapitulate the biases and limitations of the print world. Thus, although *American Memory* currently has 17 collections dedicated to African American materials, only six dedicated to Native American materials, and one focused on Chinese American history, we can hope this will change as scholars challenge narrow definitions of America. Notably, one of the early recipients of a grant from the Library of Congress was the University of Washington's *American Indians of the Pacific Northwest,* a collection of 2,300 photographs, 1,500 pages from the annual reports of the Commissioner of Indian Affairs to the Secretary of the Interior from 1851 to 1908, six Indian treaties negotiated in 1855, 89 articles from the *Pacific Northwest Quarterly* and other University of Washington publications, and 10 introductory scholarly essays. More recently, hemispheric studies has been able to attract substantial funding. In 2007, the Maryland Institute for Technology in the Humanities and Rice University's Fondren Library and Humanities Research Center were awarded almost a million dollars, which will be matched by the schools, to develop an online site that will integrate an existing multilingual digital collection (the *Early Americas Digital Archive*) with a new archive of multilingual materials to be developed by scholars at Rice University. Named in honor of Jose Marti's 1893 essay, the *Our Americas Archive Partnership* explicitly seeks to challenge "the nation-state as the organizing rubric for literary and cultural history of the Americas."[29]

The *Our Americas Archive Partnership* also provides a glimpse of an increasing interest in digital tools and the role these tools might play in race and ethnicity studies. Perhaps inspired by the radical questioning that led scholars to challenge narrow nationalist notions of culture and thus to launch hemispheric studies, the project directors proclaim that their goal is to "develop new ways of doing research" and to create "a new, interactive community of scholarly inquiry" through the adaptation of tools such as geographic visualization, social tagging, and tag clouds. Excitement about digital tools is common among digital enthusiasts who prophesy the emergence of a scholarship that is interactive, collaborative, open-ended, visual, and more likely to allow innovation in race and ethnicity studies.

One of the most impressive examples of born-digital scholarship that uses the medium to challenge how we think about race is Wendy Chun's *Programmed Visions.* Published in 2007 in *Vectors: Journal of Culture and Technology in a Dynamic Vernacular,* an international electronic journal supported by the University of Southern California's School of Cinema and Television, the site is part of a book project, *Programmed Visions: Software, DNA, Race,* in which Chun explores the paradoxical proliferation of images in the last twenty years just as there has been increasing doubt about the power of the image to index reality. Much of Chun's book focuses on programming languages, computation and information theory, and stored memory programming, but she also suggests that there are important similarities between software and race as powerful forms of visual ideology.

Chun's site focuses on the ways in which race works as an archive, as a category used to create meaning, even as the very notion of race as a meaningful category has been undermined. The result is a site that challenges our desire for an easy or invisible interface. As the editor of *Vectors* explains,

> The digitization initiatives that drive so much of contemporary online culture—from Google Books to our local universities—envision the virtual archive as a kind of seamless information machine bringing the riches of the world to a screen near you with a quick tap of the finger. Such archives privilege transparency, accessibility, standardization, interoperability, and ease of use, lofty goals all, and quite useful when confronted with reams of data. But . . . [this project] urges you to shift your line of vision and to think about the larger stakes our frenzy of digitization might likely conceal.[30]

Chun's site eschews the usual navigational tools—menu bars, an index, a "search this site" function, or even "breadcrumb trails" that mark the path taken. The site rejects the usual virtues associated with a digital archive—completeness, coherence, and transparency. Instead, it offers snippets rather than whole texts, and everything is on the move, as portions of texts float across the screen, beyond the control of the user's mouse. The words of Toni Morrison, W. E. B. DuBois, Franz Fanon, Octavia Butler, court cases, and scientific treatises collide in "an archivist's nightmare" of opacity and chaos. The site frustrates our expectations that we can move from micro to macro, from close-ups to overviews, from one well-bounded text to another, each with familiar bibliographical information. A map is slowly created that allows the user to recall snippets already viewed, but bringing faint text fully into view is not possible with just a mouse click. As one user suggests, the site "refreshes our awareness of the interface as something coded and constructed," bringing to our attention "how naturalized" interfaces have become. As a result, the site links "opacity to a complex figuring of the systematic production of race as a category of power/knowledge and, most importantly, inextricably links race (as archive) to our understanding of visuality, whether opaque or transparent or somewhere in between."[31] Samira Kawash notes in *Dislocating the Color Line,* a text included in Chun's archive, that the concept of race is "predicated on an epistemology of visibility," even as visibility is "an insufficient guarantee of knowledge."[32] Chun makes the insufficiency of visibility an integral part of her Web site and thus unsettles the clarity that race, archives, software, and Web sites seem to promise.

A very different kind of born-digital scholarship, one that taps the ease of publication and collaborative spirit many have hoped the Internet would foster, can be found in Cary Nelson's *Modern American Poetry Syllabi* (*MAPS*). The site grew out of Nelson's experience of editing the *Anthology of Modern American Poetry* for Oxford University Press, and it is a good example of how the Internet may indeed explode the boundaries of the traditional anthology. Richard Powers enthusiastically describes *MAPS* as "a living, breathing conversation between hundreds of poets, scholars, and readers" and a "clearinghouse for some of the best criticism on the best poets of our time."[33] Significantly, the site also offers an impressive introduction, intentionally or not, to the multiethnic landscape of American poetry, and pages such as "Japanese American Concentration Camp Haiku" or those on Louise Erdrich include images from the *American Memory* collections and the University of Washington's *American Indians of the Pacific Northwest.*

Surely our scholarship has changed as a result of the digital revolution and the materials now available, which are far more extensive than this survey can convey. But the change is hard to quantify. In addition to the significant body of primary sources available on the Internet for no fee, there are large databases such as those offered by Alexander Street Press in Caribbean literature, Latino literature, North American immigrant diaries and letters, North American Indian personal writings, and African American music, to name only a few of their collections. But a review of bibliographies in the journals *American Literature* and *MELUS* suggests that although scholars may be working with digital versions of primary sources, they are not often citing the online version. Librarians also know that full-text databases of scholarly journals are heavily used by scholars and that the world of secondary sources as well as primary sources has expanded, perhaps exponentially, for the scholar who has access to a university Web portal. JSTOR, Project Muse, Academic Search Premier, and other full-text databases deliver scholarly articles in a matter of seconds to teachers and scholars of American literatures, and a 2006 survey by Ithaka indicates that 63 percent of faculty are willing to see their libraries cancel print subscriptions as long as the electronic version remains available.[34]

Some speculate that as scholars do more work online, the expectation for seamless navigation will increase. Scholars will expect to be able to move effortlessly from freely available pages in a copyrighted book on Google, to scholarly journals in a subscription database, to online archives of digitized images and well-edited transcriptions of rare primary sources. The economic contexts that will make this possible are not yet clear. But while we watch individual contract negotiations and major court battles find compromises between business models, which inevitably must focus on meeting costs and generating profits, and the commitment of libraries to serving the public good through free access to as much knowledge as their budgets allow them to purchase, we should also note that the scholarly production of digital archives and born-digital scholarship is deepening and widening.[35] This is good news for race and ethnicity studies. Although the habits, biases, power centers, and economics that shaped print over the last 500 years are also shaping the digital world, this survey suggests there are more diverse materials available to a "worldwide web" of students, teachers, and scholars than ever before. Postmodern theories played an important role in undoing positivist assumptions about race and ethnicity and idealized notions about well-bounded texts. Now, by increasing the availability of materials and by welcoming marginalized voices and perspectives, digital scholarship should, in the not-too-distant future, have a profound impact on the stories and histories we tell about race and ethnicity in the Americas.

Notes

1. Christine L. Borgman, *Scholarship in the Digital Age: Information, Infrastructure, and the Internet* (Cambridge: MIT Press, 2007), 227.

2. Katharine Newman, "*MELUS* Invented: The Rest Is History," *MELUS* 16, no. 4 (Winter 1989–90): 101.

3. Mary Jo Bona and Irma Maini, introduction to *Multiethnic Literature and Canon Debates* (Albany: State University Press of New York, 2006).

4. Paul Lauter, *Canons and Contexts* (New York: Oxford University Press, 1991), xi.

5. Patricia Keefe Durso, "It's Just Beginning: Assessing the Impact of the Internet on U.S. Multiethnic Literature and the Canon," in Bona and Maini, *Multiethnic Literature and Canon Debates,* 213.

6. Stephen Pulsford, "Literature and the Internet: Theoretical and Political Considerations," in *Literature and the Internet: A Guide for Students, Teachers, and Scholars,* by Stephanie Browner, Stephen Pulsford, and Richard Sears (New York: Routledge, 2000), 171, 185.

7. See http://docsouth.unc.edu/neh/.

8. See http://docsouth.unc.edu/.

9. See http://docsouth.unc.edu/church/.

10. Joe A. Hewitt, "DocSouth 1000th Title Symposium, March 1, 2002," University of North Carolina, Chapel Hill, http://docsouth.unc.edu/support/about/jahewitt .html.

11. *Our Cultural Commonwealth: The Report of the American Council of Learned Societies Commission on Cyberinfrastructure for Humanities and Social Sciences* (New York: American Council of Learned Societies, 2006), 1, available at http://www.acls.org/uploadedFiles/ Publications/Programs/Our_Cultural_Commonwealth.pdf.

12. "About *American Memory,*" Library of Congress, http://lcweb2.loc.gov/ammem/ about/index.html.

13. Adam Banks, *Race, Rhetoric, and Technology: Searching for Higher Ground* (New York: Routledge, 2006), 135.

14. "TEI Guidelines," Text Encoding Initiative, http://www.tei-c.org/Guidelines/.

15. Jerome McGann, *Radiant Textuality: Literature after the World Wide Web* (New York: Palgrave, 2001), 91.

16. Sara B. Blair, "Changing the Subject: Henry James, Dred Scott, and Fictions of Identity," *American Literary History* 4, no. 1 (Spring 1992): 38.

17. *Dred Scott v. John F. A. Sanford,* opinion of Chief Justice Taney, U.S. Supreme Court, December term, 1856, 21; Morton J. Horwitz, *The Transformation of American Law, 1780–1860* (Cambridge: Harvard University Press, 1977), 259. For further discussion, see Blair, "Changing the Subject," 41.

18. See "Washington University Acquires Lost Documents from the Dred Scott Case," *Journal of Blacks in Higher Education* 31 (Spring 2001): 59.

19. "About the Dred Scott Case Collection," Washington University, http://digital.wustl.edu/d/dre/about.html.

20. McGann, *Radiant Textuality,* 69, 80, 71.

21. Daniel Ferrer, "Production, Invention, and Reproduction: Genetic vs. Textual Criticism," in *Reimagining Textuality: Textual Studies in the Late Age of Print,* ed. Elizabeth Bergmann Loizeaux and Neil Fraistat (Madison: University of Wisconsin Press, 2002), 92.

22. Rachel Blau DuPlessis, "Response: Shoptalk—Working Conditions and Marginal Gains," in Loizeaux and Fraistat, *Reimagining Textuality,* 56.

23. See Howard Dodson, introduction to *Digital Schomburg African American Women Writers of the Nineteenth Century,* http://digital.nypl.org/schomburg/writers_aa19/intro.html; Thomas P. Lucas, "Editorial Methods for Creation of the Digital Schomburg Editions," *Digital Schomburg African American Women Writers of the Nineteenth Century,* http://digital.nypl.org/schomburg/writers_aa19/editorial.html. Contrary to Dodson's report that the series is no longer available in print, the Oxford University Press online site suggests that it will accept orders for any of the volumes, perhaps to be filled by print on demand.

24. DuPlessis, "Response," 85.

25. "About Rotunda," University of Virginia Press, http://rotunda.upress.virginia.edu/index.php?page_id=About.

26. For commentary on the publication history of *Clotel* and its use in teaching and in scholarly studies, see Ann duCille, "Where in the World Is William Wells Brown? Thomas Jefferson, Sally Hemings, and the DNA of African-American Literary History," *American Literary History* 12, no. 3 (Autumn 2000): 452–54. For more on Brown's use of other texts, see Robert Levine's "Cultural and Historical Background," in *Clotel, or The President's Daughter,* Bedford Cultural Edition (New York: Macmillan, 2000).

27. Matthew Gibson, "*Clotel:* An Electronic Scholarly Edition," University of Virginia, http://mustard.tapor.uvic.ca/cocoon/ach_abstracts/xq/xhtml.xq?id=152.

28. Chris Mulvey, ed., *Clotel: An Electronic Scholarly Edition* (Charlottesville: University of Virginia Press, 2006), http://rotunda.upress.virginia.edu:8080/clotel/.

29. *Our Americas Archive Partnership,* Humanities Research Center, Rice University, http://culture.rice.edu/americas.html. The preliminary site can be found at http://oaap.rice.edu/.

30. Tara McPherson and Steve Anderson, editors' introduction to *Programmed Visions,* in *Vectors,* http://www.vectorsjournal.org/index.php?page=7&projectId=85.

31. Tara McPherson, "Reprogramming Vision," in *Vectors* forums, http://www.vectorsjournal.org/forums/?viewId=397.

32. Samira Kawash, *Dislocating the Color Line: Identity, Hybridity, and Singularity in African-American Narrative* (Stanford: Stanford University Press, 1997), 130.

33. "About *MAPS,*" *Modern American Poetry Site,* http://www.english.uiuc.edu/maps/about.htm.

34. Roger C. Schonfeld and Kevin M. Guthrie, "The Changing Information Services Needs of Faculty," *Educause,* July/August 2007, 9.

35. For an analysis of one court battle within the larger context of libraries' commitment to serving the public good and the obligation of corporations to serve the interests of their shareholders, see Robert Darnton, "Google and the Future of Books," *New York Review of Books,* 12 February 2009.

Design and Politics in Electronic American Literary Archives

MATT COHEN

This essay explores the political implications of digital literary archives. Its focus is on the institutional involvements and choices made by electronic resource builders, largely in the academy and largely using technologies that involve XML (such as TEI, the Text Encoding Initiative's standards for tagging literary texts). The word *archive* is here used broadly, to indicate projects that present American literature electronically and their associated storage, delivery, and community-hosting technologies (databases, interfaces, wikis, and the like).[1] Taking up a few important free archival projects—including the *Walt Whitman Archive* and the *Our Americas Archive Partnership*—the essay will discuss questions of political involvement and meaning facing American literary archives today through the lens of the internal and external commitments such endeavors must make. By internal, I mean, loosely, the sorts of ties necessary to generate and sustain an archival project (which may well be multi-institutional and transnational); by external, I mean those means by which such an archive takes its place in the larger world. Language, economics, and collaboration all emerge as important political categories as archives shape and position themselves among the different models of access available today. I argue that part of the work of responsible online American literary archival projects is to engage with these politics consciously and explicitly, even as, in turn, experimentation with the potential of electronic storage and delivery shifts the coordinates of political possibility in ways that cannot be anticipated.

Building a literary archive on a digital platform is difficult work. For

most of us, it has required learning another language (or two); mastering the differences among programming languages, scripting languages, and markup languages; encountering a world of standards organizations and their thousand-page guidelines; trying to find hundreds of thousands of dollars for humanities projects; and then figuring out how to justify all this to our colleagues in the academy. We may be driven by the ideals of a new scholarly form—one, for example, that will change the boundaries of the academy and bring previously hidden documents to an international public. But in the on-the-ground building of a project, it can be easy to accept certain disciplinary norms and consequently to make XML-based literary archives regenerate scholarly structures and priorities that we might hope to transform. Given the pace and scope of the production of digital cultural resources in the United States as compared to the rest of the world, American literary projects may be particularly susceptible to such pressures. This essay hopes to offer perspectives on the conditions in which digital archives of American cultural materials are built, suggesting questions we might routinely make part of our analyses of them.

This essay offers a précis, rather than an exhaustive or synthetic panorama. There are many other political layers that could be pursued here, including the ones taken up elsewhere in this volume. In the first place, as John Lavagnino has observed, the very use of XML is not always appropriate for a digital literary project, for formal or technical reasons.[2] *Melville's Marginalia Online,* for example, uses Adobe PDF and a regularized symbolic set to present marginalia, rather than XML stylesheets or actual page scans in free image formats.[3] XML may be unappealing for theoretical reasons: it imposes a hierarchy on a text, so it stands in a fundamental tension with the argument that imaginative literary works make meaning through inherently unstable structures. Even when XML functions relatively smoothly with a literary archival project, there persists a tension between text and image that is not in tune with the formal equality of those elements in some genres (such as children's books) and certainly within the multimedia World Wide Web interface. "Indeed, computationally speaking, the divide between image and text remains all but irreconcilable," Matthew Kirschenbaum points out, and the chasm between ASCII text and bitmap images "in turn reflects and recapitulates certain elemental differences in the epistemology of images and text."[4]

If only it were just epistemology at stake. N. Katherine Hayles's warning that electronic resources—"the prostheses joining humans and machines"—profoundly shape our identities, not just our representations, should inform any discussion about the potential of the digital to liberate or constrain us.[5] A responsible literary archive-building practice will both engage this ontological condition and heed Jerome McGann's warning that every act of remediation is an act of interpretation. The challenge then becomes to shape editorial policy with a kind of self-consciousness particular to digital storage and delivery. "Literary works do not know themselves, and cannot *be* known, apart from their specific material modes of existence/resistance," McGann writes. "They are not channels of transmission, they are particular forms of transmissive interaction."[6] This is no less true when the material modes of existence take the form of a server, XML, stylesheets, a Web browser, and a reader's computer. Most literary scholars still understand the book and its materiality better than they do the many transmissive states of the electronic text, so it can be difficult to see how form and politics get linked to each other on the way to producing an electronic literary object.

In many ways, this is a long-standing difficulty playing out in a new arena. In this essay I focus on the same kinds of questions Raymond Williams brought to the attention of literary scholars a long time ago—questions about the context of production of literature and how it influences the way human beings relate to each other through texts. "The form of social relationship and the form of material production are specifically linked," Williams wrote, but not "in some simple identity."[7] Indeed, the material and social conditions for digital work are changing so quickly that the Marxist base-superstructure analytical approach cannot make clear sense of them; what is more, the multinational and multilingual nature of our expanded audience demands attention to translation no less than to economics. The economic stakeholders in digital projects are numerous and can shift rapidly. So, too, can the sources of labor and institutional relations that make an archive possible. Given users' increasing ability to download and "repurpose" data, the line between a product and raw material is blurry (especially in the case of free-access archives). Access remains a crucial area of thinking about the political because, while dreams of universal access fuel much academic Web development, there are problems with both the ideals and the pragmatics of digital access. Literary editing is starting to become more like history writing in terms of its audience. Suddenly, much larger audiences, from beyond higher education, are able to access our richly marked-up texts. But a bigger audience usually means one less interested in the rich markup—that is, in the theoretical "angle" of the editing. If we want to keep and inform that audience, then, we must build not just new scholarly archives but new scholarly *interfaces.* Before, presses handled distribution and interface design, but now that the model for going public is less the book and more, perhaps, the museum, those processes Williams stressed in his analysis have come increasingly under the control of those who create scholarly content.

Ann Stoler argues that we should regard archives as places where knowledge is produced, not just stored or displayed; what gets kept and how it gets marked as evidence gives form to power, shaping the imagination of those who use an archive. As both editors and designers, we encode protocols of power in the systems by which our literary past is circulated and accessed.[8] In what follows, I describe important features of the landscape of contingency in which literary archives grow today, both internally, as projects shape themselves, and externally, as they take place in the digital resource realm. The distinction is merely intended as a heuristic and will begin to break down as the essay proceeds. With this gesture, I hope less to prescribe an approach than to suggest important questions and elements of strategy in building scholarly resources for literary study, so that we may attend to the kinds of knowledge our archives do—and might—make.

What *shape* should a digital project take? This question confronts every project, initially and iteratively throughout its life. In addition to the questions about what standards to use (or to attempt to develop), there are questions about the canon. Especially given the trend toward interactive Web sites, with user-contributed and user-manipulable content—collectively known as "Web 2.0"—a generation gap may be emerging that maps onto an epistemological shift from author-based literary studies to network-based literary studies. The design of each resource makes an argument about the canon and what humanities "does," even about the university and its role in society. Meredith McGill implies as much in her critique of the *Walt Whitman Archive* in a 2007 forum in *PMLA.* The archive, she writes, adheres "surprisingly closely to normative ideas of the author and the work." Why focus on Whitman (and in particular his poetry) instead of, say, transcendentalism, or American writers, or queer poets, or alternative spiritualists?[9] The boundaries of an archive are inscribed at many levels, from the way it presents itself on the Web and argues for funding to the degree of interoperability with other electronic resources built into its code.

Beyond the implications of choosing a shape for a literary resource is the question of where to lodge it institutionally. This can be much like trying to find a publisher for a scholarly monograph; one crucial difference is the importance of sustainability to a digital project. Servers, code, and software all require maintenance, and even the least-interactive project will receive suggestions for revision from users that must be vetted. Internal funding for such projects and their maintenance varies from institution to institution, as do the strings attached. Extramural federations and funding can help a project achieve some latitude, but local administrative, library, and faculty interests will still put pressure on it.[10] Perhaps most important to younger faculty initiating new forms of literary research, the degree to which digital work can be assessed as a positive contribution to a tenure and promotion case varies by department, school, and university administration. Here political goals can collide: to innovate in the form of humanities work in some situations, it might be tempting to shape a digital project around a single, canonical author. Archiving authors with both a firm place on syllabi and an audience beyond academia makes attracting funding, student labor, and attention (both within the field and from media) easier. Focusing on a theme instead of a single author may mean a longer start-up time, as more institutions, repositories, and area specialists may be involved. At the same time, pace McGill, focusing on a single author can provide models, software, experience, and a core community for other kinds of digital humanities work, as it has in the case of many of the excellent sites fostered by the University of Virginia's Institute for Advanced Technology in the Humanities. Taken together, these factors subtly create a landscape of difference with respect to where and how innovation can thrive in the digital humanities and where and how it cannot.

The labor models for archives are features of that landscape, too. Digitization is extraordinarily expensive. To save money, many projects outsource transcription and other forms of capture to overseas companies with ambiguous employment and compensation ethics. Here Marxist critiques of burgeoning global distributions of labor and new forms of alienation make odd bedfellows with nationalist critiques of offshoring jobs. The cheapness and speed of overseas digitization have, however, made archiving of certain kinds and at certain scales possible where otherwise they would not be. Since the early 1990s, medical records digitization has been performed in India, occasionally causing controversy about confidentiality and accuracy. Along the same lines, Janet Gertz argues that with inexpensive digitization offshore, the main reason a project would perform digitization in-house would be quality control and conservation of original documents. But there are also questions about how placing digitization outside the intellectual labor matrix of a project affects the self-awareness and creative development of a scholarly resource. Often the feedback between transcribers or encoders and project directors can change the encoding scheme or even some of the basic intellectual structures of a project. As a student in the 1990s, doing transcription and basic encoding of Whitman documents, I learned a lot about textual structures that I had not encountered in seminars; when discussing those observations with the project directors, sometimes new areas of concern or future development would emerge.[11]

Then again, not all schools have graduate students to perform (and learn by performing) this sort of work. The term that has been used recently as a panacea for many of the challenges, both internal and external, facing the digital humanities is *collaboration.* Long argued as the key to transforming the humanities' genius-in-the-tower, single-author model of production, collaboration is a necessity in the digital realm. It thus seems to offer an advantage that balances the difficulties of articulating literary critics, library experts, computer technicians, and code wizards together. But the necessity of collaborating on digital projects should not obscure the ways that old structures persist, shaping the rewards of such work. Two of the most frequently named inspirations for collaborative authorship in the humanities are the natural sciences and the Web 2.0 practices just mentioned.[12]

The science model relies on a relatively clear division of labor underlying attribution for published scholarly work. Coauthorship is triggered by conventions in the research process; within subfields of the natural sciences, the particular significance of first authors, second authors, and so on is recognized. Underlying that division of labor is a relatively clear funding structure, channeled through principal investigators who head research laboratories. Not attributing authorship properly when working under federal funding gets a researcher in big trouble. So while it is true that collaborations in the sciences only a few decades ago tended to be small—two or three researchers at the most—the Rosalind Franklin scandals are few and far between these days.[13] (Data theft and fictionalization, unfortunately, are not; nor, as many graduate students would respond to this, are the triggers for authorship anything more than *relatively* clear.) Most humanists are unfamiliar with the role of the principal investigator as simultaneous mentor and funding source, and there are no broad, government-funded "training grants" for graduate students in the humanities as there are for the sciences. Having them would encourage the development of a more widespread use and understanding of the many potentials of electronic mediation in humanities work. Absent these material foundations, collaboration in the humanities must borrow selectively from the sciences, with a realistic sense of the disjunctions that remain.

Web 2.0 models of collaboration are thrilling. Having hundreds of contributors create a humanities "event," online or otherwise, is inspirational, creative, and at times revelatory.[14] But realistically speaking, those who end up getting the credit—in the form of promotion, tenure, book contracts, board positions, grants, and speaking invitations—are those who *design* such events.[15] In this, we risk repeating the old theory-versus-content hierarchical divisions within the humanities. Theorists are stars; content specialists can never be. Collaborative projects sometimes have long lists of contributors (often heterogeneous with respect to academic rank), but when an article or news coverage is generated to talk about the project, only one or two people are consulted or are officially named coauthors. What is worse, the power dynamics of collaboration are often difficult to see through the hype. Using online collaboration tools to elicit responses to a draft of an essay, for example, seems the perfect embodiment of collaborative practice. But can an unknown graduate student make this move and get the same level and quality of response as an established scholar? The music industry offers a reasonable analogy here: Radiohead can give away its records for a price the customer chooses and both survive and be described by the media as innovative. But can the little-known swamp rock band The Levees do it and even get attention?

Some of what has been called "Web collaboration" is not quite as radical as it seems. Wikis, for example, are frequently cited as exemplary collaboration tools with great potential to change humanities authorship models. But wikis are not collaborative tools by nature; rather, they are iterative ones. One version is replaced by another. The authors of successive versions may not know each other, agree on changes, or agree on the final product's "correctness," much less claim a real stake in the final product. Contributions can "disappear" entirely from a casual reader's perspective, relegated to the log or discussion. Wikis *can* be collaborative in certain circumstances, and they are certainly radical as an iterative authorship model. But until coauthored articles—even, perhaps, massively coauthored articles—in leading journals in the humanities become common, little will have changed in our profession on this point. It is to social relations, as much or more than to technologies, that we must look to encourage or analyze collaboration.

Rather than trying to find a "model" in response to the current trends, I suggest that we develop ethics of collaboration. Models often risk re-creating the very hierarchies that have made it hard for digital humanities to become a widespread practice beyond the handful of institutions that have invested substantial material and reputational resources in digital humanities, such as the University of Maryland and the University of Nebraska. Collaborations can suit the conditions of a particular electronic project and its material basis while responding knowledgeably to the market conditions of academic work. This may mean that students contribute only in specific ways or to specific sections of an essay or a digital project yet still receive coauthorship credit. In some cases, it may mean that all of the collaborators shape a work equally and, thus, that the ideas of the person who originated the project morph into a different form (something that almost never happens in science, where there are generally only one or two authors who shape the overall objectives and conclusions of a paper).[16] Once people begin contributing, they should also get some control, whether or not they are leaders on a publication. Graduate students often lead innovation in digital projects, and they need credit, not just acknowledgment. The process of authorship comes to the fore in this approach and might become itself part of the considerations in promotion and tenure cases.

If grappling with the canon, university politics, and the ethics of collaboration offer challenges to the genesis of a project, others haunt it as it takes its place in the larger world. Between federal, state, local, university, and private funding sources, support and audiences flow with sometimes competing political visions or notions of what digitized literature can do in the world. Many of the questions about archival politics rotate around two issues: selection and access. Questions of selection include debates about what gets digitized and why, as well as how resources should be allocated

Wants "ethics" of collaboration rather than a "model."

for digitization. Questions of access proliferate, because it is here that the liberal ideal of free access to information is lodged. The expansion of copyright laws has made it difficult (or simply expensive) for public archives of twentieth-century media to be built, as most releases after 1923 are under copyright. Siva Vaidhyanathan, Lawrence Lessig, and James Boyle have written eloquently on the secondary effects of such extensions, including the degree to which prosecutions initiated by groups like the Recording Industry Association of America cause academic entities to be overly and often needlessly cautious about reproducing materials.[17]

Alterations of copyright laws will be assisted by evidence that scholarly digital projects leverage the freedom of the Internet to advance research and enhance pedagogy. A start toward this has been made with the creation of the easy-to-use Creative Commons licenses, which offer literary archives ways of expanding their integration with secondary materials that scholars designate as reproducible for educational purposes. These licenses help protect the intellectual property of the scholars building rich academic resources, while at the same time facilitating sharing of those resources. While our code has theoretically been protected all along, Creative Commons licenses help establish expectations on the Web about rights and usage; they also allow us to share our recent publications online while preventing their unregulated use for commercial purposes. Underlying all of these intellectual property issues is the question of the "digital divide," of who has access to the Internet, preceding the question of whether resources on the Internet should be made available for free or may be aggregated and gated for profit by groups like Elsevier. For much of the world, having reached the World Wide Web, the question will be, what language should the content be in? It is with this issue that I would like to begin, working my way back to those of selection, funding, and free versus gated resources.

American literary archives are, for the most part, still monolingual. Elsewhere I have argued about the importance of translation enterprises for this field, given U.S. linguistic demographics, the history of non-Anglophone publishing in North America, and the importance for linguistic diversity of counteracting tendencies toward "global English" and also English-language-only initiatives within Anglophone countries.[18] When literary archives tackle translation issues, they usually take care to focus on the cultural nuances of language. This is significant because efforts toward automatic translation attract a great deal of funding and attention in the digital world. Google's translation engine is probably the one known best by Web users; as a tool for limited applications, it is a time-saver, but it partakes of an old ideal of a universal language, or of conceptual equivalence across languages, that is problematic.[19] Also, literary archives are sensitive to the fact that, at least at the moment, the codes used to "tag" objects in literary archives are largely in English, with logics largely based in Western media. There are projects to internationalize code, which would catalyze the spread of standards across linguistic fields, but the question remains whether that spread will induce changes in the structure of the code itself or, at least, in standards such as TEI.

The *Our Americas Archive Partnership* (*OAAP*) offers a promising, ambitious approach to translation in an American archival project.[20] In content and organization, the *OAAP* is a transnational, hemispheric undertaking. Rather than absorbing or generating all of its content, it federates archives by porting heterogeneous data sources into a central database and query portal, through which users pass to the original repositories when they have found a document. It is thematic in focus, organized around the topic of the development of nation-states in the Americas. Necessarily, the contents of such an archive are multilingual; the *OAAP* has a translator on staff and plans to translate documents from and into Spanish, English, Dutch, French, and Portuguese. At the infrastructural level, the project will develop search technologies and protocols to address the difficulty of searching across different languages. This will demand taking into account historical and regional variations in orthography and other aspects of language, since the *OAAP* will involve documents reaching back to the seventeenth century and across the continents of North and South America.

But the archives of American nation formation will also be laced with documents featuring the hundreds of indigenous languages of the Americas. Some indigenous activists might claim, in fact, that the revolutionary era is far from over in some places in the Americas and that digital resources can play an important role in shaping political movements today—assuming those resources can be found and accessed. Questions of translation of and searching in indigenous languages have an impact on what Timothy B. Powell describes as "the struggle to identify and correct the narrative of the Vanishing Indian that lies hidden beneath the glossy surface of search engines and hyperlinks."[21] While Powell concludes that teaching American literature can be enhanced by the use of such resources, questions have been raised in Australia about the appropriateness of outside access to indigenous databases. Elizabeth Povinelli argues that the Western orientation of searching, with its belief in the completeness and clarity of information access (Stewart Brand's "information wants to be free"), should be interrogated when it comes to indigenous cultural resources, whose subjection to colonial expropriation could be extended into the digital realm.[22] To what degree should the generation of cultural resource databases be constrained by the protocols of the groups represented therein? What would interfaces informed by indigenous information protocols look like, and might American literature read differently through them? Implicit in these questions is another one, about who should be involved in the creation and curation of archives. The *Aboriginal Voice National Recommendations,* a report from a Canadian panel of First Nations representatives under the aegis of the Crossing Boundaries National Council, explicitly indicates that funding for information technology development, including electronic cultural repositories, should be structured so that it both helps link First Nations people with Canadians and strengthens self-determination through the generation of resources and networks within indigenous groups. Indigenous nations with active or potential electronic presence, whether officially recognized or not, bring the vexed questions of sovereignty together with the more familiar issues of access and intellectual property in digital humanities works.[23]

In the past, the audiences for literary archives were comparatively small. What does it mean to create a scholarly resource whose audience numbers not in the thousands but, over the not-so-long run, the millions? This shift of scale means that questions about the politics of digitization have been asked increasingly frequently in public forums beyond the academy. Anthony Grafton, in a 2007 *New Yorker* article titled "Future Reading," posed the question of digitization of textual resources using a familiar rhetorical gesture: Will physical texts disappear with the Google Books revolution? Is it, in fact, a revolution? From a historian's perspective, of course, revolutions are few and far between, so the obvious answer is no. From Grafton's perspective as a historian of books at Harvard, the library seems a permanent fixture. Grafton briefly mentions some shortcomings of digitization, including the fact that preservation efforts have been largely limited to print, texts in English, narrative or reference works (rather than government records, private works, or other manuscripts), and books out of copyright.[24] But the ethics of the archive and access to it concern him little. The ideology of "democratic access" is just that: an idea, a political platform, not something a reasonable person would consider actualizable.

Illuminating, though, is Grafton's insistence that the history of *ways of finding* information, ways of organizing it, is disjointed, heterogeneous, and likely to remain so. He reveals a critical symmetry between scholarly calls for widespread free access to information and the rhetoric of private companies promising to make information universally accessible. Google, one expects, has more to gain materially from such rhetoric (or its realization) than do scholars. "It's not likely that we'll see the whole archives of the United States or any other developed nation online in the immediate future," Grafton points out, "much less those of poorer nations." This is not news (especially in the wake of the Google scandal in China), but Grafton helpfully sees that an important reason we will not see complete digitization is that electronic archives constitute "not a seamless mass of books, easily linked and studied together, but a patchwork of interfaces and databases." The challenge under the circumstances, he argues, is "to chart the tectonic plates of information that are crashing into one another and then to learn to navigate the new landscapes they are creating."[25]

Some of the most significant scholarly digitization efforts are doing just that. Grafton cites the open-access All Patents Initiative as a boon to historians—but he does not mention SparkIP.com, a commercial research interface for the patent database built by the same folks who built the free interface. SparkIP is aimed at researchers and inventors—largely pharmaceutical companies and biotech manufacturers—who want to know what has not yet been discovered or patented, as much as what has been. The search algorithm for SparkIP is complex; it sorts by user search terms, but it also crawls through the patent files searching for commonalities, establishing links between patents based on semantic and referential links between documents. A strong link, for example, is forged when two patents cite the same two sources in their bibliographies. Thus it is possible not only to see how research clusters around certain topics but also where links have not yet been made. In a structurally similar way, researchers working on the Semantic Web are trying to come up with a metadata system to link heterogeneous bodies of digitized information through a set of umbrella categories that dynamically change as new information goes online, independent of how that new content is formatted. Groups like the Networked Infrastructure for Nineteenth-Century Electronic Scholarship (NINES) have, on a small scale, linked previously independent scholarly archival projects, across a range of disciplines, through an interface called Collex, which offers Web 2.0–style user tools for collecting, annotating, and sharing sources. The *OAAP* promises a similar federation of resources under the rubric of the development of nations and nationalism in the Americas.[26]

So areas of scholarly research are being brought together by some digitization efforts, not just tectonically separated. Still, building those bridges is expensive. Google's economic and institutional power is an important aspect of the financial context within which literary archival or analytical projects develop today. There is no common standard for choosing what should get digitized and what should not. Indeed, private entities like the Mellon Foundation have quite different priorities than does, say, the National Endowment for the Humanities. While generative in many ways, this means that there is little conversation in major venues for literary scholarship about why some digital resources get created, funded, and promoted and why others do not. Literary archives in particular face challenges to raise more money than customary for humanities projects; raising funds means tying a project to the politics of donors.

Google itself, as the biggest developer of search technologies and the engine most used by students in North America, offers potential political dilemmas to scholarly partners. Leaving aside the questions of copyright, comparative linguistic uniformity, and selection raised by critics of its book-scanning program, Google offers economical solutions for digital challenges that are tempting, building itself into the scholarly infrastructure, in bits and pieces, through APIs.[27] The *Whitman Archive*'s search engine is Google-based, temporarily solving a problem faced by many archives, which is that designing search queries and interfaces for richly tagged data sources is difficult, expensive, and time-consuming. The mass digitization project of Google Books seems also to solve a problem for major research libraries struggling to decide what portions of their budgets should go to digitization, which can appear to be a bottomless sinkhole for staff time and funds. Google Maps is beginning to appear all over the terrain of digital humanities archives, as visualization becomes more and more the focus of funders and promoters of electronic scholarship. Yet Google's collaboration with China's censorship practices is out of step with the ideals of many of the projects that use Google's tools. It may be time for scholarly archives to start finding collective solutions to the economies of developing searches; this is a matter of prioritization, not scarcity of options.

Some examples of the kinds of questions we should be asking about American literary archives in the digital age may be helpful. Rather than pick on other projects out there, I will start by critiquing the *Walt Whitman Archive,* at which I have worked for over a decade (and where many of the contributors to this volume also had their digital humanities apprenticeships). The *Whitman Archive* features translation, original page scans, standards-based markup, and free access, and it has drawn high-level attention in literary studies recently. It was the subject of an entire forum in a recent issue of *PMLA,* which does not usually devote many pages to digital work. But the *Whitman Archive* exemplifies and, to an extent, struggles with some of the problems I have just outlined.

It is surprising to see, among the criticisms of the *Whitman Archive* in the *PMLA* forum, no mention of the fact that its XML is unavailable for download, that its search engine cannot use the deep markup we have used, or that it lacks user accounts or other community-hosting capabilities. Each of these issues is crucial in assessing a scholarly resource, not because there is an ideal configuration of these elements, but because each contributes to the shape and argument of a project. The staff of the *Whitman Archive* have debated each of these issues for years and have at times had hard choices to make about them. Offering our XML remains under discussion: we do give away the code for our Spanish translation edition, under a Creative Commons license, and will, I hope, build on that precedent in the future. The search engine is a more difficult problem, because developing nonproprietary search capabilities is expensive, difficult, and time-consuming. The *Whitman Archive* has tried several approaches without finding an adequate solution and continues to try new ones. It may be partly because of the time and expense of trying to develop a rich search interface that the archive has not prioritized user accounts and interfaces for community interaction.

Less visible than these issues is the fact that the *Whitman Archive* contains a set of identifiers, called "Work IDs," that users cannot see because they are embedded in the XML tags. Together with the Document Type Definition (which defines the tags we use and their hierarchical relationships), the Work IDs materialize, in a meta-structure, the intellectual axis of the archive. Ultimately, this will be one of the most powerful aspects of the archive, because it will allow users to see the relationships—established by the editors—among different objects in the archive. It is bound also to be controversial. The public information about the Work ID structure explains that "a 'work'" is defined as "the abstract idea of a poem or book, etc. We name the work according to the last instance published in Whitman's lifetime." The "etc." is a clue to the slipperiness of the definition of the "work." What if something was not published? What establishes a subset of *Leaves of Grass* as worthy of a unique identifier? What if Whitman's contemporaries thought he wrote a piece, but we have later learned he did not? Meredith McGill is righter than she could know in her critique of the *Whitman Archive* when she says that "the effect of the archive's design is to streamline Whitman's writing so that it begins with, gravitates toward, or orbits around the masterwork *Leaves of Grass*."[28] When more prose is online, this will seem less the case, but the poetry may still predominate, since it is less the selection of texts and more the Work ID structure (which will name each poem or poem draft but not, say, each paragraph of a prose text) that encourages the eschatological orientation McGill criticizes. With this and other effects of the process of remediating Whitman's oeuvre in mind, as we continue to encode more documents and reference them from each other, the definition of the Work ID will be refined or, perhaps, kept deliberately, productively loose. It will be important for us to make public that definition, its dynamism, and how it came into being.

In making these brief critical comments, I believe I am embodying what I consider to be one of the *Whitman Archive*'s strongest points: it takes shape through conversation and difference of opinion, rather than a truly "unified" editorial theory. The appearance of editorial unity on a collaborative enterprise—including the print-based ones of the past—is partly an illusion of context and analytical framing; it does not grow solely out of the actions of editors. In truth, because the *Whitman Archive* has become an institution, a publishing venue, an editorial project, a preservation system, a laboratory for new information systems, and a training space, heterogeneity of approach is not just salutary but necessary. Different sections of the archive have different interfaces, which means different frameworks of interpretation are posited and encouraged. This heterogeneity is expensive and time-consuming to sustain, so we have implicitly, if not explicitly, made it a priority. In his response to Folsom's essay in *PMLA*, Jonathan

Freedman criticizes the "treatment of *The Walt Whitman Archive* as a product of inspired editorship by Folsom and his colleagues and elevation of database into a self-maintaining . . . genuinely collective, genre-transcending human agency."[29] This perception, I would argue, results from the fact that Folsom and Price are the dominant voices representing in print the *Whitman Archive*'s enormous staff. In fact, there is considerable disagreement within the archive about its approach and potential. What makes the archive a good collaboration is neither its editorial unity nor its databaseness but the disagreements about how to think about it and how to build it. A key advantage of the structure of the *Whitman Archive* going forward is that it is a rare collaboration in the humanities that fosters dissent within its bounds in order to help answer difficult questions both about the material and about the politics and economics of new literary archives.

Still, the bounds of that collaboration might be imagined wider. The construction of the *Whitman Archive* might systematically extend beyond the academy, might break down the (admittedly strategic) distinction I have made in this essay between the inside and the outside of an archive. The simple way of describing what the *Whitman Archive* might do would be to say that it could move from a Web 1.0 (content-focused) model to a Web 2.0 (interaction-focused) model. Yet users have been wrangling and mangling our data at the *Whitman Archive* ever since we put it out there; selections from our texts, our images, and even our background graphics can be found mashed up all over the Web. The distinction, then, needs more elaboration. Web 1.0 is not over, first of all—most of the world's manuscripts, much of its print and architecture, much of its sheet music, and so on remain undigitized. The distinction between rich markup of data and simple mass capture is one of the most important ones to keep in mind in assessing the political importance of digital archives. Weak digitization, such as the unchecked transcriptions generated through Optical Character Recognition (OCR) in Google Books or completely untranscribed images or sound files, does not move the humanities forward. So the question is not merely how to "unscrew the doors themselves from their jambs," as Whitman put it in 1855, but how to do so in a way that takes specific advantage of the value added by scholarly labor.[30]

There are a few basic things that the *Whitman Archive* can do to broaden its potential uses and impact in this light. It can make its XML freely available to users (who might make their own modifications or create their own stylesheets) under a Creative Commons license. It might even develop tools that allow users to modify stylesheets in a modular way, to look at primary texts in different ways, better to exploit the archive's XML markup. At the least, providing searches that use that markup makes sense. To create some sense of community at a time when such functionality is increasingly de rigueur on the Web, a public forum might be provided, or user accounts that allow for the caching, annotation, and sharing of archive content. The utility of audience review has limits, admittedly: most of the people in our audience will not be interested in, for example, the intricacies of marking up the ink color of one of Whitman's marginal notations on an obscure newspaper article about trains; some of the people in our audience, while loveable, perhaps kind, and sincere, have interests to promote that are persistently off-topic. Still, at least two things are worth recalling. First, standardized markup gives us the power to represent the same content in multiple ways, so we can have a spectrum of avenues into the material, among which users can toggle for different archival "feels." Second, there are ways of reaching out to audiences that will give structure to their participation without predefining what comes out of a collaboration.[31] In the era of mass digitization, whether the resources are made by scholars or by Google, creative interface design, cheap tools for analyzing vast bodies of data (e.g., data and text mining, topic mapping, the Semantic Web, and similar approaches), and carefully cultivated, integrative relationships between archives and audiences will shape humanities scholarship.

Tim Powell's work developing a resource database and interface with the Eastern Band of Cherokee Indians at the Digital Library of Georgia offers a good closing example of the multilayered nature of archival politics. For Powell, beginning to address questions about how digital archives create knowledge involves politics at three levels. Obviously, at the national level, making available the Cherokee archive helps expose a history of official policies of dispossession and their effects. At the level of the generation of the archive itself, there are local, disciplinary politics, since the archive contents are no longer solely in the hands of content experts. "Allowing the students to write for a website designed to accompany the archives turned out to be a very rewarding method of putting politics into practice and, in a small but meaningful way," Powell stresses, "improving the teaching of Cherokee culture." Finally, at the level of professional humanities work, Powell points to a politics of archive building that is familiar to me and to many other early career scholars who are involved in this work. Powell's work with the Digital Library of Georgia had no official designation for the first five years, "nor," he says, "did much of this work 'count' on my curriculum vitae or annual report." He did it anyway, because it offered "a supportive community and, although this took many years to acknowledge, a growing awareness of how digital technology's power allowed me to realize a political vision that I had written about in books but never fully implemented in academe."[32]

"We are in the midst of an event of very large proportions," proclaims Mark Poster, "an emergence that is best studied closely and incorporated into one's political choices." "In this conjuncture," he emphasizes, "discourses that rhetorically paralyze the spirit are especially noxious, however realistic and wise they might appear."[33] The questions facing developers of American literary resources in electronic form are daunting, but the opportunities to change the world, as Poster suggests, are as great as the challenges. The discourses that Poster emphasizes are certainly important, and so are actual technologies that unparalyze resources, bringing them into relation with others. So, too, are the economics of access: I would venture that there is no encoding choice we have made at the *Walt Whitman Archive* that is as significant as our decision to keep the archive freely available to all visitors.

Kevin Hearle would agree with Anthony Grafton that the revolution brought about by electronic access is not much of a revolution. Hearle has argued that for independent scholars trying to use university resources, the old open-stacks, no-login-necessary system was better.[34] Others have made this case about the expense of e-journals and their model of subscription access, in which libraries never actually own the materials for which they have paid. This could be regarded as an opportunity lost more than an injustice—universities have long been institutions that protect access to their knowledge resources more or less jealously, depending on the school. So American literary archives, if they embrace the open-access model, can potentially make a formal argument for a different kind of humanities, the digital equivalent of what Whitman famously called "the new life of the new forms" in his preface to the first edition of *Leaves of Grass*.[35] Implicitly and explicitly, such archives begin to pose the question of whether the entire social field surrounding literary study, including the role of academic authority and the relationships between "fans" and "experts," should be redefined using Web 2.0 approaches, public outreach initiatives, and sustainable funding strategies (including both federal and private capital partnerships). This level of political engagement and change is often no longer solely in the hands of slow-moving academic institutions but is in the hands of small groups of editors, historians, and archivists themselves, who will be not just telling literary history but making the spirit of a new cultural future.

Notes

For conversations that shaped this essay, I thank Paolo Mangiafico, Matt Kirschenbaum, Bethany Nowviskie, Erica Fretwell, Bart Keeton, Janine Barchas, Kevin Webb, Terry Catapano, Brian Bremen, Cole Hutchison, Lars Hinrichs, Ken Price, Daniel Pitti, Jerome McGann, Johanna Drucker, Andy Jewell, Amy Earhart, Vanessa Steinroetter, Rachel Price, Ed Gomes, Deborah Jakubs, and the Bibliography and Textual Studies Group at the University of Texas at Austin.

1. For a discussion of the semantic difficulties surrounding such work, see Kenneth M. Price, "Edition, Project, Database, Archive, Thematic Research Collection: What's in a Name?" *Digital Humanities Quarterly* 3, no. 3 (Summer 2009), http://www.digitalhumanities.org/dhq/vol/3/3/000053/000053.html.

2. John Lavagnino, "When Not to Use TEI," in *Electronic Textual Editing,* ed. Lou Burnard, Katherine O'Brien O'Keeffe, and John Unsworth (New York: Modern Language Association, 2006).

3. *Melville's Marginalia Online,* http://www.boisestate.edu/melville/index.html; see also Jennifer Howard, "Call Me Digital," *Chronicle of Higher Education* 52, no. 24 (17 February 2006): A14.

4. Matthew G. Kirschenbaum, "Editor's Introduction: Image-Based Humanities Computing," *Computers and Humanities* 36 (2002): 3–6, at 4.

5. N. Katherine Hayles, *My Mother Was a Computer: Digital Subjects and Literary Texts* (Chicago: University of Chicago Press, 2005), 64.

6. Jerome J. McGann, *The Textual Condition* (Princeton: Princeton University Press, 1991), 11.

7. Raymond Williams, *Marxism and Literature* (London: Oxford, 1977), 163.

8. Ann Laura Stoler, *Along the Archival Grain: Epistemic Anxieties and Colonial Common Sense* (Princeton: Princeton University Press, 2009).

9. Meredith McGill, "Remediating Whitman," *PMLA* 122, no. 5 (October 2007): 1592–96, at 1593; Ed Folsom and Kenneth M. Price, eds., *Walt Whitman Archive,* http://www.whitmanarchive.org.

10. Examples of such federations include both umbrella groups like HASTAC and ones that serve smaller interest groups, such as NINES.

11. Janet Gertz, "Vendor Relations," in *Handbook for Digital Projects: A Management Tool for Preservation and Access,* ed. Maxine K. Sitts (Andover: Northeast Document

Conservation Center, 2000), 151–52. For more on this and other aspects of outsourcing digitization, see the essays in the 2003 report by the National Initiative for a Networked Cultural Heritage, "The Price of Digitization: New Cost Models for Cultural and Educational Institutions," http://www.ninch.org/forum/price.report.html (accessed 29 August 2009); Daniel J. Cohen and Roy Rosenzwieg, *Digital History: A Guide to Gathering, Preserving, and Presenting the Past on the Web* (Philadelphia: University of Pennsylvania Press, 2005), especially 103–7. New NEH initiatives for international digital humanities partnerships might help address some of the questions about development raised here, by allowing scholars to leverage the infrastructural strengths of their respective regions.

12. See, e.g., Cathy Davidson, "Humanities 2.0: Promise, Perils, Predictions," *PMLA* 123, no. 3 (May 2008): 707–17.

13. Biophysicist Rosalind Franklin's X-rays contributed to the "double helix" model devised by James Watson and Francis Crick to show the architecture of DNA. The question of whether she should have been included as a coauthor of the resulting publications has been hotly debated. See Brenda Maddox, *Rosalind Franklin: The Dark Lady of DNA* (New York: HarperCollins, 2002).

14. See, e.g., the discussion and annotation of the Ithaka report "Scholarly Publishing in a Digital Age" using CommentPress, hosted by the Institute for the Future of the Book, at http://scholarlypublishing.org/ithakareport/ (accessed 14 October 2008).

15. For critiques of the structurally similar business model based on "user-generated content," see Tiziana Terranova, "Free Labor: Producing Culture for the Digital Economy," *Social Text* 8, no. 2 (2000): 33–58; Andrew Lowenthal, "Free Media vs. Free Beer," *Transmission,* March 2007, http://www.transmission.cc/node/86 (accessed 9 October 2008).

16. Legal definitions of joint copyright resulting from collaboration may be useful; see Paul Goldstein, *International Copyright: Principles, Law, and Practice* (New York: Oxford University Press, 2001); effectively, to warrant joint ownership, the contribution a person makes to a work must be copyrightable on its own—an original expression of some kind, as differentiated from, say, proofing. Collaboration on digital projects may strain these definitions going forward; debates about the copyright status of Wikipedia entries seem a preview of this. See http://en.wikipedia.org/wiki/Wikipedia:Copyrights for the latest state of copyright at Wikipedia.

17. Siva Vaidhyanathan, *The Anarchist in the Library* (New York: Basic Books, 2004); Lawrence Lessig, *The Future of Ideas: The Fate of the Commons in a Connected World* (New York: Vintage, 2002) and Web site and blog, http://www.lessig.org/; James Boyle, *The Public Domain: Enclosing the Commons of the Mind* (New Haven: Yale University Press, 2008).

18. See Matt Cohen, "Untranslatable? Making American Literature in Translation Digital," *Modern Language Studies* 37, no. 1 (Summer 2007): 43–53.

19. See also the Defense Advanced Research Projects Agency Web site, http://

www.darpa.mil, for a list of projects. Those with an interest in linguistics or translation will be particularly interested in the Global Autonomous Language Exploitation (GALE) Program; see http://www.darpa.mil/ipto/programs/gale/gale.asp. On the use of open information sources, including Google, for government intelligence gathering, see Robert O'Harrow Jr., "Even Spies Go to Trade Conferences," *Washington Post,* 13 September 2008, D01.

20. See the *OAAP* Web site, http://oaap.rice.edu/. I am a member of the advisory board for this project. It is funded by an Institute of Museum and Library Services National Leadership grant, which supports work at Rice University and the University of Maryland.

21. Timothy B. Powell, "Digitizing Cherokee Culture: Building Bridges between Libraries, Students, and the Reservation," *MELUS,* Summer 2005, par. 4.

22. Elizabeth Povinelli, "Recognizing Digital Divisions, Circulating Socialities" (talk given at Duke University, 26 November 2007); Stewart Brand, *The Media Lab: Inventing the Future at MIT* (New York: Penguin, 1987), 202. For an interface to aboriginal materials that formally challenges the Western ideal of transparency, see Chris Cooney and Kim Christen, "Digital Dynamics across Cultures," *Vectors,* Spring 2006, http://vectors.usc.edu/index.php?page=7&projectId=67.

23. *Aboriginal Voice National Recommendations: From Digital Divide to Digital Opportunity,* Crossing Boundaries Papers, vol. 5 (November 2005), available at http://knet.ca/documents/Aboriginal-Voices-Final-Report-Vol5_Doc_051122.pdf.

24. Anthony Grafton, "Future Reading: Digitization and Its Discontents," *New Yorker,* 5 November 2007, 50–54. For a somewhat panicky but usefully specific argument about what is not getting digitized, see Katie Hafner, "History, Digitized (and Abridged)," *New York Times,* Sunday Business section, 11 March 2007, 3.1, 3.8–9.

25. Grafton, "Future Reading," 53.

26. See SparkIP, http://www.sparkip.com; NINES, http://www.nines.org; Collex, http://nines.org/collex.

27. APIs, or application programming interfaces, allow applications to access operating systems, libraries, or services. See Grafton, "Future Reading"; Clive Thompson, "Google's China Problem (and China's Google Problem)," *New York Times Magazine,* 23 April 2006, http://www.nytimes.com/2006/04/23/magazine/23google.html; Jean-Noël Jeanneney, *Google and the Myth of Universal Knowledge: A View from Europe,* trans. Teresa Lavender Fagan (Chicago: University of Chicago Press, 2006); Siva Vaidhyanathan, "The Googlization of Everything," http://www.googlizationofeverything.com/.

28. *Walt Whitman Archive,* "Encoding Guidelines," http://segonku.unl.edu/whitman wiki/pmwiki.php/Main/EncodingGuidelines (accessed 30 October 2008); McGill, "Remediating Whitman," 1594. Folsom's response to McGill respecting the generic priorities of the *Whitman Archive* suggests caution about assessing electronic resources as if they are fixed, rather than evolving, entities; see Ed Folsom, "Response," *PMLA* 122, no. 5 (October 2007): 1608–12, at 1611.

29. Jonathan Freedman, "Whitman, Database, Information Culture," *PMLA* 122, no. 5 (October 2007): 1596–1602, at 1601.

30. Walt Whitman, *Leaves of Grass* (New York, 1855), 29, quoted from the *Walt Whitman Archive,* http://www.whitmanarchive.org/published/LG/1855/whole.html (accessed 1 October 2008).

31. The Advanced Papyrological Information System (APIS), extending the work of the Duke Data Bank of Documentary Papyri, has been developing a suite of tools that will distribute the labor of creating a scholarly resource even more widely, allowing owners of ancient documentary papyri to contribute transcriptions, images, and bibliographical descriptions to a centralized database. See http://www.columbia.edu/cu/lweb/projects/digital/apis/index.html.

32. Powell, "Digitizing Cherokee Culture," par. 4, par. 8.

33. Mark Poster, *Information Please: Culture and Politics in the Age of Digital Machines* (Durham: Duke University Press, 2006), 268.

34. Kevin Hearle, "Degrees of Difference," *American Periodicals: A Journal of History, Criticism, and Bibliography* 17, no. 1 (2007): 118–21.

35. Whitman, *Leaves of Grass,* iii.

Encoding Culture: Building a Digital Archive Based on Traditional Ojibwe Teachings

TIMOTHY B. POWELL AND LARRY P. AITKEN, *chi-ayy ya agg* (WISDOM KEEPER)

> The study of American literature is enhanced and transformed with the use of electronic tools and technology resources. . . . [I]ts size, richness, and multiple voices demonstrate that the study of American literature has outgrown "the book." . . . There is no longer a single point of origin with which to begin, nor a single line of literary historical development to follow.
>
> —Randy Bass, "New Canons and New Media: American Literature in the Electronic Age"

> Anishinaabe [variants: Ojibwe, Chippewa] knowledge has a beginning. Knowledge and existence were there long before humans. In the epistemology of beginnings, earth has its own knowledge. The work we are doing with this digital archive [*Gibagadinamaagoom: An Ojibwe Digital Archive*] is so important, one inevitably wonders whether they're worthy to translate wind, fire, earth sounds, bird songs, waves. I know this is hard for academics to accept, but you are the transmitter, not the originator of knowledge.
>
> —Larry P. Aitken, sacred pipe carrier and tribal historian, Leech Lake Band of Ojibwe, and endowed chair, Itasca Community College

The advent of digital technology is undoubtedly changing our understanding of the origins and story lines of American literary history, as Randy Bass suggests.[1] This interpretive shift offers a critically important opportunity to think more carefully about the place of Native American expressive culture as an integral, albeit long-neglected, part of "American literature." While most anthologies in the field now include an opening section on indigenous origins—irresponsibly reducing thousands of years of precolonial storytelling to a few pages—the selections are invariably limited to stories that fit within the parameters of the white printed page. Rather than reviewing this history of exclusion yet again, I will assume here that the field is ready to acknowledge that indigenous stories are indeed part of American literary history, whether they appear in the form of the oral tradition, rock art, narratives woven in wampum belts, or pictographic images inscribed on birch bark.[2] This may be an overly generous assumption. Nonetheless, my point is to demonstrate how digital technology can be utilized to extend the formal boundaries of the field and to create exciting new interpretive opportunities by taking seriously, at long last, the idea that the Ojibwe "epistemology of beginnings" is an intellectually valid interpretive paradigm.[3] In doing so, the *Gibagadinamaagoom* digital archive (http://gibagadinamaagoom.info/), whose name means "to bring to life, to sanction, to give authority," devotes itself to sanctioning the intellectual sovereignty of indigenous wisdom carriers, so that the question of whether American literary history begins with the Puritans or Columbus becomes moot as we set off in search of much deeper origins, wondering whether we are "worthy to translate wind" or to record "knowledge [that existed] long before humans."[4]

Although victory over Eurocentrism was declared long ago, the field of American literature—particularly in its new instantiation as digital archives devoted to the subject—continues to struggle to achieve greater cultural diversity. This is not to say that the digital archives devoted to canonical American authors are not intrinsically valuable and highly sophisticated. To the contrary, they have set the standard for this new form of literary criticism and greatly inspired the work being done on the *Gibagadinamaagoom* project. Amanda Gailey articulates the present dilemma in her paper "Digital American Literature: Some Problems and Prospects." Describing "the strange relationship between the selective canon of print literature and the body of texts digitized by digital libraries and digital scholarly editions," Gailey writes,

> Digital scholarly editions in American literature tend to focus conservatively on highly canonical authors (such as Whitman and Dickinson), and foreground compositional histories by displaying manuscript drafts, applying markup that highlights authorial process, etc. This approach asserts an author-centered view of literature and has resulted in the digitization

of minutiae by a few great authors while the major works of slightly less canonical authors (such as Poe) have been altogether neglected.[5]

From the perspective of the Ojibwe wisdom carriers with whom I work, the concern obviously extends well beyond the exclusion of Edgar Allan Poe, although Gailey's point is well taken. Again, my energies here are devoted not to another critique but to an affirmation of new media's potential to integrate cultural codes and digital codes and to expand the scope of American literature beyond "the book."

To be fair, the current focus on canonical authors derives not from a lack of critical imagination but from all-too-real constraints that continue to confine digital scholarship. As Jerome McGann writes in "Culture and Technology: The Way We Live Now, What Is to Be Done?": "Digital scholarship—even the best of it . . . [is] typically born into poverty—even the best funded ones. Ensuring their maintenance, development, and survival is a daunting challenge."[6] Given the enormous expenditures of time, expertise, and money needed to build a state-of-the-art digital archive, it is simply more financially feasible to undertake digitization projects that have already been carefully edited in paper form. The problems grow exponentially when one endeavors to design an archive of traditional Ojibwe knowledge manifest as pictographs etched on birch bark, drums, ceremonial regalia, and treaty minutes, which are enlivened by the stories of Anishinaabe *chi-ayy ya agg* (Ojibwe wisdom carriers).[7] The *Gibagadinamaagoom* project received an NEH grant in 2007, which enabled us to create several prototypes. It is still, however, very much a work in progress. Despite being in the early stages of development, we have learned a great deal that I hope will be of interest to digital Americanists and to the Ojibwe students who will use these digital exhibits to learn their language and to revitalize their culture.

Even though the term *interdisciplinary* is frequently bandied about by university presidents, deans, and faculty, this popular notion rarely translates into working with tribal historians, literary artifacts housed in museums, digital curators from the library, and humanities scholars. Yet this is precisely the partnership that needs to be engaged if we are to think beyond the legacy of print culture and to trace these story lines back to their indigenous origins. More specifically, the present essay will focus on the thought process that created a digital exhibit about one specific Ojibwe artifact housed in the Penn Museum, where I work: a pictograph of *animikii* (thunderbird) inscribed on a birch bark case. Using digital video, flash animation, and three-dimensional imaging, in conjunction with stories told by Ojibwe *chi-ayy ya agg* (wisdom carriers), the goal of the *Gibagadinamaagoom* digital archive is to bring this object to life and to listen intently to the stories it has to tell.[8]

As already mentioned, in the Ojibwe language, *Gibagadinamaagoom* (Gee-bag-ah-DEEN-ah-ma-GOOM) means "to bring to life, to sanction, to give authority." The archive dedicates itself to sanctioning the intellectual sovereignty of Ojibwe *chi-ayy ya agg,* who possess authority, conferred on them by the tribe, to tell stories that bring empowered objects (artifacts) and history to life. From an Ojibwe perspective, digital technology is valuable because its interactive qualities allow viewers to ask the elders about *their* history, to look into their eyes, and to hear *chi-ayy ya agg* speak in their own language and on their own cultural terms. Three-dimensional imaging, in turn, creates greater access to artifacts housed in museums that might otherwise never be seen by students growing up on Ojibwe reservations, and it significantly expands the meaning of the description "literary text."[9]

There are, however, many dimensions of this dynamic interchange that are simply not possible to explain within the margins of the white page. The University of Michigan Press's decision to publish *The American Literature Scholar in the Digital Age* both in print format and on the *digitalculturebooks* open source Web site creates a unique opportunity to demonstrate how digital technology makes it possible to create for the literary text a highly sophisticated cultural and spiritual context that will allow an interpretive framework that would not be available without the full partnership of the Ojibwe wisdom carriers. Thus, the digital and paper-based versions of this creative diptych work together to tell a single story—how digital technology can more accurately and artistically represent the indigenous origins and spiritual story lines of expressive culture on these continents.

Materiality and Spirituality

In all honesty, it is not easy to explain the relationship between the ancient symbol of *animikii* (thunderbird), birch bark media, and XML codes. I make no pretense to having "mastered" these complexities. Yet I do believe that there is something very special about this moment in history and the convergence between digital technology's unique tools and the Ojibwe wisdom keepers' willingness to work with this *new* technology to preserve the *old* ways.[10] Ironically, whereas the Ojibwe elders working on the project have been quick to grasp digital technology's unique powers, cybertheorists seem to be struggling to imagine how digital and cultural codes can be effectively integrated. Tara McPherson, writing in a recent special issue of *Vectors: Journal of Culture and Technology in a Dynamic Vernacular,* notes, "I am continually amazed by how easy it is to hold these two types of work [race and digital media] apart and have come to believe that *the very forms* of electronic culture encourage just such a partitioning."[11] In "Cultural Difference, Theory, and Cyberculture Studies," Lisa Nakamura makes a similar point: "*Where is race in this picture?* . . . The only way to explain this glaring omission [in cyberculture critique] is through a theory of mutual repulsion."[12] Perhaps David Silver put it best in his introduction to *Critical Cyberculture Studies* (2006), when he wrote, "Critical cyberculture studies [now] approaches cultural difference . . . front and center, informing our research questions, frameworks, and findings. The bad news is that we have a long way to go."[13]

Based on my own experience working with Ojibwe wisdom keepers, I have not found that the cultural, spiritual, and digital dimensions of the archive tend toward the type of "partitioning" and "mutual repulsion" McPherson and Nakamura describe. This surprising insight can perhaps be traced to a deeper set of meanings about "history" and "technology." To the *chi-ayy ya agg,* digital technology does not represent a radical break with the past—as implied by the term *postmodernism.* Rather, the tribal historians working on the project see this new technology as part of an ancient continuum, wherein the Ojibwe have long (for thousands of years) embraced new technology—whether it be carving new kinds of projectile points or accepting the gift of the dance drum from the Dakota—to revitalize their culture. Perhaps, then, the problem that McPherson and Nakamura describe is not necessarily embedded within "*the very forms* of electronic culture" but derives from certain *perceptions* about digital technology.

My hope that this problem can be overcome in the near future has been galvanized by Matthew Kirschenbaum's brilliant new book *Mechanisms: New Media and the Forensic Imagination.* As Kirschenbaum points out, new media has been haunted by the widely held view that digital technology constitutes a postmodern phenomenon. (Significantly, both McPherson and Nakamura cite postmodernism as a cause of the problem they seek to overcome.) Postmodernism's problematic legacy rests on two interrelated assumptions: (1) because electronic texts are infinitely reproducible, the cultural dimensions that characterize the "original" are lost in endless repetition; (2) because any and all content in digital archives ultimately ends up encoded in a "universal language" of zeroes and ones, new media's capability of representing cultural specificity is inherently compromised.

Mechanisms addresses both of these perceptions directly and, through a minutely detailed analysis that Kirschenbaum calls "computer forensics," reveals a far more complicated and heterogeneous terrain of electronic textuality. Challenging the "postmodern argument about the digital simulacrum—copies without an original," Kirschenbaum focuses relentlessly on the inscription mechanisms of the hard drive, to prove that "electronic objects can be algorithmically individualized" to such a degree that the bitstreams that encode data are "in fact a more reliable index of individualization than DNA testing."[14] This specificity productively counters the problematic "narrative" that any and all content is "reinscribed as the universal ones and zeroes of digital computation." Kirschenbaum's intent is to demonstrate how "forensic and formal materiality" restores digital technology's reliability for presenting highly specified information.[15] In light of Kirschenbaum's findings, I would argue that it is indeed possible to translate the inscription of *animikii* (thunderbird) on *wiigwaas* (birch bark) into digital form without sacrificing the cultural, historical, and spiritual integrity of the original.

Because Kirschenbaum's work concentrates so intently on the formal and forensic materiality of computer systems, detailed questions about cultural specificity fall outside the parameters of his analysis. I hope to reintroduce the question of culture by going back to a moment early in *Mechanisms* where Kirschenbaum recounts the intellectual origins that influenced his own understanding of "materiality," namely, the following passage from Johanna Drucker's *The Visible Word: Experimental Typography and Modern Art, 1909–1923*.

> The force of stone, of ink, of papyrus, and of print all function within the signifying activity—not only because of their encoding within a cultural

> system of values whereby a stone inscription is accorded a higher stature than a typewritten memo, but because these values themselves come into being on account of the physical material properties of these different media. Durability, scale, reflectiveness, richness and density of saturation and color, tactile and visual pleasure—all of these factor in—not as transcendent and historically independent universals, but as aspects whose historical and cultural specificity cannot be divorced from their substantial properties.[16]

This understanding is quite abstract, as some of my nonacademic readers will surely be quick to point out to me. Hopefully, translating Drucker's theoretical insights into more culturally specific manifestation of Ojibwe epistemology can help bridge the worrisome gap between academic prose and the incarnation of *animikii* (thunderbird) seen in figure 1. The "force" Drucker associates with the media manifests itself here with the materialism of the birch bark and the inscription of *animikii,* which are interrelated "because of their encoding within a cultural system." More specifically, birch bark is associated with Ojibwe traditional spiritual archives inscribed on

Fig. 1. Thunderbird on birch bark, Pennsylvania Museum of Archaeology and Anthropology. (Photograph by David McDonald.)

wiigwaas (birch bark) scrolls and kept by the Midewiwin (Grand Medicine Society).[17] *Animikii,* according to oral tradition, is *oshkaabewis* (messenger) of *Gitche Manidoo* (Creator). If one looks carefully, lightning bolts emanate from *animikii*'s eyes, a sign of the spiritual, literary, and social forces associated with this empowered object.

The birch bark media depicted in figure 1 invokes the sacred Midewiwin scrolls—an indigenous inscription mechanism and a form of precolonial archives still maintained by the tribe. No scrolls are depicted in the *Gibagadinamaagoom* archive, however, because the *chi-ayy ya agg* (wisdom keepers) who form the Board of Permission Givers for the project have deemed such sacred material inappropriate for use in a digital archive. In this sense, *animikii* serves as a central image for the project, both as a spiritual messenger who carries stories from Creator's world and as a powerful protector who guards the tribe's most sacred pictographic writings on *wiigwaas* (birch bark).[18]

A Digital Archive Dreams of Thunderbirds

> When we can look at an eagle and see it not only as beautiful but also as incarnate of thunderbird, who carries messages to *Gitche Manidoo*—if we can do this, we realize we are encumbered with the power to understand. But our downfall is lack of humility.[19]

What does it mean to be "encumbered with the power to understand"? From what I have been taught, it is a process that begins with a profound sense of humility—the realization that a PhD does not confer an academic with the right to appropriate this knowledge for publication or self-promotion. Understanding requires a sincere willingness to listen and to wait patiently for meanings to unfold. The reader should bear in mind that what follows is a highly imperfect translation of *animikii*'s story and that further clarification should be sought from tribally authorized Ojibwe wisdom keepers. This version is neither "true" nor "definitive." I have been authorized only to say what *animikii* (thunderbird) means to me at this particular moment in time. I want to begin, then, by stating unequivocally that because I am a novice of *Ojibwemowin* (the Ojibwe language), my understanding of such powerful symbols is limited, though I will share with you what I know.

To use the first person in the previous sentence, "*I* want to begin . . . ," constitutes the first misstep—"our downfall is lack of humility"—for the story does not begin with me, the author of this essay. According to the Ojibwe "epistemology of beginnings," the story originates with *animikii* (thunderbird), *oshkaabewis* (messenger or translator) to *Gitche Manidoo* (Creator). The story that follows begins within the familiar framework of chronological time and then gradually shifts to the spiritual temporality of Ojibwe storytelling.

In the winter of 2006, I was hired to be the first director of the Penn Center for Native American Studies. Frankly, I was overwhelmed—not because of the professional honor of working at one of the nation's oldest and most prestigious academic museums, but because I knew that many of the Indian artifacts housed there were immensely powerful sacred objects too often obtained under legally questionable pretenses. At that point, I had been working with Larry Aitken for about six years, so I was respectfully aware that these artifacts are animate beings, capable of telling stories to Native American wisdom keepers, trained in traditional ways. I also knew that no one employed by the museum possessed these kinds of credentials—although I hasten to add that the staff deeply appreciates this form of knowledge, working assiduously to bring indigenous people to work with the collections and to repatriate sacred objects through the imperfect system put in place by NAGPRA (the Native American Grave Protection and Repatriation Act, passed in 1992). I invited Larry Aitken to perform a sacred pipe ceremony in the courtyard of the museum, to honor these empowered objects and to acknowledge these animate spirits. I am fully aware that an Ojibwe *opwaaganinini* (sacred pipe carrier) cannot justifiably represent any tribe other than his own, but it was the most meaningful gesture I could make, given my own limited understanding of such complex spiritual matters.

In the winter of 2007, the *Gibagadinamaagoom* project was awarded an NEH grant. The grant paid for Larry and David McDonald, lead videographer on the project and the head of DMcD Productions, to come to the Penn Museum. We created a short film, *Weweni* (Be Careful), about Larry's interaction with *deweigan* (drum), which is the subject of a digital exhibition in the "Ask the Elders" section of the *Gibagadinamaagoom* site. In the spring of 2008, Nyleta Belgarde, dean of White Earth Tribal College (WETC) and the primary investigator for the NEH grant, came to Penn to oversee digital imaging of Ojibwe artifacts from the museum and the training of WETC staff members. It was Nyleta who first noticed the birch bark case with the image of *animikii,* flanked by *mashkode-bizhiki* (buffalo). Nyleta looked carefully at the card, which recorded information from the museum database, and observed the metadata was incorrect. The first image was described as a "fish." Looking at the artifact, then at the card, Nyleta said she was pretty sure the inscribed figure was a thunderbird, but acknowledged that she was not an elder and so could not say definitively.

From an Ojibwe perspective, the story just told might be considered intellectually impoverished, because of its overreliance on facts—chronological dates, individual names, and institutional resources—and its underrepresentation of the active role played by the spirit world. One might more accurately say that the story begins with *animikii,* who realized Nyleta was a reliable messenger (*oshkaabewis*) and entrusted her with a message to present to the *chi-ayy ya agg* (wisdom keepers) working on the *Gibagadinamaagoom* project—Andy Favorite (sacred pipe carrier, White Earth Band of Ojibwe), Dan Jones (language keeper, Fond du Lac Tribal and Community College), and Larry Aitken (sacred pipe carrier, Leech Lake Band of Ojibwe). As Larry explained later, the thunderbird appeared at this precise historical moment because *animikii* sensed our need for guidance, thus anticipating an important phase of the project.

When Larry Aitken came to the museum several months later, the embodiment of *animikii* inscribed on *wiigwaas* gave him opportunity to explain the relationship between a wisdom keeper and the empowered object in relation to Ojibwe epistemology.

> In the old days, the [pictographic form of writing used by the Ojibwe] was only one form of meaning. Actually, the invisible forces are speaking to the wisdom keeper. The empowered object recognizes a wisdom keeper and how to talk to them. The wisdom keeper is startled, surprised by the force nudging them, trying to contact the wisdom keeper. The human imagination thinks this cannot be. This feeling is not self-doubt as much as human insecurity about this higher level of thinking that goes beyond writing or the visual.[20]

Larry's strikingly honest account relates how the wisdom keeper himself is "startled, surprised by the force nudging [him]." This candor illuminates still more dimensions of what Drucker identifies as the culturally specific "force" associated with media. More specifically, we begin to see how pictographic writing on birch bark scrolls, when understood at a "higher level of thinking that goes beyond writing or the visual," invokes "invisible forces," which can then be translated by a skilled wisdom keeper into digital media (e.g., videotape).

Simply watching the videotape does not, however, begin to explain the epistemological complexity of this exchange. To understand this "content," the viewer must be provided with interpretive context, which must also be encoded into the site. When I asked Larry how we might achieve this, he explained, "We tend to focus too much on content, rather than spiritual context. You need to realize where the content originates. You need to become part of history."[21] So we set off in search of origins that go deeper into history than the digital media itself or even the birch bark medium on which *animikii* is inscribed, back to a sense of origins rooted in Ojibwe cosmology and the symbolic significance of the seven sacred directions:

East (Waabanong): new beginnings, small birds, yellow.
South (Zhawonong): warmth/healing, small mammals, white.
West (Ninagaabiin'inong): gift of sadness, flash of Creator's power, large hoofed animals, red.
North (Kiiweinong): purification/cleansing, large birds, black.
Mother Earth (Nimaamaa-aki): mother of the four orders of the earth and all living things.
Ancestor's Realm (Mishomis): the grandfathers that dwell on top of the earth.
Above World (Ishpiming): Creator's world, star world, sun and moon world.[22]

The preceding list is, admittedly, a vastly oversimplified sketch of a knowledge system so sophisticated it would take a lifetime of study with a qualified Ojibwe wisdom keeper to understand fully. Yet it provides a helpful, albeit incomplete, context for interpreting how Larry set about engaging the "invisible forces" that spoke through the image of *animikii* inscribed on *wiigwaas* (birch bark).

Larry began by addressing *animikii* in *Ojibwemowin* (the Ojibwe language), finally pausing to explain in English, "It is important to know that when you see a symbol on anything, it becomes alive, to teach you something." Here I must admit to not possessing adequate training to understand whether the invocation of Ojibwe cosmology played a role in bringing *animikii* to life or whether proceeding through the seven sacred directions was a form of ceremonial oratory, which allowed *animikii* to recognize Larry as *chi-ayy ya agg* (an Ojibwe wisdom keeper). In any case, here is an excerpt of the transcription:

> East is first and the color of yellow. . . . [Creator] said, when you want to know new things . . . look to the East. Then you look to the South. . . . The color of the South is white. . . . What do you get from the South? Healing and warmth. Not warmth in weather, but warmth in friendship. And you look to the West, the color is red. It is for the sun going down. . . . What gift do we get from the West? Sadness and sorrow. . . . But it's also a little display of Creator's power, through thunder and lightning.[23]

This is quite a remarkable moment, for it invokes so many ancient and powerful stories that it becomes difficult, perhaps even counterproductive, to disentangle them in the name of explication. The movement from East to South to West invokes the direction of prayer, this being the beginning of the proper sequence whereby to offer prayers to the seven sacred directions and/or the four cardinal points. Each of the seven directions is also associated with the Seven Grandfathers, whose gifts are considered to be the ancestral origins of sacred knowledge. The movement from East to West also invokes the oral epic of Waynaboozhoo, the Ojibwe cultural hero in many origin stories, and the historic migration of the Ojibwe people from the East Coast to the Great Lakes region, as foretold by prophecy.[24]

Upon reaching the West, in his oratorical progression, Larry then began telling a story about the origins of Ojibwe history. It was a time when the people had become spiritually lost, angering Creator, who threatened to destroy the world. *Migizi* (bald eagle) bravely took it upon himself to fly to Creator's world (*Ishpiming*). Creator spared *migizi,* who was at risk of being burned into ash by the sun. Impressed with his courage in having come so far, Creator transformed *migizi* into *animikii,* so that he could fly past the sun. *Migizi* pleaded with Creator to spare the people. Finally relenting, Creator explained, "When [the people] see giant, invisible thunderbirds, they will surely see my eyes. Now, fly back and tell the people on earth

. . . I will send them teachers . . . to teach them the good way, . . . to teach honesty, morality, legality."[25]

Although the symbolism here is more difficult to discern, this story completes the cosmological cycle. More specifically, the story begins with Larry addressing *animikii,* discussing the gifts associated with the East (Waabanong), South (Zhawonong), and West (Ninagaabiin'inong)—discreetly moving in the direction of prayer as determined by traditional codes of conduct. *Migizi,* a large bird associated with the North (Kiiweinong), then flies from Mother Earth (Nimaamaa-aki), through Ancestor's Realm (Mishomis), to Creator's world (Ishpiming). A literary reading of the narrative sequence suggests greater depths. The first part of the story emanates from Larry. As he describes the "display of Creator's power, through thunder and lightning," in the West, the imagery invokes *animikii,* embodied here by a birch bark pictograph with lightning coming out of his eyes. At this point, *animikii* takes over the storytelling, relating how *migizi* transforms into *animikii,* enters Creator's world, and returns with the promise that teachers, like Larry, will come. The two stories—one told from the memory of *chi-ayy ya agg* (wisdom keepers) and the other from the spirit world—become one. Encumbered with the power to understand, we are now prepared to take up the question of how such eminently powerful stories can be translated into digital codes.

Cultural Codes and Digital Codes: Reprogramming American Literature

> Our human shortcoming is to have animate objects not known to the academy as storytellers and wisdom keepers. If you work with us, *bizindam* [listen], you accept the body of Ojibwe knowledge and infuse it into your own work, affected by original modality. If you listen to stories, you will be instilled with responsibility.[26]

Having heard the story of the cosmology told by both an Ojibwe wisdom keeper and an "animate object," the challenge becomes how to infuse digital technology with "the body of Ojibwe knowledge" and the "original modality." I turn in this section to more practical matters concerning the integration of Ojibwe epistemology into the design of the interface of the *Gibagadinamaagoom* archive (what you see on the screen), the archive's metadata (how content is described digitally), its database (how the digital material is stored), and its navigation system (how the user moves throughout the site). Although the *Gibagadinamaagoom* site is obviously unique (because it adheres so closely to the traditional codes of the culture being archived), our hope is that it may serve as a model for other culturally specific archives and, in so doing, play a meaningful role in diversifying the digital humanities.

Interface and Navigation

The *Gibagadinamaagoom* digital archive has been carefully designed so that visitors find themselves immersed in an Ojibwe worldview the moment they enter the site. At the top of the home page, the viewer encounters the archive's powerful and daunting name: *Gibagadinamaagoom.* An audio link has been provided beside the title, so that the viewer can hear the word pronounced by a fluent speaker and can learn the English translation: "to bring to life, to sanction, to give authority." An elder thus brings the Ojibwe language to life, while the site design implicitly sanctions the authority of the wisdom keepers to speak in their own language and to guide the viewer throughout the site. In doing so, we are challenging the myth of a "universal" digital language of zeroes and ones and the assumption that all archives should conform to "standards" created by those outside the culture being digitized. This problematic, though undertheorized, notion inhibits a fuller discussion of whether, for example, Dublin Core's emphasis on "author," "title," and "publication date," which clearly derives from print culture, implicitly imposes non-Indian descriptors shaded with an ethnocentrism that does not fully acknowledge Ojibwe epistemology. This is not to say that Dublin Core standards cannot be modified, which is what we are currently compelled to do in order to be eligible for most grants. Rather, our hope is to instigate a robust interrogation of whether an Ojibwe archive would be better served by a more culturally sensitive metadata initiative. This recalibration may be over the horizon at present, but the *Gibagadinamaagoom* project nevertheless continues to explore systematic approaches to the writing of metadata based on such standards as Ojibwe cosmology, the vicissitudes of "authorship" as understood within the communal context of the oral tradition, and a more culturally accurate understanding of time as freed from the constraints of chronology.

The home page also includes a flash animation slide show, featuring a series of digital photographs carefully composed into a visual narrative. The sequence includes pictures of dawn breaking over a lake in northern Minnesota, a bald eagle soaring against the blue sky of the Ojibwe's ancestral homeland, *animikii* (thunderbird) inscribed on birch bark, and Larry Aitken with his arms outspread like an eagle as he tells the story of bald eagle's transformation into *animikii,* while collecting medicine near his home on the Leech Lake reservation. In one sense, the visual narrative reflects the cosmological story recounted in the previous section of this essay—beginning in the East (*Waabanong*), recalling how eagle is transformed into *animikii,* and depicting one of the teachers sent by Creator to restore spiritual balance. On another interpretive level, the flash animation sequence implicitly establishes this new digital archive as part of a cultural continuum that carries on in the spirit of older, indigenous archives. These include the knowledge possessed by the Seven Grandfathers/seven directions; the birch bark scrolls used by the Ojibwe to preserve their own tribal histories; the oral tradition in connection with the practice of Native medicine; and the oldest archive of all, the knowledge kept by Nimaamaa-aki (Mother Earth). The viewer undoubtedly will not be able to understand all of these meanings simply by watching a sequence of slides. This visual narrative is not necessarily meant for the viewer, however, but is perhaps better understood as a way of invoking and paying respect to the "invisible forces" that are part of the archive's living spirit. In this sense, the "force" associated with the older media—birch bark scrolls, oral tradition, *migizi* (eagle) as *oshkaabewis* (messenger)—is translated into new media.[27]

At the bottom of the home page are two video clips, designed to act as spiritual and practical guides for the forthcoming journey into Ojibwe cosmology. The first is of Jimmy Jackson, a distinguished medicine man for whom Larry Aitken served as an *oshkaabewis* (interpreter or messenger) for 17 years.[28] The prayer, asking for protection and guidance from Creator, is spoken in the Ojibwe language, without translation or transcription. The wisdom keepers on the Board of Permission Givers for the site felt that this was appropriate because it tacitly informs the viewer that some parts of the Ojibwe cosmology cannot be rendered in English and will not be shared with outsiders. For non-Indian viewers, part of being "encumbered with the power to understand" means learning to accept that the Ojibwe wisdom keepers maintain sovereign control of their own history and that, hence, the sacred dimensions of Ojibwe cosmology will not necessarily be translated, although they will be observed. Yet this does not preclude outsiders from learning about Ojibwe culture. Jimmy Jackson's prayer is meant to prepare the viewer for the journey that lies ahead, in accordance with traditional codes of conduct maintaining that such a spiritual journey should always begin with prayer.

The second video instructs the viewer about the importance of offering *asemaa* (tobacco) before asking an elder for assistance, engaging the ancestors, or embarking on a spiritual journey. Larry Aitken appears in the traditional role of *oshkaabewis* (messenger or translator). Here again, multiple interpretive layers are at play. One the one hand, Larry acknowledges his indebtedness to Jimmy Jackson, who taught him so much about medicine and traditional practices. In doing so, the site strives to replicate traditional protocol, which teaches that one should always begin by thanking the elders or ancestors who originally conveyed the story to the storyteller. The fact that Jimmy Jackson passed away many years ago reminds us that we remain connected to the spirit world and to the ancestors, whose knowledge lives on through the wisdom keepers. While this epistemological connection may seem quite foreign to some viewers, it is interesting to note how effectively the digital media conveys these meanings. The dynamic vitality of Jimmy Jackson's video reinforces the idea that his spirit is alive and plays a fundamentally important role in the teaching of future generations.

The videos of Anishinaabe *chi-ayy ya agg* (Ojibwe wisdom keepers) implicitly convey another unique aspect of the site's navigation system. Whereas most other digital archives of American literature actively encourage the viewer to search the content guided by their own scholarly interests, *Gibagadinamaagoom* works on the assumption that the viewer needs guidance to navigate their way through the seven sacred directions of Ojibwe cosmology. This is in keeping with the way traditional Ojibwe archives operated, in the sense that an initiate would be carefully taught about traditional codes of conduct, prayers, song cycles, and the interpretive techniques in order to understand the pictographs on birch bark scrolls. As Larry explains, the searcher must come to terms with the fact that they "cannot own this knowledge, but [if they follow traditional codes of conduct, they can] stir a wisdom keeper into presenting that body of knowledge."[29] The wisdom keeper must, in turn, accept their identity as a

> visionary and as a carrier and interpreter of knowledge. This higher state of consciousness is not given to everyone equally. Not everyone can read the hieroglyphs [inscribed on the birch bark scrolls]. A visionary must search for ways to explain the invisible forces' touch, without seeming "special" or aloof.[30]

Gibagadinamaagoom's relationship to the historical continuum of traditional Ojibwe archives thus gives new meaning to the technical term *search.* Archives derived from print culture conceive of searching in relation to the editorial history of the book's index, expanded into today's powerful search engines for keywords.[31] Within the spiritual context of Ojibwe cosmology, however, the term *search* takes on the connotation of a quest for knowledge guided by wisdom keepers, whose insights derive from traditional teachings and their understanding of "invisible forces."

Metadata and Database

The most difficult technical challenge in constructing the *Gibagadinamaagoom* archive in accordance with traditional codes of conduct has been the question of how to create the metadata and the database (i.e., describing the content so that it can be searched and structuring how that data is stored). This involved intense negotiations between Ojibwe wisdom keepers, the videographer, administrators of the Ojibwe Quiz Bowl (which uses the material developed by the *Gibagadinamaagoom* project to educate Ojibwe high school students about their own language and culture), Web designers, and the head of the Schoenberg Center for Electronic Text and Image at Penn. After more than a year of discussion, we decided that the best way to infuse the archive with the spirit of the "original modality" was to build the site around the seven sacred directions of Ojibwe cosmology. (Please see the digital version of this essay on *digitalculturebooks* to find a link to the navigation system.)

Before we turn to a fuller discussion of the complexities of the Ojibwe cosmology, it is important to understand the problem at hand more fully. This is perhaps most clearly illustrated by applying a standard library metadata system to one of the stories told in the previous section:

> Title: "The Story of Thunderbird" [videorecording] / Weweni Consultants; A DMcD Production; Directed by David McDonald;

screenplay by Larry P. Aitken; produced by Timothy B. Powell
Publisher: [United States]: Weweni Consultants, 2008
Description: Visual Material Videorecording
Library of Congress Subject Headings: Chippewa Indians[32]

This is accurate information by library standards but culturally misleading by Ojibwe standards. The Library of Congress heading "Chippewa" is many years out of date—an anglicized corruption of *Ojibwe* no longer in use. To say that the media of the story is a "videorecording" is certainly accurate but problematically truncates a deeper, Ojibwe sense of media history. The digital version of the story derives from older forms of media, such as archives of birch bark inscriptions and the oral tradition, which date back hundreds of years and include multiple authors whose names are not readily available to librarians. It is true the video was copyrighted by Weweni Consultants (a limited liability company founded by Larry Aitken to protect the intellectual property created by the *Gibagadinamaagoom* project) in 2008, but this chronological date distorts the depth of history involved with the intellectual ownership of the story and elides questions about the cultural sovereignty of indigenous storytelling. Finally, to credit Larry Aitken, Dave McDonald, and Tim Powell is necessary, if anyone hopes to find the video in a library (or if one of the three is seeking tenure or promotion in the academy), but to respect Ojibwe traditional teachings, credit must also go to the medicine man Jimmy Jackson, who trained Larry to be a wisdom keeper and who helped establish a precedent for using video technology to convey traditional teachings, when done in close consultation with elders properly vested with authority by the tribe. There is also the even more challenging question of how to credit *animikii,* the spirit of the thunderbird, as the originator of the story. Through this example, the need for a metadata system that more accurately describes the media in terms of its tribal genealogy and cosmological origins comes more clearly into focus, even if the solutions are not yet readily apparent.

The hidden cultural dimensions of space and time also still need to be considered much more carefully. In the library system, for example, the descriptor "United States" as the site of publication reveals the assertion of nationalism that implicitly challenges the existence of the Ojibwe Nation and its rightful claims of sovereignty. Here again, solutions remain distant, although the need to involve intellectual property lawyers and tribal lead-

ers becomes evident. This assertion of national identity can, of course, be traced back to the epistemology of colonialism, although that is outside the parameters of this particular essay.[33] The date "2008" also has its roots in the European colonization of the continents, though more subtly disguised here by the Newtonian myth that time is constituted by mathematical precision and, therefore, remains culturally neutral.[34] The way the library system identifies place and date problematically distorts a more culturally accurate understanding of how space and time function within Ojibwe epistemology as embodied by the cosmology of the seven directions.

What we are trying to describe in the construction of the *Gibagadinamaagoom* database is the way that the story lines trace the nonnationalistic space of the four cardinal directions and establish a powerful connection between Nimaamaa-aki (Mother Earth), Mishomis (Ancestor's Realm), and Ishpiming (Creator's world). More specifically, what is left out of the Western-based metadata system is the all-important relationship between the stories and the spirituality inherent in the Ojibwe knowledge system. We have attempted to rectify this oversight by mapping this spiritual geography onto the database and by designing the navigation system so that the viewer quite literally moves through the seven sacred directions. We feel strongly that the metadata system of the *Gibagadinamaagoom* project needs to be able to describe accurately the role played by Jimmy Jackson, as an ancestral presence who provides guidance about how technology can be utilized to explain traditional teachings, and to locate places such as Ishpiming, Mishomis, and Nimaamaa-aki as integral sites of the story that the database encodes. In short, we are trying to describe the space and time encompassed by the stories themselves, in addition to external factors such as copyright and publication dates.

We have self-consciously worked against both the notion that chronology is culturally neutral and the illusion that a great temporal distance separates Waynaboozhoo's time, at the beginning of Ojibwe history, from our own.[35] No chronological date can be assigned to the day that *migizi* decided that he needed to fly to Creator's world to restore spiritual balance to the Aninshinaabeg (the people), yet time is still an integrally important part of the story. To create metadata that more accurately describes the way time works in the story about *animikii* that Larry relayed on 13 October 2008 at the Penn Museum, it is imperative to understand both the chronological date *and* the temporality of "origin stories" as understood within an

Ojibwe epistemology of beginnings. These two moments—the day *migizi* set off for Creator's world and the day we filmed Larry telling the story—are not separated by a vast temporal distance but inextricably intertwined by the act of storytelling in the hands of a skilled and knowledgeable wisdom keeper.

The metadata schema and the database structure we have created thus inscribe a sacred landscape that allows *animikii* and other *oshkaabewisag* (messengers) to move freely between the realm of the ancestors and this world. In doing so, we offer a spatiotemporal paradigm that, if acknowledged by Americanists, would perhaps allow us to free ourselves of the deeply problematic concept of periodization and our seemingly endless obsession with nationalism, postnationalism, and transnationalism. It is a sacred landscape that is distinctly Ojibwe yet still part of American literary history. Sadly, many scholars of American literature have become caught up in the belief that inventing neologisms with the prefix *post-* (e.g., *postmodernism, postcolonialism, post-American*) can propel the country beyond its monocultural past. Rather than talking to ourselves in a theoretical language that we barely understand and that the rest of world finds impenetrable, my hope is that we can learn to listen more carefully to the original occupants of the land, to value the spiritual dimensions of storytelling, and to think much more carefully about the role that these eminently powerful stories can play in healing historical wounds.

Completing the Circle

One of the great joys of my personal life and most rewarding engagements of my professional life has been the opportunity to work with Jimmy Jackson, Larry Aitken, Andy Favorite, Nyleta Belgarde, Dan Jones, Florence Foy, and David and Barbara McDonald. Poignantly, to pursue the *Gibagadinamaagoom* project, I made the decision to give up tenure in the English Department at the University of Georgia to accept a job as the director of Digital Partnerships with Indian Communities at the University of Pennsylvania Museum of Archaeology and Anthropology. As Jerome McGann has so eloquently described the situation of digital humanists at a time when projects such as the *Gibagadinamaagoom* digital archive do not count for tenure or promotion in English departments around the country, "The Jordan will not be crossed until scholars and educators are prepared not simply to access archived materials online, but to publish and peer-review online—to carry out the major part of our scholarly and educational intercourse in digital forms."[36] So I conclude this essay while metaphorically standing in the middle of the river Jordan, looking back with heartfelt sadness at the field of American literature's unwillingness to recognize the origins of American Indian literature or the promise of digital technology and looking forward to continuing to do work that directly benefits Ojibwe students on the reservations of northern Minnesota. My greatest hopes are no longer for academic recognition for this work but for the grandson of Jimmy Jackson, Anthony James Belgarde, who is now maintaining the Quiz Bowl Web site, where the material for the *Gibagadinamaagoom* project is presented to help Ojibwe high school and tribal college students learn their own remarkably powerful language and to preserve their vibrant and living culture, so that seven generations in the future, we may finally understand digital technology not as a postmodern phenomenon but as part of the great continuum of Anishinaabe history.

Notes

The first person pronoun in this essay refers to Tim Powell; any and all mistakes are his responsibility. Larry Aitken inspired, participated in, and helped write the stories told here.

The Ojibwe spelling has been provided by Professor Aitken and does not, in all cases, conform to the double vowel orthography that has become the standard in the academy.

1. Randy Bass, "New Canons and New Media: American Literature in the Electronic Age," *Heath Anthology of American Literature's Online Resources,* http://www9.georgetown.edu/faculty/bassr/heath/editorintro.html (accessed 29 November 2008).

2. I have addressed these issues at some length in the following articles: Timothy B. Powell, with storytelling by Freeman Owle and digital technology by William Weems, "Native/American Digital Storytelling: Situating the Cherokee Oral Tradition within American Literary History," *Literature Compass* (Blackwell) 4, no. 1 (2007); Timothy B. Powell, "Recovering Pre-Colonial American Literary History: The Seneca 'Origin of Stories' and the Maya *Popol Vuh,*" in *The Literatures of Colonial America: An Anthology,* ed. Susan Castillo and Ivy Schweitzer (New York: Blackwell, 2005).

3. Anyone who undertakes such work owes a debt to Vine Deloria Jr. My own research has been deeply influenced by Vine Deloria Jr., *God Is Red: A Native View of Religion* (Golden, CO: Fulcrum, 2003); Edward Benton-Banai, *The Mishomis Book: The*

Voice of the Ojibway (Heyword, WI: Indian Country Communications, 1988); Thomas Peacock and Marlene Wisuri, *Ojibwe Waasa Inaabidaa: We Look in All Directions* (Afton, MN: Afton Historical Society Press, 2002); Basil Johnston, *The Manitous: The Spiritual World of the Ojibway* (Minneapolis: Minnesota Historical Society, 2001); Basil Johnston, *Ojibway Heritage* (Lincoln, NE: Bison Books, 1990); Winona LaDuke, *Recovering the Sacred: The Power of Naming and Claiming* (Cambridge, MA: South End Press, 2005); Anton Treuer, ed., *Living Our Language: Ojibwe Tales and Oral Histories* (Minneapolis: Minnesota Historical Society, 2001); Gerald Vizenor, *The Everlasting Sky: Voices of the Anishinabe People* (Minneapolis: Minnesota Historical Society, 2000); Jace Weaver, *That the People Might Live: Native American Literatures and Native American Community* (New York: Oxford University Press, 1997); Keith H. Basso, *Wisdom Sits in Places: Landscape and Language among the Western Apache* (Albuquerque: University of New Mexico Press, 1996); Julie Cruikshank, *The Social Life of Stories: Narrative and Knowledge in the Yukon Territory* (Lincoln: University of Nebraska Press, 1998).

4. Personal conversation with Larry P. Aitken, 16 October 2008.

5. Amanda Gailey, "Digital American Literature: Some Problems and Prospects" (synopsis for paper delivered at the London Seminar in Digital Text and Scholarship, School of Advanced Study, Institute of English Studies, University of London), http://lists.digitalhumanities.org/pipermail/humanist/2009_May/000439.html.

6. Jerome McGann, "Culture and Technology: The Way We Live Now, What Is to Be Done?" *New Literary History* 36, no. 1 (2005): 77.

7. I have focused, in this essay, mostly on the potential benefits of digital technology in relation to recognizing the intrinsic value of Ojibwe cultural expression. There are, obviously, many problems that arise in attempting to translate traditional archives into digital archives. These need to be discussed at much greater length, but that is another essay entirely. There are three particular issues on which we have been working that I would like to raise here, albeit briefly: (1) the issue of intellectual property rights in the context of Ojibwe sovereignty, (2) questions about the accuracy of the translation of an empowered object into a digital image, (3) the issue of how representative the views of the wisdom keepers working on the *Gibagadinamaagoom* project are in relation to the larger Ojibwe community. Briefly, our ever-evolving response is, first, that we are working diligently to address the question of what we call "the sovereignty of storytelling." A Board of Permission Givers was formed as part of the NEH grant. We have formed a Limited Liability Company, Weweni (Take Care), which will hold the intellectual property rights to all of the digital exhibits and videos produced as part of the project. Second, without getting bogged down in decades of academic arguments about the simulacrum of postmodernism, there are obviously many interpretive dimensions that get lost in translation. To take just one example, to speak with a wisdom keeper is to engage in symbolic exchange, so to speak, wherein the stories are shaped by the interaction between the wisdom seeker and the wisdom keeper. This has been lost in the sense that the stories recorded on videotape cannot possibly take into account how the

story would change if told to the viewer. The wisdom keepers are aware of this problem and have made the decision to record their stories in digital form for the greater good of cultural preservation and revitalization. Third, it should be clearly stated that the wisdom keepers make no claim to represent anyone other than themselves. Stories told by different bands of the Ojibwe Nation and even within the different bands vary widely—for example, concerning the colors associated with the four cardinal points. We are grateful to the wisdom keepers for sharing their views, but I want to state unequivocally that these views do not represent the Ojibwe in all of their regional, linguistic, and cultural complexity.

8. Concerning the goals of the *Gibagadinamaagoom* project, our primary intent, at the outset, was to create educational material that could be used in the Quiz Bowl extramural competition created by Itasca Community College. See http://www.nativequizbowl.info/.

9. There has not been a great deal written on American Indian culture and digital technology. I am especially grateful to my colleagues at the American Indian Library Association. See http://www.ailanet.org/default.asp (accessed 4 December 2008). Some of the works that have been helpful to me include Loriene Roy and Peter Larsen, "Oksale: An Indigenous Approach to Creating a Virtual Library of Education Resources," *D-Lib Magazine* 8, no. 3 (March 2002); "Tribal Archives, Libraries, and Museums: Preserving Our Language, Memory, and Lifeways," a grant project sponsored by the Arizona State Museum and the University of Arizona, http://www.statemuseum.arizona.edu/aip/leadershipgrant/ (accessed 4 December 2008); Neil Blair Christensen, *Inuit in Cyberspace: Embedding Offline Identities Online* (Copenhagen: Museum Tusculanum Press, 2003); Mark Christal, Loriene Roy, and Antony Cherian, "Stories Told: Tribal Communities and the Development of a Virtual Museum," in *Collaborative Access to Virtual Museum Collection Information: Seeing Through the Walls,* ed. Bernadette G. Callery (New York: Haworth, 2004), copublished as *Journal of Internet Catologing* 7, no. 1 (2004): 65–88.

10. My thinking here has been inspired by Jerome McGann, *Radiant Textuality: Literature after the World Wide Web* (New York: Palgrave, 2001), xiii.

11. Tara McPherson, "Editor's Introduction," *Vectors: Journal of Culture and Technology in a Dynamic Vernacular* 3, no. 1, http://www.vectorsjournal.org/ (accessed 2 December 2008).

12. Lisa Nakamura, "Cultural Difference, Theory, and Cyberculture Studies: A Case of Mutual Repulsion," in *Critical Cyberculture Studies,* ed. David Silver and Adrienne Massanari (New York: New York University Press, 2006), 32.

13. David Silver, "Introduction: Where Is Internet Studies?" in Silver and Massanari, *Critical Cyberculture Studies,* 8.

14. Matthew G. Kirschenbaum, *Mechanisms: New Media and the Forensic Imagination* (Cambridge, MA: MIT Press, 2008), 54, 56.

15. Kirschenbaum, *Mechanisms,* 6, 15.

16. Johanna Drucker, *The Visible Word: Experimental Typography and Modern Art, 1909–1923* (Chicago: University of Chicago Press, 1994), quoted in Kirschenbaum, *Mechanisms,* 9–10.

17. For more on Midewiwin societies, see Benton-Banai, *Mishomis Book;* Frances Densmore, *Chippewa Customs* (Minneapolis: Minnesota Historical Society, 1979); Ruth Landes, *Ojibwa Religion and the Midewiwin* (Madison: University of Wisconsin Press, 1968); Michael Angel, *Preserving the Sacred: Historical Perspectives on the Ojibwa Midewiwin* (Winnipeg: University of Manitoba Press, 2002).

18. For a sense of what these scrolls look like, see Selwyn Dewdney, *The Sacred Scrolls of the Southern Ojibway* (Toronto: University of Toronto Press, 1975).

19. Personal conversation with Aitken, 16 October 2008.

20. Personal conversation with Aitken, 16 October 2008.

21. Personal conversation with Aitken, 16 October 2008.

22. Personal conversation with Aitken, 16 October 2008. While most Ojibwe bands agree that the colors associated with the four cardinal points are yellow, white, black, and red, there is no consensus concerning correspondence.

23. Personal conversation with Aitken, 16 October 2008.

24. For more on Ojibwe history from an Ojibwe perspective, see Benton-Banai, *Mishomis Book;* Johnston, *The Manitous;* Johnston, *Ojibway Heritage;* Peacock and Wisuri, *Ojibwe Waasa Inaabidnaa;* Thomas D. Peacock and Linda Miller Cleary, *Collected Wisdom: American Indian Education* (Boston, MA: Allyn and Bacon, 1998); Thomas Peacock and Marlene Wisuri, *The Four Hills of Life: Ojibwe Wisdom* (Afton, MN: Afton Historical Society, 2006).

25. Personal conversation with Aitken, 16 October 2008. For a fuller account of this story, see Benton-Banai, *Mishomis Book.*

26. Personal conversation with Aitken, 16 October 2008.

27. Again, many significant aspects of Ojibwe storytelling are lost in this translation. See note 7 for a fuller discussion. More scholarly work needs to be done on this subject, and I encourage others to continue to pursue these questions.

28. The original videotape of Jimmy Jackson was copyrighted in 1987 by the University of Minnesota, Duluth, University Media Resources. We are grateful for permission from the producer of *Interview with Jim Jackson,* Iver Bogen, for permission to use the video on the *Gibagadinamaagoom* site.

29. Personal conversation with Aitken, 16 October 2008.

30. Personal conversation with Aitken, 16 October 2008.

31. For more on the history of search engines, see I. H. Witten, *Web Dragons: Inside the Myths of Search Engine Technology* (Boston: Morgan Kaufmann, 2007); Richard Rogers, *Information Politics on the Web* (Boston: MIT Press, 2004).

32. The basis of the metadata schema is *Franklin: Penn Libraries Catalog,* http://www.library.upenn.edu/ (accessed 4 December 2008).

33. For more on this subject, see LaDuke, *Recovering the Sacred;* Linda Tuhiwai Smith, *Decolonizing Methodologies: Research and Indigenous Peoples* (London: Zed Books, 1999).

34. For a fuller discussion of this issue, see Wai Chee Dimock, *Through Other Continents: American Literature across Deep Time* (Princeton, NJ: Princeton University Press, 2006), chap. 6.

35. For a fuller discussion of the problems associated with chronological time, see Fabian, *Time and the Other: How Anthropology Makes Its Subject* (New York: Columbia, 2002).

36. Jerome McGann, "The Marketplace of Ideas" (talk given at the University of Chicago, 23 April 2004), http://www.nines.org/about/bibliog/mcgann-chicago.pdf (accessed 4 December 2008).

Contributors

Larry P. Aitken is the Tribal Historian at Leech Lake Ojibwe reservation in northern Minnesota. The founder of Leech Lake Tribal College, Dr. Aitken now is Endowed Chair of American Indian Studies at Itasca Community College. He worked for 17 years with the distinguished medicine man Jimmy Jackson and is an *Opwaaganinini* (Sacred Pipe Carrier). Dr. Aitken is head of the *Gibagadinamaagoom* (To Sanction, to Give Permission, to Bring to Life) Ojibwe digital archive project, which has been awarded two NEH grants.

Susan Belasco is Professor of English and women's and gender studies at the University of Nebraska–Lincoln and a past president of the Research Society for American Periodicals. The author of numerous articles on nineteenth-century American literature and culture, she is the editor of *Walt Whitman's Poems in Periodicals* for the *Whitman Archive* and *Stowe in Her Own Time* (University of Iowa Press, 2009). She is also the coeditor of *Periodical Literature in Nineteenth-Century America* (coedited with Kenneth M. Price; University Press of Virginia, 1995), *Leaves of Grass: The Sesquicentennial Essays* (coedited with Ed Folsom and Kenneth M. Price; University of Nebraska Press, 2007), and the *Bedford Anthology of American Literature* (coedited with Linck Johnson; Bedford/St. Martins, 2006–8).

Stephanie P. Browner, Professor of English and Dean of Faculty at Berea College, is the editor of the Charles Chesnutt Digital Archive (www.chesnuttarchive.org). She serves on the Executive Council of NINES (a scholarly organization dedicated to digital research and to peer review of digital work in the long nineteenth century, British and American), and she has authored articles on digital literary studies and on nineteenth-century American literature, including *Profound Science and Elegant Literature: Imagining Doctors in Nineteenth-Century America* (University of Pennsylvania, 2005).

John Bryant, Professor of English at Hofstra University, has written on textual scholarship and on Melville and related writers of the nineteenth century, including *Melville and Repose: The Rhetoric of Humor in the American Renaissance* (Oxford University Press, 1993), *The Fluid Text: A Theory of Revision and Editing for Book and Screen* (University of Michigan Press, 2002), and various editions of Melville works. His recent book, *Melville Unfolding: Sexuality, Politics, and the Versions of Typee* (University of Michigan Press, 2008), is a companion study based on his online fluid-text edition, titled *Herman Melville's Typee,* appearing in the Rotunda electronic imprint (University of Virginia, 2006). He is currently working on a critical biography, *Herman Melville: A Half-Known Life* (Blackwell), and the *Melville Electronic Library* (*MEL*), an online archive.

Matt Cohen is Associate Professor in the Department of English at the University of Texas at Austin and a contributing editor at the *Walt Whitman Archive.* He is the author of *The Networked Wilderness: Communicating in Early New England* (University of Minnesota Press, 2009) and the editor of *Brother Men: The Correspondence of Edgar Rice Burroughs and Herbert T. Weston* (Duke University Press, 2005).

Amy E. Earhart is Assistant Professor of English at Texas A&M University. Her research interests include digital humanities, constructions of race, and nineteenth-century American literature and culture. She is the project director and editor of the *19th-Century Concord Digital Archive,* and her work has appeared in *Reinventing the Peabody Sisters* (Iowa University Press, 2006), *ATQ: American Transcendental Quarterly,* and *Resources in American Literary Study.* She is at work on a monograph titled *Traces of the Old, Uses of the New: The Emergence of the Digital Humanities.*

Amanda Gailey is Assistant Professor of English at the University of

Nebraska-Lincoln, where she teaches digital humanities and American literature. Her publications include articles on Walt Whitman, Emily Dickinson, and digital humanities, and she has contributed to several digital projects, including the *Walt Whitman Archive;* the *Edmund Spenser Archive;* and *Race and Children's Literature of the Gilded Age,* which she coedits with D. B. Dowd and Gerald Early.

Andrew Jewell is Associate Professor of Digital Projects, University Libraries, at the University of Nebraska–Lincoln; editor of the *Willa Cather Archive* (http://cather.unl.edu); and faculty fellow at the Center for Digital Research in the Humanities at UNL. He is the founding president of the Digital Americanists and the cochair of the NINES Americanist Editorial Board. He has written or cowritten several essays on American literature and digital humanities in journals such as *Studies in American Fiction, Literary and Linguistic Computing, Cather Studies, New Letters: A Magazine of Writing and Art,* and *Documentary Editing,* and, with Edward Whitley, is the recipient of an NEH Digital Initiatives Start-up Grant.

Timothy B. Powell is a Senior Research Scientist at the University of Pennsylvania Museum of Archaeology and Anthropology. The Director of Digital Partnerships with Indian Communities (DPIC), Tim is the Digital Curator of *Gibagadinamaagoom: An Ojibwe Archive,* which won an NEH grant. Tim also serves on the Advisory Board for the Leech Lake Tribal Museum and Interpretive Center. He is the author of *Ruthless Democracy: A Multicultural Interpretation of the American Renaissance* (Princeton University Press, 2000) and numerous articles, including the multimedia essay "Native/American Digital Storytelling: Situating the Cherokee Oral Tradition within American Literary History" (coauthored with William Weems and Freeman Owle), which appeared in *Literature Compass,* an online journal by Blackwell.

Kenneth M. Price is the Hillegass University Professor of Nineteenth-Century Literature and codirector of the Center for Digital Research in the Humanities at the University of Nebraska–Lincoln. His recent books include *Re-Scripting Walt Whitman: An Introduction to His Life and Work,* coauthored with Ed Folsom (Blackwell, 2005), and *To Walt Whitman, America* (University of North Carolina Press, 2004). Since 1995, Price has coedited the *Walt Whitman Archive.* In 2005, the archive received a "We the People" challenge grant from NEH to build a permanent endowment to support ongoing work. In 2008, Price received a Digital Innovation Award from the American Council of Learned Societies.

Brian L. Pytlik Zillig is Associate Professor and Digital Initiatives Librarian at the Center for Digital Research in the Humanities at the University of Nebraska–Lincoln. He has been involved in numerous digital projects, including MONK (Metadata Offer New Knowledge) Project, Evince: A Text Visualization and Analysis Tool; the *Walt Whitman Archive;* and the *Willa Cather Archive.* Brian's current research is centered on text analysis, *n*-grams, visualization of XML data, and embedded tools.

Wesley Raabe is Assistant Professor of textual editing and American literature at Kent State University in Ohio. A portion of his dissertation, a digital edition of the *National Era* version of *Uncle Tom's Cabin,* is published on the *Uncle Tom's Cabin & American Culture* site. His research interests include the preparation of a digital scholarly edition of *Uncle Tom's Cabin* and the broader disciplines of bibliography, textual criticism, and digital humanities. His teaching interests include American literature through the early twentieth century, methods for literary research, African American literature, and sentimentalism as an American and transatlantic phenomenon.

Jane Segal is a bibliographer and reference librarian at Fondren Library, Rice University. She works closely with the Department of English as well as with three other departments to develop the library's collections. She also provides instruction in research skills to undergraduates and graduate students. Jane has a master's degree in library science from Western Michigan University and a master's degree in anthropology from the University of Houston.

Lisa Spiro directs Rice University's Digital Media Center, where she helps to plan and manage digital projects, studies the impact of information technology on higher education, and oversees a multimedia lab. She created the Learning Science and Technology Repository (LESTER), founded the Digital Research Tools (DiRT) wiki, and served as PI for the

IMLS-funded Travelers in the Middle East Archive (TIMEA). A Frye Leadership Institute fellow, Lisa serves on the program committee for the Joint Conference on Digital Libraries and is the editor of the IEEE Technical Committee on Digital Libraries Bulletin. She has published or presented on a range of topics, including the history of reading and publishing in nineteenth century America, the impact of Google Books on scholarship, and the Text Encoding Initiative. Lisa received a Ph.D. in English from the University of Virginia, where she worked as the managing editor of *Postmodern Culture* and as a project assistant at the University of Virginia's Electronic Text Center. Her blog, Digital Scholarship in the Humanities, is at http://digitalscholarship.wordpress.com/.

Edward Whitley is Associate Professor of English at Lehigh University. He has written a number of essays on Walt Whitman and American poetry for such journals as *ELH, Nineteenth-Century Literature,* and the *Walt Whitman Quarterly Review* and is the author of *American Bards: Walt Whitman and Other Unlikely Candidates for National Poet* (University of North Carolina Press, 2010). He is also the coeditor, with Robert Weidman, of *The Vault at Pfaff's: An Archive of Art and Literature by New York City's Nineteenth-Century Bohemians* (http://digital.lib.lehigh.edu/pfaffs) and, with Andrew Jewell, the recipient of an NEH Digital Initiatives Start-up Grant.

Leslie Perrin Wilson has been Curator of the William Munroe Special Collections at the Concord (Massachusetts) Free Public Library since 1996. She is a writer for both general and scholarly audiences and frequently lectures before local, professional, and scholarly organizations. Her work has appeared in the *Concord Saunterer* (a publication of the Thoreau Society), *Papers of the Bibliographical Society of America, Nineteenth-Century Prose, The Encyclopedia of New England* (Yale University Press, 2005), and other publications. She is editor of the *Thoreau Society Bulletin* and a contributor to the *Oxford Handbook of Transcendentalism* (Oxford UP, 2010). Her book *In History's Embrace: Past and Present in Concord, Massachusetts* was published in 2007 (Hollis Publishing).

Index

Page numbers followed by letter *f* indicate figures.